The Immaterial Structure of Human Experience

George Lowell Tollefson

Palo Flechado Press

The Immaterial Structure of Human Experience
© 2019 George Lowell Tollefson

All Rights reserved.

ISBN-13: 978-0-9983498-9-3

Library of Congress Control Number: 2019912444

Palo Flechado Press, Santa Fe, NM

**OTHER PHILOSOPHICAL WORKS BY
GEORGE LOWELL TOLLEFSON**

Unbridled Democracy

Extracts from *Unbridled Democracy*

*Spirit as Universal Consciousness
The Thinking Arts
Ethical Considerations
Moral Democracy*

Contents

Introduction i
Section 1: Philosophy's Role 1
1. A justification of metaphysics. 1
2. Rational explanation is an intermittent but unceasing preoccupation of humankind. 3
3. Philosophical insight 4
4. A science of qualification 4
5. The building blocks of philosophy 5
6. The philosophical map 5
7. Philosophy's strength and weakness 6
8. The philosophical risk 7
9. The thing-in-itself 7
10. Empiricist and rationalist 8
11. Open-ended philosophy 9
12. Truth and fact 10
13. The philosophical matrix 10
14. The individual human mind 11
Section 2: Preliminary Thoughts Concerning the System 14
15. The tradition 14
16. Nature 14
17. Mystery and magic 14
18. Consciousness and spirituality 15

19. Spirit 15
20. The universal oneness of spirit 15
21. The material universe 15
22. One reality. 16
23. Spirit and matter 16
24. The universal oneness 18
25. The imperishable oneness 19
26. The noumenal realm 20
27. The paradoxical unity 21
28. The loss of the spiritual ground of being 23
29. The search for transcendence and unity 23
30. The sense of self and the conviction of the immutability of the self. 24
Section 3: The System 26
31. Some preliminary concepts concerning how the mind works. 27
32. The immaterialist perspective 46
33. Preliminary definitions. 56
34. The paradox of mind 84
35. Individual awareness and spirit 86
36. Berkeley and science 91
37. Kant's transcendental categories 129
38. The first three Kantian categories as intuitions explained further: from these the development and limitations of human awareness 159
39. The spiritual dynamic 199

40. The priority of spirit 209
41. The limited human mind 216
42. A review of the mapping of the precipitate 228
43. Free-form imagination...252
44. The material domain cannot be prior to spirit 254
45. Further thoughts on consciousness and its phenomenal world 262
46. The human mind..306
47. Because the concept of energy is a measure of material change, it can only be predicated of the material domain 326
48. Change is ultimately seamless within material experience 327
49. Change and the spiritual dynamic 328
50. Indeterminate change and free will 333
51. Speculative thought..354
52. Experience, individual and common 377
53. Natural insight..379
54. Spiritual insight 390
55. The indeterminate mind 402
56. The paradox of free will 409
Bibliography..413
Index of Names 417
Glossary...419

Introduction

This work represents a philosophical quest into the workings of the human mind. Its concerns are essentially epistemology and philosophy of mind. For this reason, it focuses upon experience from a subjective point of view and does not attempt the kind of empirical approach which would be centered in the senses, as would be the case with one of the sciences.

To state the point explicitly, this philosophy is immaterialist in outlook. Accordingly, what is sought is a means of broadening the scope of empiricism by providing it with a thorough grounding in subjective awareness. It is through this approach that the present work seeks to arrive at a complete analysis of human experience.

But let it be stated from the outset that the immaterialist philosophy which is the subject of this work does not in any way attempt to undermine the practice of modern science. Nevertheless, the fact remains that some observations will be made which will appear strange from a scientific perspective.

In such instances, it should be recalled that this is an immaterialist philosophy with a twofold purpose. The first, as stated, is to establish a broadened empiricism which will both include and be centered upon the experience of consciousness. The second is to demonstrate the priority of spirit over matter.

This priority of spirit does not preclude a materialist approach to science. It simply argues that, for the sake of achieving a greater understanding of the human condition, a more inclusive perspective on human experience should be taken. An illustration of the relationship (or contrast) between a spiritual and a material view of human experience is as follows.

A leaf is seen floating in a mountain stream, twisting and turning in its progress. Observing the leaf, a person wonders at its behavior. So he watches closely and begins to note that there are currents in the water which at times appear to be at odds with one another. Yet together they determine the motion of the leaf. He concludes that here are the sole causes of that motion.

Thus far, the role of the scientist in his attempt to understand nature has been considered. For him the flowing stream and the behavior of the leaf upon its surface constitute phenomena of the physical world. The currents impacting the leaf's motion represent relations within the flowing water which determine the behavior of the leaf. With acute observation and appropriate mensuration, this behavior makes possible the deduction of physical laws.

But such laws may not be all that is at work. Perhaps the observer finds his conclusions insufficiently complete and chooses to look beyond them. He does not deny the relations he has observed. So he would not forgo the acuteness of his observation and turn his back on the usefulness of the laws he has already determined.

Yet it so happens that upon further reflection, and by means of an observation of certain phenomena which have been generally omitted from his scientific procedure (but which are nevertheless a part of his human experience), he comes to understand that there may be hidden influences at work. Something lies beyond his powers of physical observation.

In other words, he surmises that there are hidden influences beneath the water which lie beyond physical appearances at the surface of the stream. These are not the currents he has observed. Rather, there are boulders strewn upon the streambed and hollows gouged in the stream banks which are undetected by the eye. And it is these which influence the motion of the currents.

This is precisely the relationship between the spiritual ground of human consciousness and the physical world of human sensory perception. Certainly the physical world has its laws, coordinated and seemingly autonomous. These, insofar as they may be readily examined, are not in dispute. For a science must be composed of that which may be readily examined. Or at least it must rest upon such a foundation.

But there are experiences which lie within human awareness that are not within the restricted field of scientific investigation. Chief among these is the phenomenon of consciousness. However, to assert that consciousness plays a direct role in influencing the outcome of experiment and observation is not the purpose of this book.

Those considerations have been put forth by those who are attempting to interpret the anomalies of quantum phenomena. Insofar as such an approach extends beyond the facts of experimental observation, it exhibits an unsubstantiated mystical approach which does not appeal to the present author.

Rather, the purpose of this book is to ascertain what the underlying role of consciousness might be in molding the human faculties of awareness and thought. In short, its focus is epistemological. It asks, why must human beings do science in the way they do? What might be the laws which govern the laws made evident to awareness?

Thus beyond the laws governing behavior on the stream's surface are other laws hidden in the stream's depths. These are the laws which sustain and uphold the general character of the stream's flow. The relations which form them cannot be seen. But where there are gaps in what can be observed, and thus an incompleteness in the physical evidence for what determines the behavior of the currents affecting the motion of the leaf, the presence of these relations can be detected.

Insofar as its presence in human awareness is concerned, the phenomenon of consciousness is governed by such laws. These are the laws of spirit, of which human and other animal forms of consciousness are limited expressions. Within consciousness lies its content. This content includes all that is generally attributed to sensory perception and thought. But in the fullness of human awareness, it also includes consciousness. For consciousness is aware of itself.

In other words, human experience involves the container as well as its contents. So may not an explanation of one be found in the other? May not the content be understood in terms of that which contains it? For it is encountered nowhere else. Beyond this consciousness, there is nothing directly apparent to human sensibility.

Understood in this way, consciousness *is* awareness. And it is originator and master of all that it is aware of. Or at least it can be said that universal spirit, in its more inclusive role, provides these functions. For universal spirit is enlarged consciousness, an expansion of awareness inclusive of human consciousness but with which human beings are not generally acquainted.

Science has failed to explain human consciousness by means of sensory investigation. Nor can it be expected that it should do so. For when such an attempt is made, certain vital phenomena in the human experience of consciousness, and in the human experience of the physical world as well, remain unaccounted for. Among these are the immaterial character of consciousness and the power of the human mind to recognize unity among phenomena.

To assert that a human being experiences the combined sensations of an apple as a single entity does not account for his innate recognition of the unity of those sensations. For, since a unity representing a combination of properties cannot be transferred to the mind by means of the senses, the recognition of such a unity must be understood to be innate.

Thus the power of recognizing that unity must already be in the mind. But a physical investigation of material properties associated with the mind makes use of the power of unity. It does not discover it. Accordingly, it is left to philosophy to investigate the matter and, in doing so, to proceed in a reverse direction to that of science. For it must determine how consciousness and sensory input might both be understood as arising from an undetected source in human awareness.

Now, given this spiritual approach and certain contradictions which might appear to arise within it, it is necessary to note that the present work exhibits a twofold character. First, the overall thrust of the exposition is immaterialist in orientation. For it is intended to support the conviction that human experience, which would include consciousness as well as sensory input, can best be explained in spiritual rather than material terms.

However, secondly, in spite of this immaterialist approach, much of the book concerns itself with a representational theory. In other words, it is asked, and repeatedly demonstrated, how it is that the human mind "maps" reality in order to interact with it. So, since both approaches, immaterialist and representational, have to do with the character of human awareness, there is a nexus to be discovered which lies between them. It is what will be referred to in this work as the "phenomenal precipitate." For it is the phenomenal precipitate which presents sensory and thought experience to human awareness.

When an immaterialist point of view is assumed, it is understood that the phenomenal precipitate is a derivative of something which is referred to in this work as the "noumenal precipitate." The noumenal precipitate exhibits spiritual influences which, at the quotidian level of consciousness, are unknown to human awareness.

In spite of this, and as explained above with the example of the leaf-bearing stream, there are certain phenomena within human experience which exhibit qualities of transcendence. This is to say that they cannot be explained by means of physical observation. Thus, since they do make up a part of human experience, they can be employed in a hypothetical context to more broadly characterize what is known and understood by more directly observational methods.

For this reason, the noumenal precipitate is clearly seen to be a speculative part of this work. As such, it departs from a sensory-based approach to the problem of mind. Nevertheless, it is designed to support the much neglected empirical evidence of consciousness. That would be the immaterial character of consciousness and the power of the human mind to recognize unity among phenomena. In addition to this, there arises a question concerning the origin of sensation.

However, when a representational point of view is assumed, the perspective shifts. For, when the representational view is being discussed, there is little or no reference to the noumenal precipitate. As a result, the phenomenal precipitate is often treated, in appearance at least, as though it were equivalent to an independent material reality.

Nevertheless, nowhere in this work is an argument made for the existence of physical phenomena which are separate from the mind. Were it so, given the immaterialist thrust of the overall work, this would indeed be strange. So, rather than leaving the matter unattended, the gulf between subjectivity and objectivity is explained in another way.

But, should the immaterialist argument be set aside for practical reasons, as opposed to the emphasis upon it which is characteristic of the overall perspective of this book, then a traditional empirical view might easily be deduced from the representational perspective. This would lend an independent value to the material phenomena within the representational point of view. Thus much of the representational approach could be found useful in contributing directly to cognitive research.

For example, it could be brought to bear on a number of questions relating to research into artificial intelligence, such as: How can emotions be explained if physiological components are rendered unavailable as explanatory material? How does a being perceive distance and the separateness of things from one another and from itself?

How would the mind provide a working map of the physical world so as to facilitate its interaction with it? In other words, how does it grow in understanding? And, in extension from this, how does thought, both imaginative and rational, mimic that which is thought about and which exists in a realm presumed to be separate from consciousness?

But, to put such considerations aside, let the principal thesis of this introduction be rejoined. Throughout this work, there is a continual shift in perspective between the immaterialist and representational points of view. So, to avoid confusion, the shift has been frequently footnoted, reminding the reader of the overall viewpoint when a narrower one is temporarily assumed.

Nevertheless, such temporary deviations into the representational perspective can be quite lengthy, as they are necessary to an overall defense of the more encompassing immaterialist view. So the fact should not be overlooked that the immaterialist argument is always prior in both scope and substance to the representational view. When properly understood, the immaterialist argument both encompasses and supports the representational view. In turn, the representational view is subordinate to and supports the immaterialist perspective.

In addition to these general considerations, the reader should also note that in various parts of the present work a specifically evolutionary point of view is entertained concerning the development of human faculties. When this is so, it should not be forgotten that any physical explanation of human development, including the evolutionary approach, should always be understood to be subordinate to the immaterialist perspective, even where the immaterialist perspective is not mentioned.

In other words, an evolutionary approach is the way in which the phenomena of experience, as presented to and understood by the human mind, can be most conveniently interpreted. But how these phenomena are initially presented to human awareness (a more inclusive category than the mind) takes precedence over their interpretation.

It is again like the above example, in which an interpretation of the behavior of leaves floating in a stream is initially explained by the visible action of currents. Only subsequent to this interpretation is the deeper influence of the stream bed in shaping those currents taken into consideration.

So a description of human mental development, involving an interactive character of mind in relation to experience, is a necessary component of the representational view. It allows for a detailed discussion of representational theory. But transcending this view remains the overall immaterialist perspective. It is a perspective in which the whole of human experience must be understood as an immediate and instantaneous expression of spirit.

July 4, 2019

Section 1: Philosophy's Role

1. A justification of metaphysics. The essence of philosophy is to provide a connection between humanity and its experience. For philosophy is the love of wisdom. And an understanding of a human being's relationship to his or her experience is what wisdom is. Wisdom is to be distinguished from knowledge, since knowledge only communicates what the experience is. It does not inform as to what should be done about it.

A classic expression of what should be done about the knowledge of human experience is aptly framed by the question: how does one live the good life? The question implies more than a narrow pursuit of ethical goals. It suggests a desire to understand broadly, cosmically, how human beings should relate to their experience. So an understanding of the principles which this question directs a person to consider constitutes an embrace of the body of concepts called wisdom.

The ancient view that philosophy embodied a love of wisdom was developed prior to René Descartes and the modern emphasis on epistemology. Humanity now lives in a post-Kantian age, where its view is further complicated by the fact that people are expected to understand that an unapproachable noumenal realm may possibly separate them from questions of being. But this does not fundamentally alter the role of philosophy. It remains the role of philosophy to retain its universal embrace of human experience. So, if it can no longer confidently assert metaphysical explanations for that experience, it should at least continue to suggest them.

For this reason philosophy must continue to endorse an examination of the full range of knowledge, which body of

The Immaterial Structure of Human Experience

knowledge is humanity and its experience. It is this relationship between humanity and its experience which elicits such responses as the appreciation of beauty, the expression of love and courage, and the pursuit of the Good. Thus philosophy cannot ignore metaphysics because, if it does, it becomes at best an objective science or a meta-science, either of which is a body of knowledge possessed without wisdom.

It becomes just another limited field of facts and objective relations between those facts. Or it becomes a theory about those facts and their objective relations. It is limited because it does not define humanity in relation to its experience. That experience becomes isolated, or objectively separated from humanity. Thus such a person may possess knowledge of the human condition. But it is simply a field of knowledge. It is not wisdom.

But it may be asked how philosophy can form a metaphysical position, when the truth or falsehood of such a position cannot be determined. The answer is that such a determination need not be made. Just as the entire mechanical structure of classical physics is founded upon the unproven concept of inertia, so a philosophy may rest upon a transcendent metaphysics.

The strength of classical physics has been that its fundamental, unproven assumption, inertia, produces a basis for verifiable results in the mechanical principles which follow from it. The concept of inertia cannot be directly verified. But the entire science of mechanics is founded upon that concept. So, even though human efforts are unable to directly confirm the concept of inertia, the mechanical relations which follow from the assumption of that concept can nevertheless be measured.

For example, how a pendulum works can be determined because an observer surmises that the resistance caused by the friction of a moving part with its ambient air (and by certain mechanical impedances as well) reduces the kinetic energy of the part. Otherwise, according to the principle of inertia, if there were no resistance, the motion would remain constant. So a measure of that resistance and its effects is obtained because it is assumed that in its absence the motion of the pendulum would not change.

So it must be with philosophy. A metaphysical theory may well involve a realm not accessible to human reason or to the senses, such as is the case with Kant's noumenal realm. But that does not mean a description of such a realm cannot be formed if it will help to bring rational order to the things which are known.

Of course, philosophy should be built upon a metaphysics which is conducive toward producing practical results. Thus, if that metaphysics creates an intellectual position which explains how human beings may relate to their experience, and if this provides an adequate foundation for an explanation of how human beings ought to think and act—in other words, if it does these things in such a way that wisdom can be pursued—then it is philosophically sound. The pursuit of wisdom may begin.

2. Rational explanation is an intermittent but unceasing preoccupation of humankind. Superstition is the uncritical acceptance of a belief. Since it is uncritical, superstition implies a neglect of reason. So pure superstition would be a purely unreasoning acceptance of a belief. Conversely, pure rationality would be the acceptance of a belief only on the condition of reason. This leads to an unacceptable dichotomy because the human mind is always positioned somewhere between these two extremes.

There is always some element of uncritical acceptance, even in something as rigorous as a mathematical proof. For, if nothing else, such a proof requires an acceptance of the reliability of a logical system of deduction and of the truth value of its immedi-

The Immaterial Structure of Human Experience

ate terms or of the axioms upon which it is ultimately grounded. Likewise, there is always some element of reason in the uncritical acceptance of a belief, since the believer must believe that it is in some way reasonable or convenient to hold such a belief.

Thus the only dependable criterion for the avoidance of superstition is a critical examination of the relationship of a particular belief to life as it is currently being experienced or as it might reasonably be expected to be experienced. However, this depends heavily on other beliefs which may be held. For a general belief system conditions a human approach to life. Some of these general beliefs are not so easy to identify.

So the process of reducing all beliefs to such a formal standard of critical acceptance is indeed a formidable, if not impossible, task. Nevertheless, though somewhat intermittently pursued, it is precisely this project which has been the principal preoccupation of an influential reflective minority throughout the recorded history of the human race.

3. Philosophical insight. Philosophers are important, not because of the elaborate systems they build, but because of the abundance of individual insights their systems contain. The systems serve to provide a framework for clearly and logically developing those insights in their multiple variations and combinations. The systems are like a strong thread upon which pearls are strung. Eventually the thread grows old and breaks, but the pearls remain to be restrung.

4. A science of qualification. Philosophy is principally a science of qualification, not of quantification. It is as much, if not more, a product of imagination as it is of reason. That is, it is to a significant degree a product of subtle associations. That is why its truths cannot be uncovered by logic alone. But once its truths have been discovered by whatever means, often imaginative, a philosophical argument may be set forth.

The truths may thus be quantified. That is, they may be demonstrated according to the form the argument takes. For it is argumentation, not the substance of the argument, which is subject to rule. This rule is what is called logic. People often associate logic with clear and insightful thinking. But the rules of logic are only that portion of the thinking which is systematic.

5. *The building blocks of philosophy*. Philosophy is an imaginative enterprise. While it is true that philosophy's principles should be laid out in a clear and logical fashion, philosophy is not mere argumentation. It is the setting forth of a consistent vision. A vision is a new way of seeing things, not simply a new way of thinking about old problems. Thus philosophy is comprehensive before it is systematic in character. That is, it is a vision before it is logical.

6. *The philosophical map.* Humankind is always in search of truth. Yet it is never truly found. Nevertheless, the fact that the approximations of human thought approach nearer and nearer to the desired goal is sufficient evidence that there is such a thing as truth. It is an indication that there is a connection between human thinking and the world of experience.

More precisely, this implies that there is a correlation between human thought representations of the world and that world itself. The many complex thought structures human beings employ in understanding their experience are systematic arrangements of symbols. They include mathematics, science, and philosophy among others. But no matter how rigorously exact the

The Immaterial Structure of Human Experience

science, its representations are never a perfect fit to what they describe.

7. Philosophy's strength and weakness. Philosophy can and should embrace ideas which the precision of mathematics would reject. Philosophy is more inclusive and less precise, mathematics less inclusive and more precise. Completeness of thought demands inclusiveness. Rigor of thought demands precision.

As an illustration of the distinction between philosophy and mathematics, let Euclid's 5th postulate be considered. There has been much controversy due to the fact that this postulate is not directly proven. Nor does it follow effortlessly from the preceding definitions given in the *Elements*, as the previous four postulates do.[1] Rather, it is imaginatively apprehended.

But mathematics ought to either prove its assumptions or they should appear to be self-evident. On the other hand, philosophy may within certain contexts indulge an imaginative construct, if it appeals to common acceptance and experience. So, from a philosophical point of view, Euclid's 5th postulate can be made acceptable because it appeals to common sense.

Unlike mathematics, philosophy may conceive what is in agreement with experience yet which cannot be precisely defined. This is its strength: inclusiveness. Accordingly, the weakness of philosophy in relation to mathematics is made evident by this inclusiveness: insofar as it is comprehensive, philosophy is imprecise, therefore uncertain.[2]

---

[1] *Euclid's Elements,* Book I, Postulates.

[2] It should be noted that the philosophical system which is to be set forth in this book will not support a common sense view of absolute space. For in the system to be presented extensions in space determine space. But neither does this system support a concept of space which is derived from energy relations. Both the concept of absolute space and that of space curvature are working

8. The philosophical risk. The great difficulty of modern times is the need for a narrow specialization in knowledge due to the limitations of a human lifespan and the massive amount of information available. This specialization comes at a cost. And that cost is the squeezing of imagination and vision into ever-smaller boxes.

On the other hand, to ignore these limitations is to allow oneself to be scattered amidst a plethora of uncertainties. It means taking ever-greater risks of becoming wrong in the details simply for the sake of a more comprehensive vision. Yet, given the increasing distance between sectors of human knowledge, the lack of a general understanding, and the social alienation this produces, philosophy can ill afford to be timid.

9. The thing-in-itself. Among British thinkers, it is not only David Hume who may have had an impact on Immanuel Kant. There is also George Berkeley. Kant's initial consideration of the phenomenal viewpoint could well have been derived from a reading of Berkeley. Berkeley's subjectivism might have suggested such an approach, since the only thing he removed from the con-

---

systems of physical science, the former including both Newtonian classical physics and the ancient Greek science, as exemplified by Euclid. The latter is the curved space of non-Euclidean geometry and General Relativity. Both the Euclidean and the non-Euclidean systems are mutually based on a belief in an independent physical reality. In contrast, the philosophy in this book is based on a phenomenal approach, which is ultimately spiritual in origin. It is clearly an immaterialist argument, as both its phenomenal and noumenal components (shortly to be defined) originate in spirit. But, though it is spiritual in origin, it does not preclude a full and meaningful interaction between the subjective human mind and the objective world upon which that mind is capable of acting. Rather, it insists that there is one unified reality beyond these appearances, and that that reality is spiritual in origin.

cept of an objective world was the thing-in-itself. And that single exception is what may have later become a basis for Kant's unverifiable noumenal world.

Anything objectively necessary for the business of life or for the conduct of science, in fact anything one might wish to conceive concerning a world known through the senses, can be found acceptable within Berkeley's immaterialism, so long as there is no insistence upon separating that world from the direct agency of spirit, or mind.

If in Berkeley's day his detractors had been willing to put aside their anxiety concerning things-in-themselves and had thus adopted his immaterialist view, they would certainly have gone on to do good science. But many thinkers and opinion holders of the time strongly opposed Berkeley because they mistakenly understood him to be denying material reality. They mistook their own solipsism for Berkeley's carefully qualified denial of the thing-in-itself. For this reason, among others, Kant was necessary.

10. Empiricist and rationalist. Plato's strength lies in his recognition that there is something in human awareness which is not material. Aristotle's strength lies in the recognition that the human mind can only grasp reality in terms of the material. That is, it is only by means of the data of sensory input that the mind can form concepts concerning experience. But this latter limitation does not mean that human awareness is confined to the material. It simply means that human reason must use material representations to express an understanding of the spiritual.

Such a dichotomy between spirit and matter, between consciousness and the content of consciousness, often forces a choice. It creates an artificial division of knowledge which encourages a person to side with one extreme or the other. A person must, it would seem, choose either the rationalist or the empirical approach to knowledge.

Even Kant, who attempted to create a synthesis of these two approaches, ended up more on the rational side and was not able to fully reconcile the issue. Such a titanic failure must give anyone pause. But go on human beings must. And they must begin by picking up the broken shards of Kant. This is how philosophy works.

11. Open-ended philosophy. Though a philosophical system is presented in this work, it is not suggested that anyone should limit his or her thinking to it. After all, as has already been noted, systems come and go. Only their insights remain. So this should not be any less true of these present efforts. However, there does exist an intuitive sense of what needs to be done. And it is this which is being translated into logical form.

The process is somewhat like that of a painter whose vision must be transformed into color and line, if it is to be communicated to others. The purpose of this work is to point the human mind in a specific direction. So it is said: consider this perspective for a moment; here are the arguments; follow their implications in your own way to see where they lead you.

This is called an *open-ended philosophy,* as opposed to a closed system. For a closed system, as it is generally conceived, demands that, if one wishes to harvest its insights independently of their place within the given structure, one must break into that structure and violate its integrity. But here in this work the only integrated goal lies in the ongoing conversation, of which this book is a part.

The Immaterial Structure of Human Experience

12. Truth and fact. Truth is not bound up in fact. It is held within the observer of the fact. This is why facts can change or be reinterpreted. But truth retains its form. The human intellect continually reinterprets the world. But what remains steadfast is the sincerity of the interpretation. The only relevant question asks how committed a person is to seeing things as clearly and honestly as she can, given the means at her disposal.

13. The philosophical matrix. All of humanity's attempts at philosophical system building have been no more than templates placed upon the face of reality. And every sincere attempt to create a new philosophical system carries on the progress of human understanding. It does so through an expansion of available insights and a rearranging of the elements of knowledge. From this, it can be seen that an emphasis is being placed upon the relationships between facts rather than upon the facts themselves, since the facts must inevitably change as their interrelationship is modified and enlarged.

It is true that relations are dependent upon facts, as well as facts upon relations. But while it cannot be denied that facts influence relations, it is the relations which are the foundations of the facts. Relations define facts. They provide the structure within which the facts must find their place.

Thus a person may, as in the case of this work, refer loosely to an empirical basis for knowledge, as though he expected to recount sensory facts. But, in making this reference, he is not implying that the concepts he forms concerning experience are inextricably correlated to a material substratum. He may be using the term empirical in a sense which includes conscious awareness. This means that consciousness itself is intimately involved in the structure of knowledge.

Experience determines how human beings think. So it is this broadened context of experience, which includes an awareness of the shaping influence of consciousness, which is the basis of knowledge. It is in this way that an empirical view of the world involves the human mind's conceptual mapping of experience. It includes everyone's carefully reasoned thoughts about that experience as something mutual and objective. Together people create a conceptual map which determines both their collective and their individual interactions with the world of their experience.

In asserting this, what is being said is that all the different relationships of facts, including those of the role of consciousness, which human beings are capable of developing in constructing concepts about experience and in putting those concepts into a logical framework—all of these relationships, once they have been collectively worked out and coordinated, must correlate in a general and practical way to common experience. Otherwise the concepts could produce no practical consequences in terms of human actions.

14. The individual human mind. For a human being there is only one framing reference for reality: the individual human mind. In this matter, one human mind is not unlike another. For what is being sought is an understanding of how it conceptualizes both itself and the world. Everything appearing to be outside the framing reference of the human mind is an extrapolation from the mind, no matter how far one's awareness appears to reach into an illusory objective realm.

The most abstract theories in physics, metaphysics, epistemology, and mathematics take their departure from this point and have their anchoring in it. In other words, the limiting parameters of the human mind determine human awareness of the world.

The Immaterial Structure of Human Experience

What is seen objectively must be acknowledged as a mirror image of the mind of the seer.

This is why Einstein could not abide the "spooky' interactions [3] of early 20th century quantum mechanics. Though he no doubt accepted an independent objective realm, he understood that the ultimate reference point for any theory is the human mind. That mind is an instrument which cannot function without a sense of order. This need for order is foundational in determining how the mind thinks, even how it perceives. It is how it *must* see things. There is no place for spooky interactions.

For instance, as Gottlob Frege points out in his *Foundations of Arithmetic*, arithmetic is grounded in the orderly logical operations of the human mind. But he does not go beyond the mathematical system which governs these operations. He leaves it in an integrated, composite state, as though one could not penetrate beyond the mysterious workings of logic. This gives mathematical logic a kind of extra-mental existence. It would appear to be something originating apart from mind, given to it innately in some mysterious way, somewhat like the eternal ideas of Plato or the transcendental categories of Kant.

However, as opposed to Frege, Kant does suggest a more fundamental unifying synthesis in the workings of the mind, something that is closer to an elemental functioning of mind itself. In doing this, he simplifies the workings of the human mind, though he does not simplify it enough. For a person is left wondering about the origin of the categories.

There is good reason for him to pursue such a simplification, insofar as he does so. For, without a unifying synthesis, such as is

---

[3] "Physics should represent a reality in time and space, free from spooky action at a distance." Walter Isaacson quoting Einstein in *Einstein: His Life and Universe*, p. 450.

found in his transcendental characterization of the mind, and without his ordering of phenomenal experience accordingly, there could be little ground for any correlation between human thought and human action in the physical world. It is a problem philosophers have been dealing with since the era of the Pre-Socratics. So the object of this present work is to determine in greater detail how the mind works, precisely how it correlates with its world, and how it comes to possess its particular categorizing powers.

For example, without a transcendental background for the logical structure of arithmetic and simultaneously for the structure of human perceptions, arithmetic would not apply to anything in the world. To do so, it must correlate both to the mind and to what the mind perceives and wishes to act upon. There can be no disconnect between the mind and the experienced world. Mathematics expresses this fact.

It is unimaginable how there could be such a disconnect, since it would raise the problem of the thing-in-itself, a paradoxical entity upon which the mind acts without knowing what it is. Thus it is the personal view of this author that Kant's tucking of the thing-in-itself into a noumenal realm disconnected from human awareness is incomprehensible. For what is fundamentally separated from the mind simply cannot exist for it. And what the mind is disconnected from cannot be acted upon. Therefore, since this cannot be the case, the mind and the world must in some sense be one.

The Immaterial Structure of Human Experience

Section 2: Preliminary Thoughts Concerning the System

15. The tradition. Several classical Western and Eastern sources hold that there is only the one, that the many is either an imperfection or an illusion. Thus there would be no such thing as space, time, energy, or mass. These concepts are no more than expressions of the material mind and do not belong to simple being. Such being is called spirit, awareness, or consciousness. From this the principles of the present work will be derived.

16. Nature. There is mystery in nature. For some things lie beyond the powers of reason. But nothing requires a suspension of reason. There is no magic.

17. Mystery and magic. A mystery is that which cannot be known by reason. This is due to inherent limitations of the human mind. If it can be known by reason, but is not accessible due to presently unsurmounted barriers to knowledge, it is not a mystery but only appears to be so at a particular stage of human progress. If it cannot be known by reason, it is, as stated, a mystery.

Magic resembles mystery in that it is also not known by reason. Like mystery it either may or may not become known by reason. But there is this difference. When not known by reason either by everyone or by the many, it is manipulated by the few at the expense of the many. This has been a cause of much misconception, retarded social and moral development, and suffering. Though many embrace it, at best it is delusional.

18. Consciousness and spirituality. There is an explanation of human consciousness which can provide a foundation for an understanding of spirit. This cannot be knowledge, if knowledge is understood to be that which is known through the senses. But, if the experience of consciousness is accepted as a ground for knowledge, much like that which is known through the senses, then such knowledge provides a means for understanding the immaterial. Such an explanation would be grounded in empirical experience without becoming mechanistic.

19. Spirit. The material universe is an expression of spirit. Just as there can be no experience of the senses without consciousness, so there is no material existence without spirit.

20. The universal oneness of spirit. Any moral conception of spirit must lie beyond the codes human beings live by, which codes are ever-changing and evolving. Spirit is moral precisely in the sense that it is beyond the materially expressed conceptions of reason. Thus it transcends the divisive and conflicting material relations of the human mind. It is approached, not for the particular, divisive, momentary view, but for the universal, inclusive, eternal relation of things about which human understanding is continually growing in experience.

21. The material universe. The material universe, as it is known to human awareness, is an expression of spirit. Spirit restricts the capacity of the human mind by means of the limited experience it provides. The human mind's experience is its universe. So in its origin the material universe of human awareness is bound by spirit and no other. In regard to this origin, the char-

The Immaterial Structure of Human Experience

acter of the material universe may be speculatively surmised. But its foundational workings cannot be known.

22. One reality. As a general practice, the Western mind tends to separate the material from the spiritual. But, whether human beings see nature as a material opponent to be overcome and subdued for their uses, or they see themselves as spiritually exempt from nature and therefore "stewards" of something which will be left behind or remade by God, the result is careless exploitation. This has placed the continued survival of humanity and the future habitability of the Earth in jeopardy.

So, since neither a predominately material nor a predominately spiritual view has worked, an alternative way of thinking must be found. Reality must be understood as simultaneously spiritual and material. In other words, humanity must acknowledge the material and the spiritual as coextensive views of one single reality.

This is not a plea for pantheism. As the human mind experiences them, it cannot be said that spirit is matter or that matter is spirit. Rather, it should be understood that material and spiritual explanations and views are concerned with the same topic, and that human experience can only be spoken of strictly in terms of one when the other is carefully excluded from consideration. But excluding something does not eliminate it. Both together are the fullness of human experience. Human beings are their total experience, whether they momentarily choose to see themselves as creatures of matter or of spirit.

23. Spirit and matter. Much of the history of Western philosophy takes the form of a dialectical argument between two opposing views. The one is rationalist, centered in the mind, which is often understood as spirit. The other is empiricist, centered in the data of the senses. But it can be no surprise if it should be discovered that they are in fact the same thing.

When a human mind thinks, it constructs the whole of its thought out of the materials of what are understood to be the senses. Even consciousness, when considered in this manner, is seen to be an entity within the whole of material experience. If it is said that a particular person is conscious, what is meant is that that person, a material entity who has hands, feet, and a head to enclose her consciousness, possesses consciousness.

Consciousness is thus referred to as though it were a material attribute bound by other material attributes, like hands, feet, and a head. For another person's consciousness is indirectly inferred through her behavior and bodily existence. It is associated with the observer's own experience of consciousness (also objectively considered) and its similarly attendant behavior and circumstances.

Yet human mental experience is not entirely material. For to be apprehended at all, all apparent sensory data must submit to a structuring mind. It must be organized by something which is not an element of sensory input, something which may be called spirit. Thus to argue for the otherness of matter on the one hand, or for the otherness of spirit on the other, is to attempt to draw a line in water. For the two are interwoven in human experience.

Insofar as human intelligence can determine a distinction, mind is matter considered without reference to its origin in matter. For that is how it is encountered: as something held apart from, though immersed in, material experience. Conversely, since matter is known only in the mind, it is an element of mind. It is spirit observed without reference to its origin in spirit. Ignoring this reference is what is meant when it is said that something is objectified.

It is only because an arbitrary distinction is drawn between spirit and matter, now in this context or again in that context, that any sort of an investigation of human experience can be established at all. That is why human beings draw such distinctions. It is not because they know them to be so.

24. The universal oneness. There is a state of mind in which the oneness of all things is recognized. To attain it, a person must acknowledge that his view of himself, the world, and how he relates to the world are determined by how he organizes the data of life. He generally does so discretely, in bits and pieces, which he puts together into mutually delimiting concepts. This leaves him with a sense of the divisibility and separateness in all things. He is limited, cut off from other things both spatially and in time. So he comes to see himself as a limited being in competition with others.

But this view is determined by the *content* of conscious awareness. If a person shifts that view to a consideration of consciousness itself, he obtains a different input. He perceives that consciousness is unextended in space and time. It appears to his awareness as a great, clear glass bowl in which he can view the contents but not the sides that hold the contents. He can neither determine the limits of consciousness, nor a divisibility of it. It is pure unity, pure spirit, indivisible and whole.

This view comes from looking into what one might call the "core" of oneself, since consciousness is prior to its content. The only being a person can look into the core of is himself. That core is called spirit, since spirit is by definition indivisible, unlimited, a simple unity. Through empathy a person discerns that in the emotions and actions of others lies the reflection of a consciousness which resembles his own. Through the same process and to a lesser extent, he also recognizes it in other forms of sentient life.

The fact that he does not see it in plants and inanimate objects does not convince him that their core is not in some way the same. They simply lack the means of behaving as a medium of expression articulating that core to the outer world. They neither think nor feel. But this does not mean that at the base of their nature there is an absence of that which either does, or at least can be, a potential means of doing so.

Spirit, being indivisible, must be one and the same everywhere. That which is whole and complete in an individual being must be whole and complete in all beings taken together. That is, there is but one single unity within and encompassing all things. It is also whole and complete in *each one* of those things.

25. The imperishable oneness. The will to be, to overcome, to survive, etc. is sometimes referred to as the survival instinct. But what is meant by it? Why should any creature wish to preserve itself as opposed to not doing so? Not to do so requires less effort, less pain, no attachment to things, and no cunning. Such detachment and indifference is therefore less likely to cause physical and psychological setbacks with their accompanying privations in circumstance and wounded sensibility.

So what drives life to push forward into life, rather than dropping out of it? Why should the hare run so hard, squeal so loud, when pursued and captured by a coyote? There must be something in its experience which commands it not to perish either in body or (were it human) in reputation. Something that

The Immaterial Structure of Human Experience

contradicts the material evidence of death and decay which lies open to experience.

That something is simple consciousness. Consciousness defies materiality. It cannot be divided, counted, measured out into proportions. It is this consciousness which supplies the manifold of human experience. So that which encompasses experience may be said to be greater than that which it encompasses.

Unlike the manifold of experience, consciousness demonstrates no proclivity towards limitation. A simple unity about which neither external limits nor divisible parts can be perceived, it appears to itself as indestructible. It is this consciousness and its apparent indestructibility which is associated with a person's sense of self.

Because of this, human beings in particular, with their conceptual awareness, find themselves in an attitude of defiance toward the reportage of sensible experience and toward the limited material expressions it represents. Accordingly, they are unable to accept an inevitable, but in important ways illusive, sense of descent towards perishability and oblivion.

26. The noumenal realm. The principal difficulty which an attempt at an understanding of the nature of spirit presents is the human tendency to use modes of thinking that belong to experience which is not spiritual. This is what Immanuel Kant would refer to as moving intellectually from the phenomenal to the noumenal realm.

Extension, duration, quantity, etc. belong to the phenomenal realm, that which is presented to human experience as limited. As a person can only form concepts in terms of limited phenomena, she cannot be certain as to how to form spiritual concepts. Nevertheless, though definitions drawn from such circumstances must be tentative, she tries. For it is better to grope with inadequate lighting than to abandon the search.

27. The paradoxical unity. A human being may be said to express the whole of universal spirit. Yet universal spirit's presence in each separate person would imply a division of some kind, much as the human race is divided into individuals. This presents a conceptual problem. So it must be asked how it is that the nature of both matter and spirit can be understood.

Matter can be defined as limited being, spirit as unlimited. Since matter is limited being, it can be seen that a human understanding of material reality might be the problem. With its appearance of division between one thing and another, the concept of this reality is in conflict with the concept of the unity of spirit. But perhaps the sense of limitation is simply an illusion. If so, it can be concluded with Parmenides and the *Upanishads* that the true nature of being is oneness.

But this is not a satisfactory conclusion for a contemporary Westerner to reach. With her emphasis on individuality and on the empirically verifiable nature of the material realm, she will not relinquish limitation. For example, she would not give up her right to a concrete, individual self. Nor would she be willing to do science without some assurance that what she is working on is both measurable and real.

But, since she may not wish to choose one alternative over the other, such a person might proclaim the dual and complementary nature of the material and the spiritual. She could then specify the limits of her ability to see one or the other. Together, she would say, they are like a mirror with its glass surface and reflective backing.

The Immaterial Structure of Human Experience

The reflective backing with its silver coating can be equated to the limits of her awareness. It stops the penetration of her vision and returns it to her. Thus she sees things in the limited terms of the material. The backing she does not see. If she did, she would see the whole, both glass and silver. That whole would be the nature of spirit.

Now there is only one glass and one backing. And together they are one. Perceived together they are spiritual awareness. But they can also be understood separately. The glass is her material awareness. And the backing is what puts a limit to that awareness. The backing might thus be referred to as the unknown spiritual foundation of the material.

When a person gazes into the glass, she does not see the same thing as another person. What each person sees differs according to the angle of her individual vision. Yet each of these perspectives is in itself an expression of the unified character of the mirror. For it takes the whole mirror to receive and reflect an image back to whomever may be looking into it. The mirror as a whole is universal spirit. So, understood in this way, each individual perspective is at once spiritual and individual.

Thus the limitation in a person's ability to see is not a fragmentation. For at each sighting she gets the whole expression of the mirror, of its glass and silver backing. Her vision is therefore spiritual in character but limited in such a way that it does not see all that spirit has to offer. Spirit within her, the backing, limits her vision. For this reason, her experience is limited to the material realm. And she believes herself to be limited in the same manner. This limited perspective is what is called material awareness. Material awareness causes someone like her to think of herself as materially limited.

In this illustration, the mirror is in fact the person who is aware of her own experience. What she sees when she looks into the mirror is the range of her experience. For, as a knowing person, she is both her awareness and her experience. If she could see through the whole mirror, including its backing, she would see what spirit sees. She would see what the mirror is, what spirit is, what she herself is. In other words, if she had full spiritual vision—if she could see all that spirit is as it is expressed through her individually—she would see herself as unlimited spirit.

28. The loss of the spiritual ground of being. Every human being is spirit. Without this being so, he or she would not exist. But humanity does not do well with a spiritual view of itself because a sense of limitation cuts it off from such a view. To recognize themselves as spirit, human beings must be able to see past the divided world reported to them by human sensibility. This unfragmented unity can only be discovered within consciousness.

But the material perspective which limits human sensibility seizes upon a person's attention and convinces him of divisiveness and alienation. Fear then permeates his being. And, in one fashion or another, self-preservation becomes his obsession. From that point, he can no longer see the wholeness of things. He is unable to have confidence in the spiritual ground of his being.

29. The search for transcendence and unity. Superstition is difficult to define, particularly in an age when spiritual life is considered by many to be a form of superstition. But there is a difference between spiritual life and superstition. Spirituality is a search for transcendence. It is an attempt to find that which is more permanent and unified than the flux of daily experience.

The Immaterial Structure of Human Experience

This is true of religion in general, even animistic religions. All at bottom are a search for spiritual transcendence and unity.

But superstition takes a different tack, often affecting an established religion. It is a kind of shunt between the desire for transcendent meaning and the need for a sense of security. By reaching out to take hold of something concrete, say an anthropomorphic representation of spirit, a person loses the transcendent meaning. When this is lost sight of, even for a moment, the result is superstition.

30. The sense of self and the conviction of the immutability of the self. Humankind is endowed with both a fundamental awareness and a conviction which do not express limitation. The awareness is an experience of self. And the conviction is a recognition of the immutability of that self. Human awareness is experienced as unlimited in character because it is consciousness. And simple consciousness is unlimited and indivisible.

It is the content of consciousness wherein all limited perceptions are experienced. But consciousness is not dependent upon its content. It is founded upon itself. In other words, human beings do experience a consciousness of limited things. But, insofar as human beings are referencing themselves, their consciousness is prior to those things of which they are conscious.

For the latter could not exist without the former. There could be no content of consciousness without a consciousness. Thus consciousness is not subordinate to the various perceptions of the mind. On the contrary, it is that which makes possible an awareness of the perceptions, since the perceptions are its content.

It is this simple consciousness then which grounds the sense of self. And it is also by means of this consciousness that a conviction of the immutability of that self is acquired. For there is a recognition that consciousness, being prior to its content, does not partake of the changeable character of its content. Consciousness is experienced as unlimited, indivisible being.

The Immaterial Structure of Human Experience

Section 3: The System

As discussed in the introduction, please note that in what follows two points of view will be considered alternately. The discussion will move from one to the other then back again, depending on the issue being discussed. Such a procedure is unavoidable, due to the fact that the two points of view represent different interrelated levels of consciousness, the one human, the other transcending human awareness.

These two levels of consciousness are human awareness and what will be referred to in the forthcoming discussion as secondary mind. Though a mature human being is not aware of the role of secondary mind, human consciousness is itself an expression of it. This is to say that it is grounded in secondary mind. It is a product of it.

For this reason, the perspective of secondary mind must be periodically invoked when elaborating upon the limits of human consciousness. For human consciousness and its content are an immediate expression of spirit (the primary mind which also expresses itself as secondary mind) and are therefore ideal in character.

But, when such a reference to the overall philosophical idealism of this discussion is not necessary, and when it is more expedient to elaborate on human mental processes from a human point of view, that human awareness may then be treated in a manner which does not appear to be idealist in character. Rather, the human mind will be made to appear to function in such a way as to create imaginative representations of an independent sensory experience.

As anyone knows, this is how human beings experience themselves and their world. They see the physical world as being independent of their subjective awareness. For, without deep reflection, they cannot acknowledge their intimate relationship with spirit. So the fact is that such an unreflective viewpoint precludes a full understanding of the total grounding of human experience in spirit. That is what this work attempts to rectify. It points out the means by which the transition between universal spirit and material human awareness involves an extraordinary transformation from the infinite to the finite.

31. Some preliminary concepts concerning how the mind works. This book is an attempt to develop a project in which a firm connection may be established between mind and matter. Accordingly, it begins with two philosophically idealist assumptions. These are: (1) mind in its fundamental character is spirit and (2) all that is known of matter is that which occurs within mind.

Matter is often conceived as that which a human being experiences through his senses. But a human being's perceptual capacity, as well as his powers of imagination, abstraction, and conceptualization, require the experience of spirit. For it is the experience of spirit which makes these faculties possible. Spirit, understood in this sense, is what is generally referred to as consciousness, or awareness.

An experience of spirit is not simply a capacity for being conscious, but must also involve an awareness of the character of consciousness. Such an awareness of the character of consciousness—i.e., an immediate and non-conceptual apprehension of the fundamental properties of consciousness—produces an intuition which accompanies and makes mental phenomena possible. For

The Immaterial Structure of Human Experience

this intuition is a sense of simple unity, which must lie at the foundation of all thought and of all but the most primitive perceptions. Thus this intuition is prior to and necessary for any form of figural representation or conceptualization to take place in the mind.

Accordingly, the full range of experience apprehended within the human mind must be conceived both in terms of the content of consciousness and in terms of spirit, or consciousness itself. When conceived independently, consciousness is the mind independent of its content. It can be experienced as such. Thus consciousness can be conceived as mind without reference to its content. It will be referred to as pure consciousness.

So consciousness and perception are things which can be conceived and contemplated by the mind as though they were independent of one another. But perception, conception, and contemplation cannot exist apart from consciousness. Whereas it is possible to put these elements of the content of consciousness out of mind. This allows consciousness to stand alone in human experience. It is thus prior to its content.

However, it is together that consciousness and the content of consciousness constitute a full range of human awareness. For this reason, and particularly since an experiential approach is being undertaken in this work, the project must be considered empirical in character. That is, it is empirical but more than sensory. For its empiricism must include consciousness as an element of experience.

At first glance, such a procedure does not appear to be unlike the approach of John Locke. For Locke's empirical approach encompasses what he calls "ideas," [4] which are derived both from

---

[4] John Locke, *An Essay Concerning Human Understanding,* Book II, Chap. I, 1 & 2, p. 121.

impressions received from sensation and from "the perception of the operations of our own mind within us." [5]

But he does not reduce the operations of the mind to consciousness, which is experienced as a simple, indivisible unity. Since consciousness is apprehended in this way—i.e., as a simple, indivisible unity—and since it is the only source for a sense of unity, such a recognition of its fundamental character functions as a mental framework for the intuition of simple unity.

Thus it is this intuition which provides a means for the unification of sensations in terms of mental representations of combined sensory experience. A common experience would be the taste, texture, and appearance of an apple. The taste, for example, may be experienced independently. But without further mental association in a unified image, it cannot be assimilated as experience. For the nature of any meaningful experience is that it is contextual in character.

So, by means of an association of sensations, the intuition of simple unity supplies unity to the elements of experience. These associations constitute independent objects or properties of objects, which are inscribed upon the mind by means of thought representations. Such initial elements of thought are images.

In either case, object or property, whichever is focused upon by mental attention, that is what is perceived as a thought image. For it is mental attention which focuses the sense of unity over a greater or lesser content. It is as if a person were to say, "I am conscious of all this," or "I am conscious of only that."

The properties of an object, when these properties are selected as independent thought images, may also be separated in the mind from the object and recombined with other properties to

---

[5] Ibid., 4, p. 121.

The Immaterial Structure of Human Experience

produce a new image. Thus the new image originates in the mind, but is composed of sensations derived from experience.

This is a secondary process of abstraction. For it is a compound abstraction from experience. First, a direct image is produced in the mind, no doubt leaving out a few details as a result of focus. [6] Hence the fact that it is an abstraction. Then a modified image is constructed from the properties of one or more of these direct images. This latter procedure can, if so desired, continue in an unlimited progression of imaginative reverie.

Representations in thought do not only involve images of single objects or properties. There may be collective representations as well, as is the case with a mental apprehension of several men or of several individual instances of human intelligence. Moreover, a thought can be about another thought. In other words, an apple may appear initially as an image in the mind, subsequent to which a person may contemplate the image itself as a mental representation.

But this process of abstraction, or mental distancing from direct experience, may ascend to a even more rarefied state. For, whether the properties of a thought image belong to a direct representation of experience, or whether these properties belong to a modified thought image, the image can be brought under the discipline of a definition by means of a precise accounting of certain of its properties. When this occurs, a concept is formed.

---

[6] Here is an example of the representational perspective as opposed to the idealist view. However, it should always be borne in mind that the idealist view predominates, even when it is ignored for the sake of expository clarity. Were the idealist view being expounded at present, it would have to account for those sensations which are supposedly omitted from the mental image. This would involve an immaterial explanation for sensation itself. Such an accounting can only be made at a level transcending human awareness. What this level transcending human awareness is will be explained further along in the work.

Now concepts can represent individuals, plurals, or universals, such as "a man," "several men," or "mankind" respectively. Individuals and plurals are simple concepts referring either to what is, or to what ostensibly could be, encountered in direct experience. But a universal, such as mankind, constitutes yet another level of abstraction.

It is an abstraction derived from individual and plural concepts. Thus the concept, "mankind," refers to "a man" and "several men" universally—that is, in specific recognition of the conceptual, or definitional, properties belonging to them. In other words, these properties are recognized as being held in common by all instances of that type. A universal cannot therefore be encountered in direct experience, except by a recognition of its definitional relation to the specific referents from which it is derived.

So, regarding such examples of the flexibility of mental focus as have been given, a person may (1) refer to an object as an object, or (2) to a thought as a thought, or (3) to several objects or thoughts, or (4) to a property or several properties of one or more objects, or (5) to the universe of objects and thoughts, or (6) to a universe of one or more properties.

Thus he may consider (1) a man, (2) his thought about that man, or (3) several such men or the thoughts about them. Or (4) he may consider what that individual man's or several men's characteristics are. Or (5) he may consider all men as such (as in mankind) or the totality of thoughts about the latter (as in human knowledge of mankind). Or (6) he may consider one or more of the properties of mankind as a general property in itself, as when he contemplates human intelligence in general.

All this depends upon the application of mental focus in the exercise of the intuition of unity. Thus it is the intuition of simple unity which supports the character of mental operations which

The Immaterial Structure of Human Experience

contribute to the structure both of material experience (the mental representations of associated sensations derived directly from experience) and more complex and varied thought about that experience.

Now, when referring to the content of consciousness, it does not matter whether that content be understood in terms of physical experience or in terms of the perceived operations of the mind which organize sensation into associated representations which are designated as thought. For, whether it be considered as physical experience or as thought representations of that experience, what is being considered is the content of consciousness.[7]

Not only is pure consciousness held to be independent of and prior to this content. The intuition of simple unity, grounded in the nature of consciousness and intimately associated with it, is also held to be independent of and prior to the mind's content. For this intimate association between consciousness and the intuition results from the fact that the intuition arises from consciousness spontaneously experiencing itself.

Thus the intuition is immediate in experience and prior to any mental operation. It is not imagined or thought about. It simply is. For it is a fundamental characteristic of self-limiting universal spirit, which is the progenitor of the human mind. The self-limiting of universal spirit is that which separates the finitude of human awareness from the infinitude of spirit. But this is not to say that these are two different things. It is only to assert that they appear to be so.

Self-limiting universal spirit is what confines the operations of the individual human mind to a specific content. Thus the specific content of human consciousness is constricted in both its

---

[7] Will, feeling, and emotion are more complex matters which will be discussed later.

inclusiveness and in the individual character of its perceptions and representations. In this way, the human mind is rendered finite in awareness.

So it can be seen that, in creating these limitations through the imposition of focus, self-limiting universal spirit is limiting itself. One could say it becomes incarnate. And the fact that *infi*nite (i.e., *not* finite) spirit is given a carnal character implies that it assumes a character of finitude. Understood in this way, the limited, finite human mind is nevertheless universal spirit operating under self-imposed limitations.

This transformation is accomplished by means of spirit's, and likewise the human mind's, exercise of focus, a focus turned in upon spirit, making it an individual limited mind, while turning it away from a universal perspective. In other words, the human mind's range of awareness is limited through the limitation of its content. It is this limitation which provides the human mind with a sensory content which is finite in character.

So, be it either pure consciousness, focus, or the intuition of simple unity (which is focus exercised *within* the limitations of human awareness), it is understood to be independent of the mind's content. Thus neither consciousness nor its intuition are dependent. It is the mind's content which is so. For there is nothing of which consciousness is aware which is not contained within it and known only through it.

Therefore, in addition to the location of any content of awareness in awareness itself, it is focus, both prior to and subsequent to its becoming the intuition of simple unity, which circumscribes whatever constitutes the content by means of its limiting of perception both in part and in whole. For each sensory

The Immaterial Structure of Human Experience

perception[8] (or percept) is experienced as finite, either individually or in association with other percepts. Consequently, the sum total of what can be materially experienced must be assumed to be finite, insofar as may be determined from its constituent elements.

Altogether then, consciousness, its exercise of focus, and its employment of focus as an intuition are closely allied to one another in being prior to and independent of the mind's content. For they are responsible for the sense of finitude in human experience and are not themselves subject to it. They are only perceived to be finite because of the mind's limited content. Freed from this content, human consciousness would assume the unlimited dimensions of universal, infinite spirit.

Moreover, since the content of the human mind cannot be apprehended independently of consciousness, it cannot be independent of universal spirit. Rather, as indicated above, a human mind is universal spirit compartmentalized. In other words, it is a product of universal spirit compartmentalizing itself in order to create individual entities (conscious and otherwise) which are nevertheless each grounded in its fullness.

But, since this is so, it is not only the case that the sensory content of human experience cannot be understood to exist apart from consciousness. Neither can this sensory content be assimilated to human understanding without an exercise of the intuition of simple unity. For the human mind's operations are an expression of the intuition of simple unity's handling of mental content.

So, given the fact that this intuition is founded upon the capacity of consciousness, or spirit, to recognize its own character as a simple unity and apply that character by means of an exer-

---

[8] "Sensory perception" is here and elsewhere employed simply in the meaning of "that which is perceived." It does not indicate the use of physical senses.

cise of mental focus on perceptual content, the human power of an imposition of simple unity upon phenomena is understood to be an immediate exercise of consciousness itself. It is not a result of intellectual awareness.

Human consciousness, then, is the sole source of an immediate intuition which is independent of the mind's content. Moreover, as this intuition is closely allied to consciousness—being a veritable act of that consciousness—it can be understood to be a function of self-limiting spirit. And, if the spiritual view itself were to be taken under consideration, then the mind's sensory content must also be understood to be dependent upon a universal consciousness which is beyond human awareness. For all things are an expression of spirit.

Nevertheless, this is not the same thing as saying that, within human experience, the mind's content cannot be understood by the mind to exist apart from its consciousness. For quotidian events do appear to posit an objective realm, separate from the mind. Rather, it is saying that, in a manner which is prior to human awareness, the mind's content originates in spirit, which is the very ground of human awareness. Thus reality, both subjective and objective, is ultimately one in spirit, however it may be perceived within the limitations of a human mind.

Moreover, it is within the context of human awareness that the intuition of simple unity, as a necessary constructive element converting immediate sensory perception into thought representations, must be seen to constitute a foundation for any form of thinking (i.e., for imagination, concept development, and reason). For it undergirds the representational perception of sensation.

Without this imaginative representation, placing images of associated sensations before the mind, sensation could not be understood to be experienced as objective in character. For there

The Immaterial Structure of Human Experience

would be no mental illusion of a separation between subject and object, the mind believing a sensory object to have supplied the percepts of the image. Nor, upon such objective circumstances being accepted as valid, could sensation be understood to be experienced in any but a fundamentally disparate and meaningless manner, until gathered into a mental image.

But all this is the mind's belief, not its character. Not only the intuition of simple unity, which makes thought representations possible, but the content of consciousness is a direct product of consciousness. Both originate in spirit. The content does so because, unbeknownst to human awareness, consciousness is the source of the elements of sensation in its awareness. Consequently, the sum total of awareness may be understood to lie within consciousness. Thus consciousness, as the ground of the thought forming intuition of simple unity, together with its content, is what completes the perceptual and the conceptual activities of the human mind.

For this reason, it can be said that consciousness not only is, it encompasses. Moreover, it acts within the domain of its encompassment. Thus consciousness is more than a ground of human awareness, a whiteboard upon which something might be written in erasable marker. It is the dynamic of that awareness, creating its content, limiting that content, and making possible an assimilation of the result to an understanding rendered limited and finite by these very same activities of spiritual and mental focus.

Hence, consequent to the mind's limiting of its own content is its sense of finitude. For this reason, human understanding does not apprehend the full creative role of consciousness, or spirit. And that is why human consciousness must be referenced to spirit, yet appear to stand apart from it. For intellectually it does not know its origin.

In addition to these fundamental operations of the mind, human consciousness, as the source of the intuition of simple unity, must also be seen as being responsible for the creation of a sense of space and time. That is, it must be seen as such from a representational viewpoint. For, from this viewpoint, associated sensations become extensions when represented to the mind as images. Thus space and time only exist for sentient purposes. They do not pertain to spirit.

So it is by means of its construction of the extensions both of the mental representations of material objects and of more complex thoughts, that the intuition of unity may be understood to establish a mutual exclusion of objects and thoughts from one another. Accordingly, because these extensions are individually differentiated associations of sensation in mental experience, they are mutually exclusive and must compound to create space.

Such a differentiation among associations of sensation also helps to emphasize (though not originate) a sense of differentiation among individual sensations. For individual sensations of a particular kind must exist apart from one another in order to exist together with other sensations in separate extensions. However, these individual sensations are not extensions. So they do not constitute building blocks of space. Rather, they are the sensory elements of those extensions which do.

Now a recognition of change is dependent upon the existence of space. For change is relational in character. A change in a property within an extension of space expresses an alteration in the character of an object. A change between the extensions of space (i.e., a change of relative position between objects) constitutes motion. Thus changes occur both within and between the

The Immaterial Structure of Human Experience

extensions of space. It is these which make possible a measurable perception of time. For measurable time is an expression of change.

Therefore, in light of these considerations, it cannot be overemphasized that objects are experienced as representations in the mind. The representations are thoughts. And thoughts are extensions in the mind. For it is these mental representations of sensation which are figured forth as extended images. And it is these extended images which are believed to be physical objects in objective space.

But, when thoughts themselves are considered as thoughts, where the emphasis is not upon what they represent, they must be conceived simply as extensions in time. For, though each thought represents an association of sensory elements, it either precedes or follows another thought and cannot coexist with it, as would be the case in physical space.

Thus a thought extension cannot be compounded with another and be held to occupy physical space. However, in spite of this fact, a thought may, in a certain sense—i.e., as an extension—be referred to as an extension of mental space. For, though when considered as a thought it does not participate in an objective physical domain, it is experienced as occupying a space in the mind.

Thoughts are composed of sensations. The associated sensations within a thought are the object of that thought. So, because a thought is composed of sensations, its object is understood to represent an entity or property of an entity which either is or could be in the physical domain. For it is either directly or by indirection (thoughts representing other thoughts which represent things), that thoughts are understood to represent physical objects.

This understanding of their physical origin is reinforced by the seemingly independent character of material events. For material events cannot be altered with such ease as thoughts in the mind. They are therefore assumed to exhibit an existential priority. And sensations are assumed to arise originally from an encounter with physical objects. But this distinction is a necessary illusion, the peculiar character of which will be explained in due course.

So, given the foregoing paragraphs, it can be seen that neither space nor time are intuitions. Rather, space is a mental construct of the intuition of simple unity working upon individual sensations to create a domain composed of extended entities of associated sensations. And, though time in its most fundamental form is a more subtle element than measureable time, it is nonetheless closely allied to the manner of presentation of the sensory content of the mind.

Measureable time arises from relations among spatial extensions (i.e., physical entities), each extension originating in an association of percepts (or sensations). But the most fundamental form of time is that which accompanies the mind's recognition of individual sensations before any awareness of associations among them emerges.

It is expressed in terms of variations in the initial presentation of sensory data. For the mental apprehension of each percept of sensation, as it is recognized in distinction from the next, is necessarily sequential, since one must be acknowledged prior to the next by the limiting faculty of mental focus.

At such a primary level in the presentation of sensation, time is expressed without regard to spatial extension. Rather, it is prior to it, and thus prior to the manner in which a mature human mind

The Immaterial Structure of Human Experience

experiences its world. For a mature human mind experiences a world of space and measurable time.

Thus the most fundamental form of time is neither presented to the mind in terms of images nor conceptually recognized in human understanding. However, it can be deliberately configured in imagination for the purpose of such a discourse as this. Otherwise, it would not be spoken of here.

So, at the level of human awareness, another expression of time is necessary to make it recognizable. This is its measurable form, which is an indirect product of sensations being presented to the mind in a continuously varying order. In other words, sensations are not delivered to the mind repeatedly in the same order without exception. If they were, no changes would occur in human experience. For human awareness, this variation is reflected among the extensions of space. Spatial entities occur, change, and depart from human awareness.

Extensions in space are derived from associations of percepts (sensations). These associations occur in the initial presentation of percepts. So it is a variation in the order of presentation of associations of percepts which changes a spatial extension in its spatial relationship to another spatial extension. This is motion as it is generally observed. It is observed as such because the associations of percepts are immediately transformed by the mind into the extensions of space. It is this transformed state which constitutes mature human experience.

In a similar but more subtle manner, each variation in the presentation of percepts *within* an association of percepts alters the character of the association and thus the character of its expression as an extension. Wood burning or water transforming into ice are examples of this. As a result of both these kinds of modifications, there is a correlative expression in the relations of time. For its measure is determined by a recognition of these changes.

In any case, the fact remains that it is the associations of sensation which govern the character of their expression as spatial extensions. For the relationship between a particular association of percepts and its representation in a corresponding spatial extension does not change. They are one and the same, differing only in their manner of expression in the mind.

Thus the fundamental form of time, which is registered in the initial presentation of sensation, is indirectly expressed in measurable time. But, because the spatial extensions are arranged differently from the initial lineal presentation of the associations of percepts, measurable time is perceived somewhat differently from the fundamental form of time.

The principal point being brought under scrutiny here is that the intuition of simple unity is prior to imaginative representation and concept formation and their consequents. This means it is prior to a recognition of space and measurable time. For this reason, it is neither space nor time, but the intuition of simple unity alone which resembles Immanuel Kant's intuitions of space and time.[9] For the intuition of simple unity, which is mental focus, creates the sequence of percept presentation which brings about the fundamental sense of time. And the intuition of simple unity also forms, or isolates, the associations of sensation which become the extensions of space.

As has been shown in this discussion, consciousness is highly versatile. It is no dead thing receiving life from what might be played out upon it. For it is spirit. So, as the ground of the intuition of simple unity, it not only makes imaginative representation

---

[9] Immanuel Kant, *The Critique of Pure Reason*.

The Immaterial Structure of Human Experience

and concept formation, and thus thought, possible. It gives thought its means for classification.

In making possible the formation of mental images and in supporting the abstraction of concepts from those images, it is consequently responsible for the logical workings of thought. For a concept is a classification. And so are propositions and systems of thought. Each of the latter can be conceptually summarized—i.e., brought under a concept. So logical operations are further developments in classification. In other words, the operations of the intuition of simple unity are prior to what Locke referred to as "the operations of our minds."[10]

The intuition of simple unity is instrumental in perception (which involves the presentation of images in the mind), image formation beyond perception, concept formation, and logical operations expanding the use and interrelationship of concepts. For these are all combinative operations forming unities.

This is no more than to say that the process of an abstraction of sensations to an image, and then a further abstraction to a single classification, and finally to broader classifications demands a prior intuition of unity which is needed to combine these sensations in an image, abstract an image into a more rigorous combination which is a concept, and bring concepts together in the elaborate logical operations of classification. The image or the classification of whatever level is thus an expression of that intuition of unity.

Now, overall, the aforementioned intuition of unity makes possible Kant's first three transcendental categories, which are gathered under the heading, "Of Quantity."[11] These are: unity,

---

[10] John Locke, *An essay Concerning Human Understanding,* Bk II, Ch I, 4, p. 121.
[11] Immanuel Kant, *The Critique of Pure Reason*, p. 42.

plurality, and totality. They do operate within the mind as means of perception and classification, which is the role Kant gives them. But they are intuitions, not categories. For Kant's first three categories are no more than the intuition of simple unity operating under three modes.

The first mode is simple unity. The other two are subtle variations of the first. The intuition of unity recognizes simple unity. In addition, it recognizes that any such unity is a form of limitation. For it has focused upon this and not that. Yet it may also focus upon that and not this. As a consequence, the same intuition, functioning as an intuition of plurality, is enabled to recognize a multiplicity of focus by means of a juxtaposition of limitations. It thus recognizes a plurality. Again, operating as an intuition of totality, it recognizes greater unity in a plurality of unities. Thus the greater unity is a totality of the lesser.

Consequently, all three must be referred to as intuitions and not categories. Moreover, there are no more intuitions than these three. For Kant's first three categories are conceptual reflections of these intuitions. And his other nine categories can be accounted for in terms of the first three, understood as intuitions. [12]

The material content of consciousness is comprised of sensations, or percepts. [13] Percepts provide the matter of human experience. They are what is associated within spatial extensions, which is to say that they are what is abstracted to imaginative imagery and classified in concepts. For in either case, image or con-

---

[12] No argument will be made here as to whether Kant's categories are sufficient to cover all mental operations. It is enough that they stand in illustration of them.

[13] Henceforward, sensations shall with increasing frequency be referred to as percepts. The designation, "percept," emphasizes the fact that what appear to be sensations emanating from a thing-in-itself are in this philosophy considered to be mental phenomena.

The Immaterial Structure of Human Experience

cept, a thought is extended in time and may in a certain sense be said to be extended in mental space.

So it can be seen that the term "matter" may at times refer to thought as well as to an objective realm. This applies, of course, when a thought image is directly representing a perception. In such a case, the thought is the perception. And the thing perceived is a thought. Thus a distinction between matter and thought simply indicates an emphasis.

Since it does not appear evident that Kant pursued his transcendental analytic beyond the logical categories, other than to have previously posited intuitions of space and time and to make some reference to a unity of consciousness, the present work, in its search for mental origins, is forced to deviate considerably from his perspective.

As has already been indicated, this must be done particularly in regard to the three closely integrated intuitions of simple unity, plurality, and totality, since their assertion as independent categories would produce an untenable divide between spirit (i.e., mind) and body. For the categories act as a backstop beyond which any probing into the origins of mind can go no further.

Moreover, to assert that space and time are intuitions, and thus independent of representations, causes a conceptual dilemma because such independent intuitions as this cannot be accounted for in experience. They cannot be referenced to awareness without further qualification. For the questions arise: where do they originate, and of what do they consist?

In both these objections to Kant's position, the dilemma is that of the old Cartesian divide between mind and body, as yet unsatisfactorily reconciled in philosophy. [14] It is, of course, a

---

[14] René Descartes, *Discourse on the Method of Rightly Conducting the Reason* and *Meditations on First Philosophy*.

problem that is of deep concern in the present work, since this work seeks to construct a comprehensive empirical foundation for philosophy.

So it is from a concern with this divide that a broadened empirical approach arises, an approach sufficiently enlarged to encompass consciousness as a form of experience equally valid along with that of the senses. This approach allows a person to conceive a human being as an integral part of the totality of human experience.

Human beings can therefore be conceived as products of nature, differing from nature's other sentient life forms only in a matter of degree but not kind. Thus conceived, they are in one sense material. But it can also be maintained that they are spirit, though only inasmuch as it is understood that the concept of spirit is sufficiently enlarged to include matter.

However, this does not mean that matter is a part of spirit or that spirit is a part of matter. These are mutually exclusive means of understanding the same phenomena of experience, which may be spoken of either in terms of matter or spirit. But neither does this imply a parallel equivalence between matter and spirit, in which both are individual attributes differentiated from one another while each arises from and expresses an identical source.

So these two modes of experience, matter and spirit, do not resolve themselves into the dual attributes of Benedict de Spinoza's pantheistic vision. [15] If they did, such a vision would restore the unity of experience. But it would also unnecessarily preclude the possibility of a free will and of an independent personal relationship with spirit. An alternative solution to this problem is what will be further elucidated within the text of this work.

---

[15] Benedict de Spinoza, *Ethics*.

The Immaterial Structure of Human Experience

32. The immaterialist perspective. If one should begin from a perspective based on the material limitations of human awareness, it can be said that human beings are animals. They are a product of nature. Any perceptual or conceptual response a human being exhibits toward the physical world—that is, any expression of a person's faculties, including her intellect—is limited by that physical world.

At best, her intellectual response to the physical world is a template thrown over it, a template which is itself a construction limited by the physical world. Yet it is neither a full expression of that physical world, nor does it apprehend the completeness of reality. There are in both cases relations which cannot be fully determined by the human intellect.

The fact that much of the physical world escapes human awareness may be illustrated by the following problem. No human being can fully grasp the relationship between motion and location. Hence the need for a calculus to minimize such a discrepancy. This calculus is used at the macrophysical level in calculations concerning motion. Distance, which involves location, is inherently involved in motion. But a particular location for a moving object cannot be designated (except by a very close approximation) so long as the motion of that object is understood to be in progress.

Likewise, there is also a need for a mathematical science of probability. One of its many functions is to establish a connection between momentum and location at the microphysical level. Thus it can be seen that the relationship between motion and location remains problematic throughout the physical world.[16]

---

[16] These statements are being made for illustrative purposes. They will be addressed in greater detail elsewhere.

According to these examples, physical reality may be seen to be elusive in particular circumstances. But the fact that reality transcends human awareness altogether may be expressed by the inaccessibility of future events. These events remain stubbornly indeterminate. They are referred to as potential, rather than actual. For this reason, the need for a mathematical science like probability becomes apparent once again. It is by means of this science that the rationally inexplicable may be reduced to fit within comfortable parameters.

Take the problem of determining the behavior of gases. In such a case, what might have remained uncertain is comfortably replaced by what is probable. Thus the law of entropy as it relates to the behavior of gasses. Here, through the use of probability, the macrophysical and microphysical worlds are brought into a measure of accord with one another.

Hence, through uncertainties of this kind, there emerges a reality which stands mysterious and unapproachable beyond human awareness. A few of its relations and events may be brought under a partial domestication, as has been suggested above. But the whole remains inscrutable. However, let it be said that what is being considered is not Kant's noumenal world. For other than as represented by the potential experience, or expectation, of a human perceiver, it cannot be asserted by a human being that such a world exists.

Human beings may predict events with varying degrees of accuracy. But they cannot guarantee their occurrence. In short, there is no such entity as a thing-in-itself lying inert just out of reach of human consciousness. There is no quasi-material reality subsisting independently of awareness. But there is something expressive of potential, albeit that this reality may not be proximate to human awareness.

The Immaterial Structure of Human Experience

To state this as George Berkeley argued it in *The Principles of Human Knowledge,* there is nothing that exists which is not known to a mind, whether that mind be a human consciousness or the universal mind that is spirit. Thus what is not proximate to human awareness, must yet subsist in spirit if it is to exist at all.

So the question which must be asked is, can the distance between these two realms ever be bridged—i.e., the conceptual distance between material experience and that which transcends it? As a minor illustration of this problem, it might be asked, can a bumblebee see a yellow flower as a human being does? Or conversely, can a human being see what a bumblebee sees: an ultraviolet flower instead of yellow?

It is evident that neither can transcend its material limitations. Yet a human being can think ultraviolet, while it is assumed the bee cannot. What is this thinking that a human being does? And how is it that she does it? In other words, how is it that she can think the existence of something she does not experience? How does she think at all?

Human beings are conscious beings. Let it be assumed that the bee is also. Is consciousness thinking? Clearly it is not. It is simple awareness. Then what is thinking? Let it be assumed that thinking is a process, or at least one expression of the processes, by which an organism internalizes environmental relations. If thinking is defined in this broad way—that is, simply as an internalizing process—then under such a heading can be included much that is not normally considered thinking.

The processes involved in the absorption of nutrients, metabolism, and growth are means by which an organism internalizes its environment. Yet it is not assumed that a plant can think. The movements of an organism also appear to take energy, or the power of producing change, from the physical world to place it at the disposal of the organism.

An organism can move itself. It can create change of place without an immediate reliance upon something else first imposing that change upon it. A woman can walk of her own will. And she can build a fire. In building a fire, she not only takes possession of the process of change, but controls the power of producing it. For a fire produces change in other things.

A bird can follow a migratory route, build a nest, or care for its young without having been taught. But this is not thought. It is instinct. Yet instinct is like frozen thought. For, though it is not a fluid process, since it remains unaltered for extended periods of time, it can on occasion be modified by the organism which possesses it.

New habits may be learned, such as a new migration route for birds. And these may be acquired as new instincts which displace the old, much as one thought replaces another. Most importantly, this can be accomplished in a few generations—much too quickly to be considered a product of a blind physical process, such as random variation.[17]

So what is meant by higher thought—that is, reasoning? Many animals appear to reason in varying degrees of similitude to human beings. A young wolf learns to associate the smell of a rabbit with the satisfaction of a meal. In time, it also learns the evasive habits of rabbits. So, when in adult life it encounters the scent of a rabbit, it recalls and sequentially associates these learned responses. Thus it can be said that the wolf thinks a cer-

---

[17] The older Darwinian, or Lamarckian, use of the term "acquired" is employed here. This is opposed to a neo-Darwinian emphasis upon a strict regimen of mutation and natural selection. More on this will be discussed elsewhere.

The Immaterial Structure of Human Experience

tain detected odor—that of the rabbit—will be followed by the possibility of a range of evasive behavioral options on the part of that rabbit. Furthermore, these, if carefully attended to, may lead to the satisfaction of a meal.

Need this series of likely events become a chain of language or symbols in the animal's mind before it can be labeled reason? More to the point, need these symbols become logically ordered concepts? If the process which takes place in the wolf's mind is assumed to be no more than an associative chain of images, it nevertheless resembles what generally happens in the human mind prior to a logical reorganization of such thought.

In many everyday situations, human beings associate images charged with emotional significance. Guided in this chain of thought both by an associative relationship between images and by their comparative emotional weight, a human being will arrive at an end of the chain, having made her selection.

Then, recollecting the train of thought which has just taken place, she will convince herself she has reasoned, as if the original chain of thought had been a logical process. She will most likely reorganize and replay this train of thought to herself in logical form, as though it had been a logical chain of reasoning from the beginning.

Nevertheless, though human thinking may often prove not to be a logical process, human beings do reason in more complex ways than one is accustomed to associate with other animals. Reason itself then—i.e., logical thinking—is what is at issue in any discussion of the internalization of environmental relations by human beings.

While most organisms appear to specialize in internalizing this or that group of environmental relations, including, among the more highly organized sentient organisms, making use of mental processes of association, human beings specialize in the process of internalization itself. That is, they become reflective concerning the matter. They know they are thinking. And they think about the fact that they are thinking and about what its possible consequences might be. This is what is called higher thought. And it is what is generally meant by thinking.

Hence human disappointment in other animals, which appear to reason but fail to make a point of doing so. But what further complicates the issue is that such a large proportion of humanity also refuses to do so. For most human beings, reasoning is simply a means of functioning advantageously within an environment. It is not an intentional means of organizing environmental relations within themselves. This is done only by the few. Yet these few have become the definition of the race. They are Homo sapiens: rational man. Thus people call themselves reasoning beings.

At issue is an examination of how this higher thought process might have come about. However, it is not necessary to pause at this point to examine the prehistoric development of the species. For this is beyond the scope of the present discussion. What lies open to immediate examination is the mind of a human being in its existing state.

The problem is how to understand this mind. So, as was the case in the previous essay, an examination must be made by looking directly into it. For it is by searching into the human mind that both the things which are known and the means by which they are known will be discovered. Keeping at the center of this search the idea that these two things must be intimately related, each can come to be understood in terms of the other.

Neither reason nor nature should be enthroned, one at the expense of the other. For reason is not prior to nature. It is, at least in part, a product of nature. For in common human experi-

The Immaterial Structure of Human Experience

ence both the causal and logical relations of reason may be understood to parallel physical events, where experience appears to teach that causal relations hold. Moreover, logical relations appear to be structured much like these causal relations. So this certainly indicates at best a complex interrelationship between human experience and the workings of the human mind.

Yet, inasmuch as all human experience appears exclusively in consciousness, which is an expression of spirit, nature itself must be understood to be a product of universal mind, or spirit. This is not to say that it is equivalent to universal spirit, though in practical terms it is often considered to be synonymous with human awareness as human beings experience it.

In other words, physical nature is generally thought to be the cause of human awareness. For much that is encountered in consciousness can be affected by physical manipulations of the brain. However, were this equivalence between the mind and physical processes truly the case, it would require an omission of the important role of consciousness in structuring human awareness. That role has been given a brief explanation in the previous essay.

So, on the one hand, it should be asked, by what other means could human beings know the physical world than through their minds—i.e., through consciousness, or spirit? Do they know anything beyond their own minds? If they do not know anything beyond their own minds, nature cannot be predominant over spirit.

On the other hand, if nothing spiritual should be assumed in directly accounting for the operations of the human mind, if everything concerning the human mind can be understood in terms of physical nature, how else could this mind apprehend its world but in such a manner that it is itself a derivative expression of that world? In other words, viewed in this way, reason must be considered to be a product of the biosphere.

The mind would thus be at best only an indirect product of spirit. Spirit is responsible for the material. But the mind, being a product of the material, is indirect in its relationship to spirit. Thus it does not transcend the material in any way. In fact, it does not even quite come up to it. For human knowledge is generally assumed to fall short of human experience, even when that experience is considered only in material terms.

So, given the present influence of scientific materialism on the public outlook,[18] it is understood by most people that human beings are material creatures. This point of view is held in regard to most of their affairs, even when they profess a religious view which conflicts with the general outlook. Consequently, as a result of this outlook, they live with a sense of limitation and fear—a dread of annihilation—which further testifies to the true character of their understanding.

This sense of impending annihilation is derived from a recognition of the perceived all-encompassing material condition, a situation in which everything in their experience, including themselves, is found to be limited and subject to change. The inevitable result must be an eventual reduction of every individual existence to extinction by means of the ascendancy of other things in their turn.

Yet at the same time a person senses something different within herself. That something different is the simple unity of an indivisible, immaterial consciousness, which, being unlimited, is

---

[18] This is an influence George Berkeley battled against three hundred years ago. He was not successful, both because he was misunderstood and because more analysis was needed to support and clarify his position. This further development of the immaterialist perspective is what the present work attempts to supply.

The Immaterial Structure of Human Experience

imperishable and therefore spirit. Having thus recognized consciousness as spirit, a person finds herself to be grounded in spirit. So she can go on to indulge an extended inference.

By means of that extended inference, she can begin to recognize within all things, particularly other human beings and all sentient forms of life, a spiritual ground of being. In each case, this spiritual ground of being is concurrent with the material expression of being. So together these two perspectives, material and spiritual, express the full range of her experience. Whereas either one of them alone falls short of this completeness.

It is in this way that a person may begin to philosophize in the manner which is being done here. For, when considered in terms of spirit, each existent thing may be conceived to be an expression of something common to others, as all are expressed within one unity of spirit. But this idea can only be entertained so long as it is not assumed that each individual being is compromised by others in its unique character. The possibility of the absence of such a conflict arises from the fact that the perceived individual character of each material being is understood to be a product of the material view. This view is opposed to the spiritual.

So the spiritual view is monist in character. But the material view is not. It is necessarily fragmented. Accordingly, spirit, which is an unlimited unity expressing the ground of existence, cannot be encompassed by the material view, which in all its manifestations is an expression of limitation. Spirit is thus conceived to be fully present in each material thing. Moreover, there is only one universal spirit, wholly present in each, as well as wholly present in all.

The apparent paradox of this latter point could not be maintained within a material perspective. There a single entity cannot be wholly present both in one thing and in all things simultaneously. For it is the essence of the material perspective that one thing obtains its individual being by excluding and thus limiting another. This is the character of finitude.

So how does the material perspective come about? What is the source of the experience of limitation? Spirit, since it is not finite, can only be limited by itself. This is accomplished by means of a focus of universal mind. For mind, any mind, in its fundamental character, is an expression of spirit. Thus it is the self-limitation of spirit which brings about the material mind.

But this introduces a problem. It is a problem of immaterialism in general, which is that it presents the possibility of the commission of a solipsism. At least, this is what many people conceive to be a problem with immaterialism. For there is a suggestion, albeit false, that an immaterialist view of reality implies that the material does not exist. In other words, if the physical world were conceived to be contained only in a single human mind, it could not be accepted as existing collectively and coordinately in multiple human minds.

On the other hand, if human consciousness should be conceived to be an epiphenomenon of the material world, as some materialists would have it, this consciousness would appear to be nothing more than an illusion. Given such a circumstance, human beings could not truly be understood to exist independently as mind. They would be utterly determined and without free will.

Since from a practical standpoint human beings are incapable either of denying the reality of the physical world or of denying the reality of themselves as knowing, free-will beings, and since a duality between mind and spirit offends the human desire for a single, unified explanation of reality, a way must be found to accept both interpretations and allow them to support a single

The Immaterial Structure of Human Experience

system of thought. As will be demonstrated, that acceptance does involve a complex form of immaterialism, one which will neither infringe upon the practice of science nor the maintenance of moral responsibility.

33. Preliminary definitions.

Primary Mind. Primary mind is universal spirit. It is characterized by actuality, or being. However, in relation to human experience much of its activity is characterized as potential, since the future is unknown to people. A simple analogy for the activity of primary mind might be found in a contemporary theory of the behavior of gases in a closed system.

The specific whereabouts of individual molecules cannot be determined, though the behavior of the collective whole can be. Yet the activity of the whole is dependent upon the behavior of each individual member of that whole. Likewise, in regard to matter and spirit, natural events appear to human intelligence to be expressed in some semblance of an order. But a possible means of human intelligence explaining that order in reference to its source is completely lacking. For the activity of spirit is inaccessibly more complex than the elements of human experience.

This analogy is of course, merely a human representation, reflecting the material limitations of the human mind. Although it is only natural that the human mind should seek analogies for spirit, it cannot be understood in material terms. Thus the "relations of its parts"—if such a material expression may be pardoned—are incomprehensible to the human mind.

Yet the human experience of spirit is daily and intimate. It is the experience of a person's own consciousness without reference to the content of that consciousness. For this reason, when described in terms of an analogy to human consciousness, primary mind might be thought of as universal consciousness. Such an analogy is supported by the recognition that consciousness is without material bounds and is therefore indivisible.

That is to say, consciousness is not extended within what is generally thought of as the material world. This unbounded, indivisible character is the general nature of spirit, be it universal consciousness or human consciousness. Universal consciousness is, of course, a speculative extension of human consciousness. It cannot be directly apprehended. But it is not an unwarranted conceptual extension, considering the lack of satisfactory alternative means of accounting for the experience of human consciousness.

Nevertheless, to be fair, a possible material explanation for human consciousness ought to be briefly considered. It could be said that there is a general electro-chemical activity in the human brain which "surrounds" or accompanies whatever more specific electro-chemical activity the brain is focused upon. This surrounding activity is felt as an environment within which the focused activity occurs. Thus the surrounding activity is experienced as an envelope of consciousness.

The problem with this explanation is that it supports a conceptual circularity which leads to a deterministic conclusion. It works as follows. The human capacity for grasping a unity, such as the environmental condition just described, cannot be explained unless such a unity is presupposed. That presupposition must be innate, *a priori*, or prior to material experience. Thus the simple unity of consciousness is prior to the experience of any material unity which may be described.

If one were to go on to say that the collective material environment of synapses in the brain creates consciousness and thus the felt sense of simple unity, which in turn allows human beings to apprehend the material unity, such reasoning fails. For the

The Immaterial Structure of Human Experience

mind cannot be demonstrated to experience such a physical unity qua unity as it does the unity of the mental state of consciousness.

But if this reasoning should be accepted, it could then be said that consciousness is an illusion derived from material circumstances. It is no more than an epiphenomenon. However, it must be conceded that this would not be an unlikely explanation of consciousness, if it did not lead to a further problem. It supports a strictly material explanation. And, as such, it precludes the concept of free will. The lack of such a concept undermines any assumption of moral responsibility.

If there is no moral responsibility, then why should human beings care about civilization, ethics, philosophy, science, or anything else? They should allow one another to be left to graze in bovine peace. Unfortunately, without moral responsibility or concern, and given the fact that human beings are not a peaceful species, such neglect would most likely cause them to do more harm to one another than they presently do. And the harm they presently do is already more than is good for them.

Secondary Mind. From the human point of view, primary mind becomes secondary mind. Secondary mind is not perceived as such by human awareness. But it forms the basis for human awareness. Thus, if it is looked at conceptually from a human perspective, secondary mind may be understood as primary mind conceived in terms of change. It may also be referred to as *the dynamic*. For change is a dynamic.

Pure consciousness, considered only in terms of itself and not in terms of its content, is primary mind. Its unlimited content cannot be known by human agency. For it is universal spirit. But the human mind is consciousness confined to a limited content. In its outlook, it is strongly influenced by the dynamic of change which informs its content and appears to dominate the range of its experience. Thus it attempts to see all things in terms of change. Accordingly, it is inclined to see itself as existent within its own content. That is, it is inclined to see itself as limited being.

In other words, human awareness does not generally conceive, nor indeed even perceive, itself as either primary or secondary mind. Rather it becomes subject to its own illusory focus on change. This tendency is reinforced by the fact that the entire content of human consciousness is present to that consciousness as being in a perpetual state of coming into and going out of being and not as an immediate and permanent expression of fully actualized being. Thus the human mind understands itself in terms of its own content.

Conceptually, human beings account for change in terms of space and time. This is because the expression of change is made possible in the human mind by means of temporal alterations in the relations of space. Change is thus the means by which human beings perceive what they generally refer to as reality. For this reason, considering the matter from a human perceptual and conceptual perspective, the world appears to be bound up in space and time.

In this way, space and time become the human mind's constructs for limited being. Consequently, limited being is understood as an expression of space and time. That is to say, space and time are not only constructs for perception, but form the basis of concepts by which limited being is recognized.

But, as has been pointed out, the dynamic of secondary mind is either change, or it is in some way directly responsible for change. Human awareness is determined by secondary mind. Therefore, it must be concluded that the human awareness of space and time is derived from its awareness of change. This

The Immaterial Structure of Human Experience

must be so, since change, a direct product of the dynamic, is prior to space and time.

Nevertheless, for purposes of ordinary human comprehension, change may be graphically represented as space limited by time. For an event would seem to occur in space over a duration of time. Hence the apparent unfolding of change, or events, in space and time, as if space and time were prior in occurrence. However, when considered in order of precedence, this is the reverse of what is the case.

Primary mind, as universal being and the universal ground of being, is the source of all things. But when all things are considered in terms of the content of consciousness, particularly as revealed temporally to human consciousness, primary mind's expression of itself is as a dynamic of secondary mind.

As a dynamic, secondary mind may therefore be conceived in terms of change. It is this change which appears to separate, limit, and thus delineate the percepts which are the sensory elements of human experience. For this reason, secondary mind may be regarded as limiting being, or that which is the cause of the finite human world.

Thus the expression of limitation is what distinguishes the human world from universal being. Universal being is understood simply as universal awareness, spirit, or the actual as opposed to an unfolding potential. The human world is the temporal actualization of that unfolding potential. Its actualization is therefore always incomplete.

But a confusion appears to arise from these two descriptions of universal spirit, which have been referred to as primary mind and secondary mind—the one universally comprehensive and the other limiting (but not limited) in character. That confusion comes from the limited perspective of the human mind, not from the nature of spirit. Universal spirit is simply that which encompasses all in the actual, a unity which is dynamic in an incomprehensible and ineffable way. Secondary mind is primary mind, or universal spirit, as self-limiting spirit.

To continue this investigation of spirit from a human perspective, let it be said that universal spirit is universal consciousness, or universal being. In contradistinction, limited being is limited consciousness—i.e., consciousness brought under some kind of a constraint. For illustrative purposes, this distinction may be conceived in the following way.

Universal mind might be likened to a prism refracting and transmitting multiple wavelengths of light. Thus light of a single wavelength, passing through this prism, would resemble the perspective of a limited being. This is a narrowing of focus. But, if this narrowing of focus were all, and the focus did not itself produce a further limitation, such a being would not truly be limited. It would be secondary mind, or self-limiting spirit, not human consciousness. For it would remain in possession of a universal awareness, however restricted its present focus.

Now a specific wavelength of light passing through the planes of a prism in one direction would nevertheless inhabit the same medium as a full spectrum of light passing through the prism in multiple directions. The single wavelength of light would, at least potentially, have access to all the resources of the medium. For it is a mere branch of the full spectrum of light. It is not something entirely distinct from it.

But, as stated, due to its self-imposed restricted character it would proceed in only one direction. So it is here that the role of the dynamic, or secondary mind, limits human perspective by adding a necessary progression of change. This progression is the

The Immaterial Structure of Human Experience

human sense of time. And it is the sense of time which truly limits human awareness.

Universal mind is thus converted by this progression of change from a mind which possesses knowledge which is immediately present to it into something more limited. It is converted to a mind which receives knowledge as revealed through a progression. This is how a single human consciousness is derived from universal awareness. It is that awareness under self-imposed limitation.

The same conversion which limits the human mind is also a means by which the material realm perceived by that mind may be understood in terms of spirit. For the material may be understood as an expression of limitation within that which is not limited. In its unity, the material is an immediate expression of spirit. But in its temporal revelation to human awareness, it is a progression from spirit, from which it is differentiated by the presence within spirit of an internal limitation. That internal limitation, brought about by focus, is change.

Change is both perceived and conceived by means of its revelation through time. For this reason, a human being has a divided nature, limited by time. This is why a person cannot be understood simply as being, but must be understood as both actual being and potential being. Those of his decisions and acts which have been actualized—as well as the progression of changes which have already been revealed to him within the flow of time—constitute his actual being.

Those of his decisions and acts which have not been actualized—as well as the progression of changes which have not yet been revealed to him—constitute his potential being. The common terms for this distinction are past and future. But, as already mentioned, these distinctions are derived from change and are not productive of it.

The Dynamic. The dynamic has been described in terms of secondary mind. However, it must not be overlooked that the dynamic may also be described from a universal perspective—that is, from the perspective of primary mind. It may be considered strictly in terms of its role within primary mind.

For though it can be readily conceived that universal consciousness, or universal spirit, fully expresses actuality, it must also be acknowledged that it is unlimited in potential as well. This potential encompasses not just what will be actualized in the material realm, but what might be actualized and perhaps never is.

In other words, this potentiality is not only the limited kind revealed by change within a sequence of time, when a possibility either does or does not become actual through a person's individual choice or through happenstance. Either of these cases would appear to have resulted from a material cause. It is also the potentiality which allows for that change, and for those changes which do not occur, or may not even be known to a limited awareness. Such potentiality is perceived at once as actual by primary mind. Yet it retains its characteristic of actualized potentiality within that mind.

It is this union of the potential and the actual which characterizes the dynamic as an expression of primary mind. Such a contradictory combination is, of course, beyond human understanding. But it is a conceptual conundrum which is necessary for avoiding a deterministic interpretation of the character of universal spirit. For should one succumb to a deterministic view of universal spirit, he must also surrender human free will.

The Immaterial Structure of Human Experience

As previously explained, there is a sense in which secondary mind is also a dynamic, though when considered independently as such, it is of a more limited scope. It should be remembered that secondary mind is primary mind with the added condition of an individuated focus. Other than that focus, it lacks nothing of the universal character of spirit.

The individuated focus is the means by which secondary mind is able to create the perspective of individual, limited being. As secondary mind transforms itself by means of focus into an expression of a limited dynamic, and thus an instrument of limitation, it becomes the source of material change. Or, more precisely, it becomes the source of the perception of material change, which is the stream of time.

But spirit is mind. Thus, this being the formation of human consciousness, the consciousness itself retains the character of spirit. Yet it also exhibits all the limitations associated with that focused character which it has received. Accordingly, human consciousness perceives itself as being immersed in and limited by change. It is change which necessitates the formation of a "phenomenal precipitate," which is the human mind's expression of limited being.

It can be seen that material change necessitates the expression of time, since material change is time. [19] So it is that such change necessitates the expression of limited being in general because, were only physical space and not time to be considered, there would nevertheless be an exercise of mental change in distinguishing one percept from another, one object from another. This is in itself an imposition of limitation onto experience.

Thus the phenomenal precipitate is perceived as an expression of limited being by a consciousness which is limited as to its

---

[19] A further development of this will occur later in this work.

content—i.e., human consciousness. So, other than when in the act of contemplating itself, it may be said that such consciousness knows only limitation and change. It is the mode in which a human being experiences life.

The Phenomenal Precipitate. The phenomenal precipitate is human awareness in the sense that it is the content of human consciousness. It is, of course, also the awareness possessed by any other sentient being, however further limited that being may be in its faculties of perception and knowledge. Thus an ant or a bumblebee experiences some form of the precipitate and possesses consciousness as well. Insofar as this sentient awareness takes place within consciousness, it is material. But the consciousness itself is spirit.

Spirit is unextended and indivisible. Thus it is not finite. It is infinite, or without the finite characteristics of limitation, such as extension and figure. For though it may be thought that consciousness is extended in such a manner as to sufficiently encompass its content and perhaps a bit more, this is not so.

To be materially conscious is to be conscious of something as opposed to being conscious of something else. It is confined to this focus, even when that something is nothing more than itself. Consequently, if it is conscious of itself, then it is only conscious of itself. If it is conscious of some portion of the phenomenal precipitate, it is only conscious of that. Thus it is not conscious of itself and the phenomenal precipitate at the same time. So what this means is that consciousness is sufficient to and never in deficiency or excess of its content. For its scope is a function of mental focus.

Now, in contradistinction to spirit, the phenomenal precipitate is extended and divisible. Thus it is inherently limited. So, when awareness is focused upon the phenomenal precipitate, it

The Immaterial Structure of Human Experience

takes on its limitations. In other words, it perceives a limited world and therefore conceives of itself as limited. For this reason, human beings are divided between matter and spirit. They cannot experience themselves as both simultaneously.

The phenomenal precipitate is the realm of quotidian human events. It is the domain of perceived human activity. So it is the sphere of common focus. Within it is the all-pervading presence of limitation. This presence implies division, plurality, multiplicity, something other than, etc. It is an environment of a progression of events and decisions.

It follows from this that material change, which brings about the progression of events, must be understood by a limited being as proceeding according to a process of division, boundedness, and addition. This is because division and boundedness produce finite distinction and difference, which are in turn compounded by addition. These distinctions can and must be recognized in material change. For they express the character of limitation.

It should be pointed out that change is recognized in the sentient mind in a way that it is not recognized in primary mind or secondary mind. In primary mind, change is actual. Its various conditions are present to universal spirit at once. In secondary mind, it is also actual but formed for delivery to the sentient mind as potential. In the sentient mind, it must be potential prior to *becoming* actual.

Thus potentiality and actuality do not coincide in change as perceived or conceived by the sentient mind. Rather actuality is derived from potentiality. Therefore, an individual case of an alteration in the content of consciousness is experienced as a change from that which is to that which has not yet become.

An illustration of this material change can be taken from common experience. Imagine a billiard ball which is stationary, or in a state of rest, until a moving cue ball makes contact with it. At the moment of contact, the state of the billiard ball is changed from rest to motion. Accordingly, its state of rest has been replaced by a motion which did not previously pertain to it.

Where there is a consistency in such an order of events, the perceived "effect" is the motion which has been introduced into the previously stationary billiard ball. It follows a perceived "cause," which is the motion of the cue ball making contact with the billiard ball. The contact is the nexus between the two states of the billiard ball. It is the moment when motion is transferred to it from the cue ball.

So, insofar as the billiard ball is concerned, the perceived effect exists as an unrealized potentiality prior to the moment of contact. This is a causal relationship which exists between the potential and the actual in human experience. That is to say, it exists between the spiritual potential—which has not yet occurred—and the material actual which is the occurrence of that potential. It is accordingly not a relationship between two physical phenomena.

A material causal connection, on the other hand, is recognized by a regular association between a material precedent and the repeated appearance of a particular material consequent to that precedent. In the case of the stationary billiard ball, the material precedent for a change in its state of rest is the motion of the cue ball at the moment of its contact with the billiard ball. The material consequence is the motion of the billiard ball.

Yet, insofar as the power to produce a material effect is attributed to a material cause in this manner, it is an illusion. For the relationship between potentiality and actuality is the true cause of the change. And any spiritual potential is hidden from human awareness. Moreover, it exists not only when a consistent

The Immaterial Structure of Human Experience

material nexus between two phenomena appears to be the case, but where there is no such regularity of occurrence.

It is for this reason that the sentient mind does not ever "see" a causal relationship between material phenomena. For, from a strictly material perspective, its apparent manifestation is fortuitous. Regular in some cases, but still fortuitous. Yet, in spite of this accidental character which obtains between physical causes and effects, the drive toward order in the human mind will, where there is a consistent appearance of a cause-and-effect relationship between two phenomena, come to expect the experience of a material effect from a material cause. That expectation, when ratified by repeated experience, may even seal the connection with the epithet of a material law.

This view of material relations would seem to throw a wrench into causal relations within the precipitate, since it implies that a material cause does not produce a material effect. For the actualization of the effect lies within the domain of the potential, as opposed to the actual. But to the human mind, appearances are otherwise. For human awareness does not experience the mind of universal spirit with its awareness of the potential as spiritually actual. It only experiences the materially actual.

What it experiences is the phenomenal precipitate. Thus it establishes relations within the materially actual alone. So an orderly appearance of change within the precipitate allows for the material assumption of a causal connection. Not spirit, but the observed motion of the cue ball and its contact with the billiard ball, is understood to make the billiard ball roll.

But such a material relationship is tenuous. It remains in doubt because the power of a material cause to produce a material effect cannot be explained in terms of the human experience which asserts it. Nevertheless, the tenuous character of the connection does not suggest that, in assuming its validity, a person should be described as exercising no more than a mental habit, as David Hume has envisioned it.[20] For Hume deliberately restricted his investigations to what was observable from a sensory perspective.

But, allowing for the activity of consciousness in shaping human perception and thought, and thus the activity of spirit in doing so, there is, in fact, an order to the change in material phenomena which may be understood as causal. However, this order is unexperienced in human awareness and consequently cannot be understood in material terms. For it is grounded in universal spirit.

Moreover, having once recognized the all-inclusive activity of consciousness, it can be understood that material causal relations are in fact spiritual. This is attested to not only in the role of consciousness in the formation of thought processes, such as perception, imagination, and concept formation, but in the supply of percepts to human awareness. For it is spirit in the role of secondary mind which is also responsible for the manifold of sensation in human experience.

Consequently, there is no reason to assume that the appearance of an actual effect in material awareness does not, in the mind of spirit, arise in full view of the material cause, though it might not be understood as such were its pre-phenomenal relations to be observed in spirit. The potential and the actual exist together as actual in the mind of spirit.

That is to say, all things actual in human experience are, from a human perspective, potential prior to their material appearance. But all things, which from a human perspective are po-

---

[20] David Hume, *An Enquiry Concerning Human Understanding* and *A Treatise of Human Nature*.

The Immaterial Structure of Human Experience

tential, are actual in spirit. So any appearance of a causal relationship in the material realm is determined within spirit. Thus the causal relationship exists prior to its recognition by human awareness as a physical phenomenon.

Now, in addition to the spiritual order of individual changes, all change in human experience is grounded in the potential of spirit. Even when a change appears to be occurring in one place while not in another, as when at a particular moment the hands of a clock are observed to move, but not the clock itself, this does not mean that the actualization of change is selective, occurring here and there but not to the whole. Rather, change is unfolded in time. And time *is* that unfolding of change. For the whole of human awareness is conditioned by sequence and is thus a manifestation of continual change.

In other words, from beginning to end in any one person's experience, the entire content of the phenomenal precipitate originates as potential in spirit prior to his mental recognition of it as actual. But it does not appear all at once. Every percept of it must appear before his mind as a change in sensation, even though the change may only be recognized in terms of associations of percepts, or sensations, which are whole properties, objects, and thoughts. For, if all change appeared together at once in human experience, the various positions of the hands of a clock could not be distinguished from one another.

Individual percepts and groupings of percepts are continuously being realized within consciousness. Should a person sweep his eye over a forested ridge, noting first one tree then another, each is being realized in his mind either for the first time or once again. But, though it should be a repeat experience, the fact is, its position in experience is immediate. For it is its realization at that moment which is the experience. Thus a recall from memory is in this sense no different from a perception.

Every perception, every event, every thought, every decision, every act is rendered actual to human awareness by the phenomenal precipitate. This precipitate brings these phenomena into being not only for, but as a product of, perceptual and intellectual recognition. For from infancy the human mind is engaged with secondary mind in the formation and development of the phenomenal precipitate. But with increasing maturity, the human individual is largely unaware of this. The initial formation of the phenomenal precipitate in infancy is forgotten. Thus the phenomenal precipitate acts increasingly as a screen between secondary mind and the human mind.

This screen is a product of secondary mind and human understanding working together to form a grid work of spatial relations and spatial-relations-dependent temporal relations. For it is a restructuring of what is made present by secondary mind alone. That which is made present by secondary mind alone is the unacknowledged *noumenal precipitate* of secondary mind. However, it is the phenomenal precipitate, as it is formed within human awareness, which constitutes the *actual* environment and events of a human life. It is always arising from the potential, from spirit, by means of an orderly noumenal presentation of sensation.

None of this should imply a solipsistic conclusion. While it is the case that all the constituent elements of an individual person's phenomenal precipitate arise in a single human mind through spirit, spirit is nevertheless one. And it is that one which supplies each mind according to it peculiar condition. Thus it is the ground for an integrated coordination between one person's experience and another's.

The Immaterial Structure of Human Experience

It is also the means of the independence of much of experience from an individual human will. For that which is the common experience of all should not be easily modified by one. So it is from this universal ground that so much of material experience gains its consistency and otherness to form a collective human sense of objective reality. To describe it from George Berkeley's perspective, it is all in the mind of God.[21]

The Noumenal Precipitate. The unacknowledged *noumenal precipitate* is the manner in which secondary mind presents percepts, or sensations, to the human mind. The human mind converts associations of these percepts into extensions which are the spatial relations of the phenomenal precipitate.

Changes in the spatial relations are due to variations in the flow of the noumenal presentation of percepts, where alterations occur among associations of these percepts. The time relations which are recognizable by human awareness follow upon the changes which occur among the spatial relations.

Together, the spatial and time relations are recognized and developed in the phenomenal precipitate by means of an intellectual conversion process involving the formation of mental images, concepts, and systems of thought. These progress from an emphasis upon images in the early formation of the phenomenal precipitate, to concepts and conceptual systems in the developing phenomenal precipitate, as the human mind matures and grows more complex in experience. Thus intellectual conversion is a process which involves both precipitates. For it draws upon the noumenal to create the phenomenal.

This occurs in the following manner. Secondary mind presents to human awareness a stream of percepts, which are limited

---

[21] George Berkeley, *The Principles of Human Knowledge* and *Three Dialogues Between Hylas and Philonous.*

in presentation by secondary mind's employment of focus. That is, because the percepts are recognized sequentially—i.e., focused upon one at a time—they are rendered finite. For they become discrete entities in the mind's eye and delimit one another.

So, insofar as human awareness is concerned, as opposed to the spiritual comprehensiveness of secondary mind operating within itself, these percepts are experienced not only as discrete, but as occurring in an order. The order is expressed sequentially as a result of secondary mind's focus upon one percept at a time.

Secondary mind and human awareness are one mind understood to function in two simultaneous states. The principal distinction between them is expressed by the two precipitates. Secondary mind lays down the noumenal precipitate. And human awareness converts its content into that of the phenomenal precipitate. The conversion process is immediate. So, for a mature human awareness, there is no discernible separation between the two states of mind. This is because the operations of the first are overshadowed and obscured by those of the latter.

But for a newly developing infant mind, there is some awareness of the distinction, albeit that it is an awareness which is imaginative and not intellectual. As its content is imaginative, the early phenomenal precipitate initially formed by the infant mind is strictly associative and imprecise. Objects are easily confused and tend to blend into one another. Thus the transition between the two states, noumenal and phenomenal, is momentarily fluid.

But, as an increasingly intellectual development begins to supplant the purely imaginative, concepts and, eventually, systems of concepts arise. Thus the phenomenal precipitate becomes more carefully delineated and, as a result, more clearly established in the mind. As this occurs, the noumenal origin of the

The Immaterial Structure of Human Experience

percepts is subsumed within the complex buildup of the phenomenal structure.

Accordingly, the noumenal process fades from human awareness. Thus all new additions to experience are instantly recognized as phenomenal. This latter state of mind is what is generally referred to as human awareness. But it should not be overlooked that human awareness is, in fact, secondary mind, with this unique qualification, or limitation: it exhibits a loss of awareness of secondary mind's origin in universal spirit.

The outcome of such a mode of presentation of the percepts is a sequential order in both precipitates, albeit that there is some difference in the arrangement of the two. For the phenomenal precipitate must make adjustments to accommodate spatial relationships. Thus much of the linear sequence of the noumenal precipitate is exchanged for a contiguous multidimensional relationship amongst objects in space.

The sequential order in the noumenal precipitate becomes a temporal succession. The initial experience of this succession may be referred to as noumenal time, or *non-incremental time*. For it is not subject to measure. And, as stated, it is a matter of one percept following another according to the mind's focus in recognizing each percept individually. It is in this way that the following of one percept by another expresses duration in the mind.

If the percepts are repeated in identical orderly groups, the combination of percepts, as occurs in such groups, is imprinted upon human awareness as an association of percepts. Here it is the repetition of the group in being presented to the mind which makes the grouping a recognizable association. And it is these associations which are converted into extensions in the phenomenal precipitate.

The extensions are apprehended as thought images. As the mind continues to develop in experience, the thought images are distinguished objectively and subjectively. This bifurcation divides experience into a realm of physical objects and one of objects of thought. As all the thought images, objective and subjective, appear in an order of relation to one another (spatial and temporal in the case of the objective and temporal in the case of the subjective), they constitute the phenomenal precipitate, which includes both physical objects and objects of thought.

So within the order of percepts introduced by the noumenal precipitate are the associations of percepts which are converted by the human mind into the extensions of the phenomenal precipitate. A spatial understanding of those extensions which are to be recognized as physical objects is, in some cases, modified in experience. To give a crude example, what had at first been recognized as a lagoon may upon further experience be identified as an estuary. Or what is apprehended as a general polygon, may be refined into a quadrilateral.

Now, in general, this ordering of associations of percepts as spatial extensions provides a basis for the human sense of time. For the phenomenal precipitate continually undergoes modifications in its extensions. And it is these modifications which are a means of the measuring of time. In other words, the modifications can be taken under observation and compared with one another, as the progress in the movements of a sprinter is compared to the motion of the hands on a stopwatch.

Excepting certain changes of qualities, as in a change of color or taste (the source of such changes being generally hidden from observation), physical change is expressed in two types of motion which provide accustomed measures for time. Either an extension (an object) changes its position relative to contiguous

The Immaterial Structure of Human Experience

extensions. Or it undergoes modifications of its properties. A change of location alters an object's spatial relationship with contiguous objects. Likewise, modifications of the properties of an object, though this is not always the case, may upon occasion do the same.

If the latter does alter an object's spatial relationship with contiguous objects, the change exhibits a different instance of motion than that of a change of location among objects. For an extension, modified in its properties in such a manner as to alter its own figure, changes its relation to other extensions in a minor way. It does not move in terms of its general location. Rather, it has only moved some portion of itself *within* its location. Nonetheless, it is spatially not in the same situation. It, or a part of it, has undergone a type of motion. Chemical change is one expression of this.

In the case of either type of change (displacement or figure), the process becomes a registry of time when it alters spatial relations between extensions and when its changes occur independently of any adjustments in human understanding. The adjustments in human understanding being referred to here are like the example of the estuary given above. The lagoon does not become an estuary. The latter was simply mistaken for the former. Thus this does not constitute a physical change. It is a change in the understanding of an unchanging phenomenon.

Since phenomenal time is measurable in terms of changes in spatial extensions, it is referred to as *incremental time*. For it is founded upon increments of physical change. Nevertheless, it is grounded within and reflects non-incremental time, though it differs from it somewhat in character. For its measurable changes arise from a conversion of the linear sequences of associated percepts in the noumenal precipitate into the spatial relations of extensions in the phenomenal precipitate.

Now it is the case that, following an initial mental construction of spatial relations in the phenomenal precipitate, the process is not static. It evolves. That is, it involves an ongoing reconstruction of some of those relations. Where this occurs, there is observable change. Such change will appear to occur in one place and not another.

Other extensions, standing seemingly unperturbed in human experience like granite mountains, maintain, or at least seem to maintain, their original character. But this relative stability is only an appearance. For all is flux. And even a diamond undergoes change, given sufficient time.

What is notable about the conversion of noumenal, or non-incremental, time into the modified phenomenal form of incremental time is that, though the two forms of time are ultimately one, they must be distinguished from one another. For, given the modified ordering of percepts in the phenomenal precipitate, time based upon that order differs somewhat from time based upon the noumenal order. It differs not in substance, but in the way human awareness experiences it.

In the first place, it is in the noumenal precipitate that time establishes its origin in human experience. For here the simple sequence in the presentation of percepts is in an order which could be said to demark time, if it were not for the fact that it does not lend itself to mensuration. So it is the phenomenal precipitate which must provide the spatial relations which render time measurable.

Because this latter expression of time is the one which is measurable, it is the one which is recognized by human intelligence. It is recognizable by human intelligence because the finite

The Immaterial Structure of Human Experience

mind must analyze and fragment knowledge in order to reconstruct it in a manner which it can apprehend conceptually. This capacity not only for analysis, but for a comparative analysis, is what the extensions of the phenomenal precipitate provide.

As stated above, the sequence in the noumenal appearance of percepts is somewhat modified in the development of the phenomenal precipitate, due to the fact that the human mind, in organizing associations of percepts into extensions of space, must create spatial contiguity. Where there is contiguity, there is simultaneity instead of sequence. This conversion must, of course, take place. Otherwise objects and the properties within objects could not be understood to coexist with other objects and properties in human experience.

So this requires an arrangement and assignment of place for the associated percepts which initially appear sequentially in the noumenal stream. And this arrangement and assignment of place is what appears to distort time relations from the noumenal to the phenomenal expression. But it does not distort time so much as it displaces it, truncating it here, lengthening it there in the phenomenal precipitate, as opposed to its appearance in the noumenal precipitate. Yet nothing of this strikes the human understanding as out of order. For it is only phenomenal time which is the time that is consciously experienced by the maturing mind.

Nevertheless, the measurable time of the phenomenal precipitate remains grounded in the non-incremental time of the noumenal precipitate. The former progresses as the latter does. For its increments of change refer to modifications in percept associations, which initially appear in the noumenal stream of percepts. These are what become the extensions of the phenomenal precipitate, where the change is observed. So it is the measurable time of the phenomenal precipitate which is referred to as incremental because it can be measured in units of physical change.

The noumenal precipitate and its non-incremental time constitute the operations of secondary mind. As such, they are increasingly masked from human awareness by the phenomenal precipitate and its incremental time as mental maturation occurs and the phenomenal precipitate grows more complex and settled in character. The noumenal precipitate and its non-incremental time are therefore not directly present to human awareness, particularly in a mature awareness.

Nevertheless, they are the means by which self-limiting spirit establishes the limits of that awareness. By supplying sensory material to the phenomenal precipitate, and supplying it sequentially, they provide it with its incremental time. For the phenomenal precipitate is a working up of the limitations in the sensory material which is presented to human awareness by secondary mind. These limitations in the noumenal flow of sensation result in a sequence of presentation of percepts before the mind. And that sequence in presentation is the product of focus on the part of secondary mind.

It is in the character of focus to limit. To focus upon something is to limit attention to that something. Thus focus limits the noumenal stream of presentation of sensation to one percept then another. And that limitation is what not only establishes the sequence of presentation of percepts before the mind. It establishes finitude by delineating each sensation from the other.

The human mind is self-limited primary mind. The transformation from primary mind to the human mind is a transition from the *in*finite (the *not* finite) to the finite. This is brought about by means of the agency of secondary mind. Secondary mind is primary mind, or universal spirit, which has rendered itself into a

The Immaterial Structure of Human Experience

self-limiting mode. It limits itself to the content of human consciousness. So the product of that self-limiting process is human awareness with its limitations. Thus, by means of this process, human awareness is made unaware of its spiritual origin.

Consequently, though the faculty of human focus is an expression of the focus of secondary mind, the former must be described as a different kind of focus from the latter. For, insofar as human awareness is concerned, human focus is independent of the focus of secondary mind. Human focus is perceived as taking place within the phenomenal precipitate, not prior to its initial formation.

Because the noumenal precipitate with its non-incremental time underlies, and is therefore obscured by, the phenomenal precipitate with its incremental time, it is the latter which constitutes human awareness. Thus, with the increasing maturation of human awareness, it is within the phenomenal precipitate that human decisions and actions are experienced as occurring. There is thus an illusion that free will occurs within this restricted domain. But, in fact, human will transcends the temporal and physical limitations of human awareness.

Free Will. It must be admitted that the present discussion has so far placed the problem of free will in a precarious position. For it would seem that thoughts and acts are given by the phenomenal precipitate and that the material for that precipitate is given by secondary mind. In other words, all sensory input is provided to human awareness by secondary mind. And human awareness constructs the phenomenal precipitate from this input in accordance with the manner in which it is given. Consequently, it does not appear that any freedom is implied in the individual's interaction with the events which occur in his experience.

So where is the role of an independent will to be established? What is meant by "independent" is that which should be capable in some measure of acting free of any process or circumstance in which it is found. It must determine its own course, even if that course should be limited to specific choices.

But, in fact, this need not be a problem. For will may be recognized not to subsist within the limited circumstances which are created for the human mind by spirit. Rather, it can be understood to have its origin directly in spirit. For this to be understood, it must be recalled that the content of human consciousness is derived from universal spirit by means of its passing through modifications in focus which are created by secondary mind. These modifications create the finite and temporal conditions of human experience.

But it is not within this modified content that the elements of the content derive their origin. Rather, it is within universal spirit that they do. Recall that the roots of causation are spiritual rather than material. Moreover, within universal spirit, which is neither temporal nor finite, all the elements of human experience may be said to coexist as though simultaneous. For in universal spirit they are determined instantly, prior to the temporal, piecemeal delineation of them in human awareness.

So what a human being understands as an act of his will which appears to him to be revealed in the sequence of time and within the sphere of his individual awareness, is, in fact, an act of his will which lies outside the limitations of his awareness and prior to any consideration of time and its sequential character. That is to say, the will itself lies outside this awareness. But the awareness remains limited.

How can this be? Timeless, or instantaneously determined, though such a will must be, it remains individual. For the agency

The Immaterial Structure of Human Experience

of secondary mind has expressed it independently of other individual wills. But it cannot be overlooked that secondary mind is universal spirit, which is one and indivisible. Thus it is that all individual wills coexist in the unfathomable complexity of one spirit.

Understood in this regard, each individual will, independent of the others, is a full expression of universal spirit. It is as though in its exercise it were the single will of spirit and there were no others. Yet there is a plurality of such wills in spirit, which collectively is also a unified expression of spirit.

Spirit is a unity which is infinite. It is infinite precisely in the sense that it is not finite. For it is materially unbounded and indivisible. Therefore, it is not governed by the relations of finitude. Rather, it exhibits a division in unity which is not subject in any way to a material delineation. Thus the expression of will within universal spirit is individually unique, yet collectively multiplex and entirely subordinate to the whole, as are the varied currents of a mountain stream.

How can this occur? To understand it, one must set aside the material mind and its means of imaginative and rational thought. In their place must be inserted the character of pure consciousness: consciousness unbounded and materially indivisible. There is but one consciousness: universal spirit.

Human consciousness is limited only in its content, not in its essential character as spirit. This limitation in content is the domain within which an individual will is expressed. But it is not a limitation which pertains to the unity of spirit. Spirit, considered as spirit alone, exhibits no limitation of itself.

Rather, the content, as well as the seeming isolation of that content, is within spirit. And, insofar as spirit is concerned, any individuation of this content is but one of many simultaneous streams of thought in a single, universal mind. This is a mind which is not in any way like a human mind. For its thoughts are not human thoughts.

As to human moral responsibility and its relationship to the unity of universal spirit, this can only be understood in terms of purpose. Insofar as human beings are concerned (as individual experience is seen, or will come to be seen, from a human perspective), the purpose of spirit in a human being is the realization of its spiritual unity. For the overriding influence of consciousness is unity.

It is a purpose which is registered, however dimly at any particular time, deep in the awareness of each person. For he is, above all things, conscious. And consciousness is a unity. It is the foundational character of that person. In fact, that unity exists in every conscious being and in the collectivity of all things. But it is human beings which are rationally able to understand this unity and thus act upon it in varying degree.

So the unity is brought to fruition through them, each acting his part, however faintly or profoundly the greater purpose is understood. This is so even when human acts appear to be at cross-purposes with spirit. For in the sum of individuals and in the sum of time, the character of spirit is realized.

So what is the nature of an individual human will? When understood as spirit, that person exhibits an immaterial character. All his decisions are expressed instantaneously, as though they were a single integrated act. For they are the timeless but independent thought of spirit. But, within the independence of that thought, they remain the acts of a finite being, confined to a finite awareness. For that is what the thought is about. Thus, inside his own awareness, the acts of a person derive from temporally isolated decisions involving a dim understanding of spirit. Yet that

The Immaterial Structure of Human Experience

dim understanding is understanding enough. The person is responsible for his acts.

34. The paradox of mind. Human thought cannot be described as creating something out of nothing. For its efforts do not produce an endless upward progression of knowledge, like a geyser from the hidden bowels of the unknown. Rather, these efforts may be described as a spreading of understanding through experience.

Thus human knowledge is more like an inundating sea than an ascent into ethereal realms. This is because conceptual thought is subordinate to nature, or the phenomenal precipitate, which is responsible for its content. For human thought is drawn from experience. So this thought can only adjust to what it contemplates. It cannot transcend experience. Even should its speculations advance into metaphysics, it must be referenced back to experience, for which the metaphysics provides an explanatory means of unification.

Material nature's most important contribution to the human thought process is this: human thought content is limited by the laws of nature. That is to say, the human mind in its experience of the material is governed by the relations of the material. Though the material is subject to modification in its conceptual interpretation, the groundwork of its relations is laid down by the earliest contributions of the noumenal precipitate. So, should the mind try to advance beyond the material, it must reflect back upon it. For this material domain is grounded in perceptual awareness.

However, it does also include subjective feeling. Thus nature, as that which is perceived—i.e., as that which is generally understood to be prior to conceptual thought—is subjective as well as objective. Accordingly, for it to function at all, thought must use the building blocks of nature, its internal impressions, its external objects, and their relationships to one another, as initial content for its intellectual constructs.

But what must not be overlooked is that which lies beyond the human mind, which is indicated in human experience by the presence of consciousness. Consciousness is indivisible and unbounded. So it is not material. Nor is it limited to the human mind. Thus beyond the material content of human awareness is a more fundamental level of awareness which encompasses both the human mind and its experience.

This more fundamental level of awareness is secondary mind. Secondary mind is responsible for material nature as it is represented to the human mind prior to any human conceptual thought about it. It is of course ultimately responsible for that thought as well. But, in its initial acts, the material nature which it presents is the human mind's immediate perceptual experience.

It is this representation of nature to human awareness which is the earliest manifestation of the noumenal precipitate and which involves the most rudimentary imaginative foundations of the phenomenal precipitate. These are what serve as a basis for the phenomenal precipitate's subsequent intellectual constructs.

Beyond secondary mind is *primary mind*. Primary mind is universal spirit. Secondary mind is self-limiting primary mind as regards the content which it will present to human awareness. This self-limitation in content is the focus which creates the noumenal precipitate and ultimately the phenomenal precipitate. The phenomenal precipitate is the experience of material nature, both subjective and objective. As it develops toward maturity, it grows in complexity to include the conceptual thought which appears to reflect upon it.

The Immaterial Structure of Human Experience

Primary mind, or spirit, is human consciousness, when that consciousness is considered without reference to its content. But within human limits, human consciousness does not function as universal spirit. For it is limited to a knowledge which is the human experience of material nature. It is in this way that human consciousness, though originating in the unboundedness of universal spirit, is positioned within nature.

From this the paradox of mind arises. For the very consciousness which is limited to material nature at the level of human awareness is that which serves both as the ground of human consciousness and as the source of its limited awareness. As the ground of human consciousness, it is one and the same with it. But as the cause of its limited awareness, it is differentiated from it.

35. Individual awareness and spirit. Human knowledge of the physical world is both limited and unlimited. It is limited in capacity and unlimited in ingenuity. What does this mean? It means that, since the line of demarcation between the material and spiritual realms is not a clear one, the materially oriented human mind must find a way to fill in the gaps it encounters in its attempt to understand its experience. It uses imagination to do this.

The finite human mind is restricted in knowledge to what it can perceive and, even more pointedly so, to what it can conceptually process. It cannot know what lies beyond its faculties of perception and thought. In fact, to attempt to envision such limits would not be unlike comparing a human being to a frog.

The frog cannot appreciate the sensual beauty of a person in the way a human being can. Neither can a person envision the sensual delights of a frog. This is because neither has the means of experiencing the other's biological impulses. Thus the mental and emotional capacity of human beings and frogs differs. And both are limited in what they can know.

But, though limited, the human mind is nevertheless unrestricted in its flexibility. It succeeds in finding a way around whatever obstacles may obstruct its understanding. In other words, when confronted with inconsistencies, the human mind makes imaginative adjustments. Such was the case in physical science, when a single referential inertial system was replaced with multiple inertial systems of equal referential value. Such was also the case when the ability of a shaman to use spells to ward off sickness was replaced by modern medical technology.

This characterization of the mind can be illustrated by a long tube enclosed within a circle:

The cylindrical walls of the tube represent the mind's natural limitations. These are the limitations which are imposed by the phenomenal precipitate which is made present to human awareness. Yet the cylinder is indeterminately long, for this indeterminacy is an expression of the mind's unlimited imaginative flexibility. The mind finds a way around obstacles in its search for knowledge, advancing up the tube without foreseeable limit.

Nevertheless, though it is through the use of imagination that the mind can indefinitely extend its powers within its precipitate-imposed limitations, it cannot transcend those limitations. Be-

The Immaterial Structure of Human Experience

yond the human mind's capacity for material knowledge lies a vast domain: it is the range of possibility. That domain is indeterminate, just as imagination is. But the range of possibility extends well beyond the reach of imagination. For they are not at all akin to one another.

The greater domain of possibility which encompasses the phenomenal precipitate is an indeterminacy which expresses a far more extensive field than the mind's imaginative response to what is either actual or probable within the precipitate. From the human mind's perspective, this greater domain may be conceived as an extension of the two precipitates (noumenal [22] and phenomenal) into an unknown realm which extends beyond them both.

This is to say that, where they are concerned with potential events, the precipitates appear to partake of that which can only be tentatively accessed by human faculties. For there can be no certain knowledge of what has not yet occurred. Even the predictable is in some measure uncertain. This is due to the fact that causal relations, as human beings know them (and as recognized by Hume), are an expression of uniformity, not necessity.

The necessity lies elsewhere than in the human mind. For other unseen relations correlative to what humans think of as causal may be formed in the mind of universal spirit. It is these which determine the appearance of causal relations within the phenomenal precipitate. This larger realm is what is encompassed by the circle in the figure above.

Thus the distinction between what the mind can know and what it cannot know, or cannot know with certainty, is not a distinction between what lies within the phenomenal and noumenal domains. These together are the material world. They are recog-

---

[22] As can be seen, the use of the term "noumenal" is a nod to the pervasive influence of Immanuel Kant. But it is used in a much more restricted sense.

nized by what is actual and by what appear to be the materially determining circumstances of what is probable.

All else, including the probable occurrence itself and its true spiritual determinants, belongs to the greater domain of possibility, which is the realm of spirit. This distinction lies between the faculty of human awareness, which is created by secondary mind, and the ground of all being which is primary mind.

It should be observed again that what the above mentioned frog experiences is different from a human being. The frog's material domain may have a range correlative to the human. But it nevertheless differs uniquely from that of the human, giving the frog a different frame of awareness and, accordingly, a different cast of mind. Thus there is a line of demarcation between primary mind and the frog's awareness which is in varying degree opposed to the one that lies between primary mind and a human being's awareness.

What links the frog with humanity is spirit—i.e., primary mind, or general awareness. Spirit, as understood by a human being, is consciousness without regard to its content. In respect of that content, there may be more or less of a correlation between the material domains of a frog and a human being. But these domains are unlikely to be identical, due to differences in perceptual and representational capacity. Most importantly, there is a considerable difference between a frog and a human being in the range of their mental operations.

From this it can be seen that all forms of awareness proceed from spirit. Spirit *is* awareness. And it is spirit in the role of primary mind that links and coordinates the phenomenal worlds of the frog and the human. These phenomenal worlds correlate, or overlap, because primary mind, acting through the various con-

The Immaterial Structure of Human Experience

figurations of secondary mind, creates a single, integrated material realm.

Secondary mind configures awareness differently for a frog than it does for a human being. In each case, primary mind, functioning as secondary mind, renders an array of percepts which is fitting to the awareness that will be expressed through it. An example would be the awareness of a frog or a man, or even the awareness of one person as opposed to another. Thus this is a distinction which holds not only between species, but between frog and frog and person and person. Each individual is unique.

Secondary mind may again be described, as in a previous essay, as a prismatic limitation of primary mind. What is in primary mind passes in a unique way through secondary mind. Through secondary mind, which is the prism, all things material, or phenomenal, are made present to a finite individual mind—that of a frog, a human being, or some other form of sentient life. These individual material domains are the phenomenal precipitate of each finite mind. Thus each of these minds expresses the same universal spirit in a unique way.

But one can also refer to a general precipitate, a general expression of primary mind made collectively available through all the universally coordinated configurations of secondary mind. For living human beings, there is potentially but one unified reality of spirit. And all its configurations of expression through secondary mind are referenced back to that unity.

Other sentient forms in the material realm experience other unified realities, which are closely linked to the human reality, but not identical with it. The distinct realms are linked but not identical because they are integrated and distinguished by the unlimited capacity for both relation and diversification within the one universal spirit.

Let the conclusion to this discussion be extended to every object, even to every percept. All things, whether conscious or unconscious, whether considered in their individual existence, in the kindred relations of a type or species, or in a collective unity of being, all these are the expression of one indivisible spirit.

Each individual is a full expression of that spirit, as are all together. This is as true individually and collectively of the color green, a tree, or a rock as it is of a frog or a person. That is why a philosophically immaterialist view can be reasonably maintained without fear of falling into solipsism.

There should be no fear of such a view posing a threat to the progress of science. This view may question the intellectual foundations of science as not being absolute. But it will not deny their functional utility. Moreover, the problem of the thing-in-itself, which originally came glaringly forth out of Descartes' dualism of body and mind and was of such deep interest to the British empiricists and to Kant, need not be of concern. For all things exist in the mind of spirit. In other words, spirit is the ground of material being. Thus material being is mind stuff. But this does not make it less experientially real for human and general sentient awareness.

36. Berkeley and science. Many thinkers have had a problem with Berkeley's immaterialism, though he has influenced some, such as Hume and Kant, without converting them to his point of view. When he first published *The Principles of Human Knowledge,* informed people of his time came out in vigorous opposition to the system he proposed.

But the problem does not seem to lie in the incorrectness of his argument. On the contrary, given an acceptance of its initial principles, the argument is airtight. Nevertheless, a problem does

The Immaterial Structure of Human Experience

exist. And it can be found in two places. One is in the opinions of non-philosophic people, who do in fact generally support the notion of things-in-themselves, whereas Berkeley believed they did not. The other is the apparent conflict between Berkeley's system and the way people do science. The latter presents the greater objection.

For instance, a person might observe that a bumblebee sees an ultraviolet flower where a human being sees a yellow flower. The person can do experiments to verify this. That is, by masking the yellow without removing the effects of the ultraviolet, she can test the bee's reaction to it. Then, given positive results, she might ask, what causes the discrepancy between what the human sees and what the bee sees?

She decides that it is not as though the flower were untrue to itself in separate instances, appearing yellow here, but not ultraviolet, and ultraviolet there, but not yellow. For the flower exhibits both effects simultaneously. Rather, it is a divergence in perception which is the issue. Humans and bumblebees are sensitive to different levels of the color spectrum. [23]

So she reasons that the divergence is principally caused by something more fundamental in the flower than is apt to be superficially detected. It is this something which permits the flower to reflect more than one wavelength of color. Of course, the difference in perception would also be caused by a variation in the functioning of the organs of the human and the bee.

But the explanation centered upon a divergence of effects coming from the flower raises a philosophical question. It is thus the more interesting case. For it would seem to indicate that the flower in its full character is something other than what either the

---

[23] Whether or not a bumblebee also sees yellow, the present author does not know.

person or possibly the bumblebee perceives, and that this is not primarily due to a subjective difference in perception. Rather, it is due to the fact that each perceives the flower differently due to characteristics found in the flower. Such a conclusion would challenge the immaterialism of the philosophy presented in this work.

From a material perspective, a scientific hypothesis has been offered for this discrepancy in the one object. It is, as indicated by the two colors reflected, that the flower is both yellow and ultraviolet at the same time. In other words, as already noted, it has fundamental qualities (as in Locke's primary qualities) [24] which support each of the two different perceptions. Human beings see a yellow flower because they cannot see reflected ultraviolet light. Bumblebees, apparently, can see the ultraviolet and either ignore or cannot see the yellow.

Given this hypothesis, it would seem that nothing more need be done than to apply a an experimentally verified theoretical construct which, from a human perspective, would more fully account for the bumblebee's uniquely different perception. Such a theory has been supplied. It asserts that a bee senses frequencies of light, and therefore color, which lie outside the range of human sensory organs.

But this explanation does not resolve the philosophical problem because it suggests an argument for the existence of what is philosophically referred to as a thing-in-itself—i.e., something which exists apart from perception. It was precisely this concept of a thing-in-itself which Berkeley was anxious to refute. It is why he created his system in the first place.

---

[24] John Locke states in *An Essay Concerning Human Understanding* that primary qualities reside in the object, while secondary qualities reside in the perceiver but are caused by the primary qualities.

The Immaterial Structure of Human Experience

So, since it is a human intellectual perspective which provides an explanation for what a human being cannot see, another question must be asked: if it is true that human beings cannot directly perceive the color ultraviolet through their senses, what exactly is meant by the term ultraviolet? How is it known that it exists? Perhaps the experiments supposedly confirming its existence have not demonstrated what people think they have.

That brings the discussion to the theory of electromagnetic energy. Light is understood to be electromagnetic energy. Its frequencies, or wavelengths, provide the different colors, both visible and invisible, to human and other creatures' perception. But what is electromagnetic energy? As a theory, which at best is indirectly supported by experimental evidence, could it not be described as a convenient and useful mapping of a particular portion of the field of human experience?

Convenient because it provides a tool for organizing certain processes of nature for the understanding. And useful because it supplies a means for manipulating those processes. The theory might be compared to a terrain map. As is generally known, a terrain map is not the terrain itself. Likewise, neither can it be ascertained with certainty that the theory of electromagnetic energy, which works so well at a practical level, is an accurate or full statement as to the precise nature of the phenomena it describes.

The electromagnetic theory is a creation of the human intellect. An impressive one, to be sure, particularly when one considers the simplicity and comprehensiveness of Maxwell's [25] equations and all the discoveries which have followed upon them.

---

[25] James Clerk Maxwell, a British physicist who developed his equations concerning electromagnetic phenomena in response to the experimental data of Michael Faraday.

So, to systematically link together the bewildering array of the myriad of perceived phenomena which they encounter, human beings do need such intellectual constructs. And there is no practical reason to assume the constructs are false. As suggested in the preceding paragraph, it would be more accurate to say they are incomplete.

Thus they may be modified over time, as the general history of science indicates. Occasionally they may even be discarded for a more effective explanation. The point is that scientific theories, however powerful, are maps. They inevitably fall short of describing all the features of the terrain of human experience. That is why modifications do occur.

Allowing for the limitations of the human mind, any theoretical construct is restricted to the range of the percepts which are given in human experience. What is meant by percepts is the sensations made available to awareness. These sensations are not only individually finite. They are collectively finite. And, in the case of a mature human being, most of these, having been presented to the mind in associations in the noumenal precipitate, have been further organized to become extensions exhibiting various properties in the phenomenal precipitate.

The extensions, in turn, collectively make up the phenomenal precipitate. But the percepts of the phenomenal extensions are yet the same as those which are initially presented to human awareness by the noumenal precipitate. So they are prior to any development of the phenomenal precipitate. In other words, they alone are what might be called the ground elements of material experience. And this experience arises solely in the mind.

Now extensions encountered in the physical (or "objective") portion of the phenomenal precipitate are believed to be physical objects. They constitute the substance of physical events. But, in

The Immaterial Structure of Human Experience

fact, they are perceived strictly as mental representations, or images. Thus images are the mind's initial figuring forth of the physical extensions which are understood to be physical objects.

A sequencing of these images in the mind as mental extensions, or thoughts, is what provides a delineation among them. They may be recognized as either images or objects. But it is the focus of the mind which individually differentiates them. And it supplies a register of the changes which occur among them. This change may express a transition in thought or a physical modification, depending on the function of the image, or the manner in which it is understood.

Thus some of these mental extensions are one and the same as what are believed to be physical extensions. But not all are. For others are recognized as simply being mental images. All mental images are composed of percepts. So it is images composed of percepts which are understood to be physical objects composed of percepts.

Aside from this, any concepts are also composed of percepts, since they are abstracted from images. Thus images are the fundamental means of mental representation in human awareness. Without them, nothing material is represented as a thought. And, without thought, there is no representation.

How does a belief that some images are physical objects occur? It occurs as a child develops. A bifurcation of her mental content into subjective and objective components creates a sense of two realities, mental and physical, which are separate from one another. Thus she experiences herself subjectively and her world objectively.

In the objective realm, where mental images specifically represent perceptual experience, two dimensions establish the fundamentals of extension. A third adds depth of field. So the three spatial dimensions of the physical reality, particularly the addition of the third, are projected in such a manner as to enhance her sense of independence within her environment. This allows her a personal sphere of action, which permits her a freedom to react in response to circumstances and events in the objective realm.

The objective realm is productive of this functional advantage because it is necessitated and brought into existence by those things which she cannot easily alter in her experience. These are the associations of percepts which resist modification in the noumenal stream of percepts. They appear again and again before her mind in an unmodified or only slightly modified form.

Nevertheless, such objective events, which she can neither easily effect nor disavow, are introduced to her mind in the same noumenal stream of percepts as those which are more frequently modified in their presentation and over which she accordingly experiences herself to have a subjective control. She identifies these easy modifications with her inner life, while identifying physical phenomena as separate from that life. But both are in a deep sense translated out of her consciousness.

So it is in this way that images of physical things are assumed to be sensory, detached from the mind. And what are added to this peculiar compounding of experience into two spheres are the concepts which can be derived from some of the images, regardless of whether those images are understood to be perceptual or imaginative in origin. In other words, concepts are mental extensions which, like the images which ground them, are also composed of associated percepts. So, as another type of thought, they, along with images, belong to the subjective sphere.

Consequently, beyond their mutual origin in noumenal associations of percepts, it can be seen that the various extensions of the phenomenal precipitate differ in significant ways. An image,

The Immaterial Structure of Human Experience

which is composed of these percepts, is a mental representation which is understood to be either perceived or imagined. A perceived image is believed to be a direct representation of something objectively existent. But, in fact, the image *is* the object. For the object cannot be otherwise determined.[26]

In contrast with a perceived image, an image which is a work of the imagination is much more free in its arrangement of percepts. For, in representational terms, it may be said to be initially drawn from images of perception, whose percepts are then freely dissociated and recombined in new ways.

Of course, in immaterial terms, perceptual and imaginative images are both understood to be presented to human awareness in the noumenal precipitate. So, from this perspective, it can be seen that the representational viewpoint is part of the illusion of material awareness. But the representational view is nonetheless necessary for understanding human experience in human terms.

In either case, images may be understood to vary somewhat in their function, depending on whether they are recognized as perceptual or imaginative, or, in other words, whether their composition is humanly perceived as regular and sustained or as arbitrary. Again, it should be noted that perceptual images are those which exhibit less variation in their repeated appearance in the noumenal precipitate.

A concept, on the other hand, is neither free and variable in its composition nor thought to be objectively determined. Rather, it is experienced as an independent and disciplined work of the mind. It is a set of images supporting one image. Each of the images in the set is rendered as an independent extension, exhibiting

---

[26] Here it should be observed that, though mental images are generally predominantly visual, there are percepts of touch, sound, etc. which can contribute in part or in full to mental representations.

a particular property. The combined images support a more inclusive image which is purported to jointly express these properties.

The set of images is brought into prominence by a definition which indicates that these properties are essential to the supported image. In this way, a classification is created. For a classification defines something in terms of its salient properties. These defining properties cannot vary without altering the classification, or concept.

The concept thus pertains definitively to this and not to that. The set of images supporting the general image of the concept is what grounds it. For a concept, however abstract, is arranged in a particular manner by qualifying determinants. These determinants are its properties. And the properties are figured forth by images. Images inevitably represent percepts within extended objects, however unrecognizable in physical experience such a mental object may be.

The common origin of percepts in human awareness is the noumenal precipitate. Yet, in spite of this, mental images representing perceptions of physical objects, mental images which are independently imaginative, and concepts formed from either are each understood by a mature human awareness as being separately distinguished within the phenomenal precipitate.

Nevertheless, they are all extensions within that precipitate. Thus thoughts, which are recognized in terms of both images and concepts, are presented in the phenomenal precipitate as extensions possessing equal validity with physical extensions, which are understood to be something other than thoughts.

It is because of the possibility of a confusion between thoughts and physical objects that they must be differentiated in this manner. That is why a person recognizes a perceptual image as a representation of an object, though, in fact, it is the object.

The Immaterial Structure of Human Experience

For it is in this way that the object becomes objective and real for the experiencing person.

In the early development of the human mind, physical objects come to be understood as constituting something independent from the perceptual images deemed necessary to represent them. The objects are imprinted upon a growing sensibility as things-in-themselves. And concepts are also distinguished from the images upon which they depend. They are distinguished by the rigor of their definitional limitation.

Yet, though it is reasonable, and therefore acceptable, to acknowledge the origin of concepts in images, the distinction between a physical thing and its representation cannot be verified by reason. The reasonableness in accepting the origin of concepts in images results from the fact that both are thoughts. So they have their subjectivity in common and need not cross an indemonstrable barrier to be joined.

But physical objects, which are believed to be objective in character, are understood to be perceived by means of images which are subjective in character. Thus an indemonstrable barrier to a joint relationship between the image and the thing supposed to be represented by it remains. How is it to be demonstrated that the representational image corresponds faithfully to the thing represented?

Moreover, as the term "impenetrableness" indicates, not all percepts related to physical objects are visual. They may be tactile, aural, etc. The extended object is a combination of these. So, when the matter is subjected to a close analysis, an unlabored explanation for such a unity between disparate sensations separated from consciousness also becomes problematic. If they exist apart from the mind, how are they understood to be unified? Their appearing to be in the same close relationship when the object is examined or encountered multiple times does not necessarily affirm their adherence to one another.

Yet, in spite of these possibilities for doubt, the objectification is carried further in the human mind. For it is by means of a plurality of physical extensions that the human mind recognizes physical space. It would be so even if there were an independent intuition of space. Space would still be recognized by what occupies it.

This is reinforced by the fact that, in practical terms, whatever appears to be empty space is either bounded or assumed to be bounded by something which occupies space. For, to human perception, space is a conjunction of figures, sensible or otherwise. A demonstration of this can be supplied by the illusion of a painting. The only unbounded areas of the painting are the edges of the canvas, which do in fact act as boundaries. Outer space is no exception to the rule of boundedness, except in a theory which deliberately ignores the rule.

So, to be more precise, and regardless of viewpoint, the mind can be said to operate in the following manner. It is through an imagery of contiguous extensions, and through their incorporation into a conceptual framework concerning relations of the same, that the human mind constructs *quantifiable* space, *incremental* time, and those *proportional* relations describing change which are rendered into the equations of force and energy.

From a representational perspective, objects of thought, even when ideal and abstract, are reflections of objects in physical space. For that is the only way in which a mental image can be formed. In this way, the individual sensations which make up both physical objects and thought content are combined into extensions which constitute the whole of physical and thought experience, but not the whole of material experience. Though

The Immaterial Structure of Human Experience

physical objects and thoughts are both expressed as extensions, material experience includes feelings and emotions as well. And these are not extensions.

More important than these material considerations is the problem of consciousness in human experience. An immediate experience of pure consciousness is not only excluded from direct representation, as are feelings and emotions. It is excluded from material experience as well, which is not the case with feelings and emotions. For, though it is certainly experienced, pure consciousness is not at all perceptual in character (i.e., there are no percepts involved). Rather, consciousness is that within which perception must occur. In other words, perception only occurs within consciousness.

Thus the conscious mind should be characterized as being the source of all percepts which are experienced. It expresses every subjective and objective datum for human awareness, insofar as such data are introduced by percepts. The human intellect, in turn, organizes this data for a developing human awareness.

It is in this way that the phenomenal precipitate has come to be construed in this philosophy as the mind's map, or general representation, of the extended portions of material experience. The three-dimensional character of space, as commonly perceived, is the manner in which the objective realm of physical objects and events is distinguished from the subjective realm of thought. But, if both objective and subjective extensions constitute the whole of the phenomenal precipitate, feelings and emotions, which are also subjective, must be added to round out the full range of material experience.

So, since the construction of physical space is the work of the phenomenal precipitate, it is responsible for the distinction between subjective and objective experience. For it is physical space which separates the objective from the subjective. It separates extended objects from extended thoughts by expressing contiguity among the extended objects and thus enclosing them in extended space.

Feelings and emotions are then associated with thoughts, and the physical cause of them attributed to objects and events. The objective ground for a feeling or an emotion is the animal body. An event within this body is a series of changes which is generally attributed to physiology. This, in turn, is understood to be put in motion by thoughts representing events either within or without the body which are, or have been, experienced as pleasurable or painful.

However, while remaining within the representational viewpoint, the issue continues to become ever more complex. For, though a person's thoughts are commonly considered to be subjective in nature, their content is not. Their content is derived from the objective data of perceptual experience. Therefore it is objective. This is so because thoughts either directly or indirectly represent aspects of physical experience.

Conversely, if one were to entertain a thoroughly immaterialist outlook concerning human experience, consciousness must be given a status superior to that of material awareness. As a result, the whole of experience would be rendered immaterialist in character. Consequently, thoughts would be counted among the extensions of the phenomenal precipitate, as though they expressed a validity comparable to that of physical extensions and were not derived from them.

Whereas, when once again considering matters from a representational perspective, where a clear distinction is made between the objective and subjective realms of experience, thoughts are held to occupy "mental" space only. And physical extensions—

The Immaterial Structure of Human Experience

i.e., physical objects—occupy "physical" space. From this immaterialist and representational opposition of perspectives it can be seen that an understanding of human experience is variable, depending upon which viewpoint the topic is approached from.

Now, according to the representational viewpoint, perceptual content is the only content that a thought can possess. For thoughts are either images or concepts, both of which are extended associations of percepts. This is as true of concepts as it is of images because a concept is supported by imagery. It is a definitionally controlled arrangement of images. So, in spite of the seemingly unbridgeable gulf between human mental life and objective spheres of activity, the perceptual content of thoughts is derived from objective experience either immediately or by derivation.

In addition to its possessing perceptual content, a thought, understood in the representational way, must ultimately reference something which is physically extended. For this is how a thought is understood to obtain its material characteristics: its percepts. The percepts are gathered in an "object" of the thought. The object is the means by which the thought becomes an extension. This is so, even should the thought be quite fantastical or profoundly abstract. Otherwise, it could not be imagined to have any objective reference to life.

For example, if a thought about a feeling or an emotion is to be made concrete before the mind (i.e., if it is to exhibit perceptual content), it must have a material object, which becomes an object of the thought. Consequently, it must be a thought about a body in which that feeling or emotion occurs. Whereas, for a person to simply make a statement about a good, bad, happy, or sad feeling, as though it were an independent entity, does not present an image to the mind.

Likewise, a thought about such things as pure consciousness, chaos, or the infinite is not possible. To be a thought, it must be about what these things are not. Such thoughts as these are therefore indirect. Thus, in the first instance, the thought may be about an awareness which is aware of nothing but itself. But to register anything concretely before the mind in that regard, the thought must be about the absence of all those things which are normally present to awareness.

It is these normally present things which are understood not to be present. So it turns out that it is the things normally present to awareness which are the true focus of the thought. Though consciousness may be simply aware of itself without any representation in the mind, it is only in the way of an indirect representation that it can be imaginatively or conceptually aware of itself. For a thought about consciousness, involving any kind of imagery, can only be expressed in this indirect manner, not as a direct reference to material experience. Thus consciousness cannot be directly thought.

In the case of a train of thought which begins with a normal condition involving order, and proceeds to imagine that order as being presently in a state of disorder, the latter thought is simply about the absence of order, which is unimaginable. So, to render it concrete before the mind, the original exemplar of order must become the focus of the thought. Then it is understood that such a state of order does not pertain to the situation under consideration.

Or again, a direct thought about the infinite would be a thought about something which has no bounds. For the infinite is neither extended nor undergoing limited duration. Thus the thought is about nothing. For these conditions cannot be conceived. So, to form a concrete conception of the infinite, the

The Immaterial Structure of Human Experience

thought would have to be about things which are both individually and collectively finite. Then it is these which would be considered not to be the case, the finite entities becoming the focus of the thought.

These three types of thought take on a negative character because, to be thoughts, they must be expressed in percepts. And the percepts must be, or must initially have been, encountered in experience in some form of physical limitation and relation—i.e., as belonging to or suggesting a physical extension in space. For even a thought limited to the color blue must be a thought about a blue "space," as in a blue sky. The blue sky is bounded by horizons or the blackness of non-blue space. Thus it is an extension.

If a person should envision only the blue of the sky or the blue of a blue surface without including any bounds in her mental image, the fact remains present to her mind that there must be such bounds. If she considers the matter closely and insists on no bounds, she will still think of these bounds as the bounds of her thought. That is why a thought itself is an extension in the mind. As such, it simulates a physical extension, though it lacks contiguity with other thoughts and exhibits only a temporal sequence.

A thought about anything suggests the possibility of a relationship between at least two extensions. This is because a thought concerning extensions requires that any one extension be limited to make room for another in order that it be finite. So there must be limitations for these relations to occur.

In other words, in any imaginable context of space, there are contiguous extensions, each limited by the other. Moreover, due to the ubiquitous experience of change, measurable durations of these extensions are exhibited within a context of differing durations. In other words, every extension is limited, or finite, in duration as well. Besides material experiences which exhibit these limitations, there is nothing humanly imaginable.

And should a universal concept asserting every member of a class, but no particular member of that class, cross a person's mind, it too is no exception to this rule, since even a universal concept, insofar as it has reference to concrete experience (i.e., is not about the infinite), must both include and exclude definable properties. It must therefore be limited.

This requirement holds for human awareness because material experience is experience of one thing as opposed to another—i.e., one thing limited by another. So, as a thought image, whatever is under consideration must be imagined in this way, whether it be as an individual sensation which is a quality of a physical extension, a physical extension itself, or an event involving a change in the relations between extensions or their properties which serves to register a limited duration of time.

So, in brief, the problem with the three negative concepts mentioned above is the following. For the first, there are no percepts to be encountered in any attempt at a direct consideration of pure consciousness. Thus there are no extensions either. For the second, there is no means of understanding chaos in terms of disorder alone, since there must be relations of some sort, and therefore order, between the extensions concerned. And, as regards the third, there is simply no possibility of conceiving the infinite, when all the mind's experience is of the finite.

Consequently, following upon the implications of this discussion, it can be seen that all mental images are comprised of the perceptual content of thought, as that perceptual content is figured forth in physical extensions. Thus thought images will often resemble these physical extensions directly. Or, in imaginative thought, the content of these direct images is reorganized to

The Immaterial Structure of Human Experience

become images which are seemingly independent of physical experience.

Furthermore, it is from both these types of imagery that concepts are derived. These concepts may be concepts of experience. Or they may be concepts of imagined experience. Concepts of imagined experience would include even the most abstract and seemingly non-experiential ideas. For they must express some measure of concreteness—i.e., perceptual content—in order to be represented to the mind.

For example, if a person were to entertain the concept of an isosceles triangle, she would concretely envision a figure. This figure is an extension. It is a mental extension of thought, resembling a physical extension. As such, it stands as an exact rendition and support of the concept in her mind.

It would of course have been learned by her. For, in its abstract form, it was originally conceived in a past epoch: that of the early Greeks. However, its original form was suggested even to them by any one or all of the inexact physical counterparts of it which had been encountered by Egyptian farmers in practical experience.

So, having engaged the figure in her mind, the person recalling it would envision the pertinent lines and vertices of the figure, which are the properties that define it. Or at least, she would know that she could call these properties forth in her mind when required. For, though she can simply state the concept while holding its imagery in abeyance, that imagery is never beyond the possibility of immediate recall.

The equality of two sides and of two base angles are the specific properties which make the triangle isosceles. So, in accordance with this image, these properties would be understood in terms of a sameness between each of the like properties. This would be the sameness in length of the two lines which make up two sides of the triangle. It would also be the sameness in angles of the two vertices at the base of those lines.

Now it is a portion of the perceptual which is set aside by the human mind as objective reality. For objective reality is restricted to perceptual experience. Moreover, from a representational point of view, objective reality is considered to be extended outside the mind. But feelings and emotions are also perceptual. Yet they are not extended outside the mind. So they are generally considered to be subjective in character. Therefore, not all perceptual content in the mind represents the objective.

This disparity between the objective realm and the subjective character of the perception of feeling and emotion can be corrected. It is corrected through the special case of a person considering her body to be a physical extension which is objective and separate from her contemplating mind. Her feelings and emotions are then understood to occur within this objective body. In this way, as belonging to her body, they are considered by her to be objective.

But, however much adhered to in practice, this exception is an imaginative construct and does not constitute a felt reality. Normally, her feelings and emotions are considered to be subjective. It is her body which is considered to be objective. Somehow it appears to her to be mysteriously affected by changes in the general physical realm which affect it in such a way as to seem to bear an influential impact upon her personal feelings and emotions.

Conversely, when brought under the closest scrutiny, mental images and concepts are, it is to be observed, objective in content. This is so, even when they are freely imagined or recalled from what is understood to be memory. For their percepts are

The Immaterial Structure of Human Experience

those of experience. And the form of such thoughts is mental extension, which is not unlike the extended form of objects.

Thus objectivity would seem to be intermixed with subjectivity. For images and concepts are thought extensions which are subjective in form (i.e., mental), while their content remains objective in origin (i.e., perceptual). In other words, as thoughts, they are extensions within the mind. But as thoughts representing experience in terms of its perceptual content, they are composed of the percepts of objective, physically extended experience.

However, this apparent crossover between subjectivity and objectivity can be rectified. For the problem can be easily identified. It is that the present discussion exhibits a representational perspective, which, however useful and necessary to daily living, is inherently contradictory. For it assumes a subject/object distinction which is unsupported by evidence.

Whereas the immaterialist viewpoint is more inclusive. For it treats all experiential phenomena as alike in character—i.e., as existing in the mind. In other words, since all percepts are mentally perceived, the more inclusive immaterialist viewpoint does not recognize a subject/object distinction.

Ironically, when the representational perspective is retained but brought under greater scrutiny, the issue does ultimately resolve itself. For objective reality, as understood from a representational viewpoint, must be represented in the mind to be perceived. This representation arises from the fact that objects presumed to be encountered in objective physical sensation must take the character of images when brought before the mind for recognition. Hence the phrase "representational viewpoint."

Since sensory data must form an image to be recognized in a context of experience, and since images are subjective in form, everything may be said to be subjective in character. For there is no other means of recognizing objective extensions (i.e., physical objects) but through mental representation. Thus it is in the mind that all percepts are revealed to a consciousness prior to any subject/object distinction being made between them.

So, when the subject/object distinction is observed, it must be acknowledged to be illusory. For, even from a representational viewpoint, the objective cannot ultimately be distinguished from the subjective. Thus the immaterialist viewpoint conveniently eliminates this troublesome subject/object distinction. And, as a result, subjective feelings and thought extensions stand in their true relation together with physical extensions in the mind, the physical extensions being themselves experienced as thought extensions.

However, in human experience it is generally assumed that there are physical sensations which are omitted from perceptual images which are cursorily formed. This occurs when someone looks at a car and only registers bumpers, doors, wheels, and a general shape, while omitting many other details. Thus the image is thought to be an incomplete representation, which would indicate its independence from the object.

But, of course, an apparently incomplete observation need not indicate an incomplete relationship between the image and the object represented by that image. In the case above, the image reflects what is to be represented at that moment. It is a representation of an object which must be regarded as complete precisely in terms of the representation which is made. Further images representing other details may, in this sense, be considered to be representations of other objects.

It is a combination of these images in the mind which fleshes out the presumed greater object composed of all these representations. In spite of an overlapping of details between these repre-

The Immaterial Structure of Human Experience

sentations, such a whole object does not exist in observation. It exists only in a hypothetical combination. However, multiple encounters with such a train of experience, involving a variant but consistent series of related observations, will inevitably set up an indelible belief in the integrity of the whole.

So, if it should be further insisted that most observations are observed to be incomplete, that there is almost always more to an object than can be encompassed in a single representation, the obvious response must be that the more complete object is a product of a mental adjustment made through a compounding of fragments of experience. For no one ever sees a complex object in its wholeness.

Even when a person presumably knows what an object should be, she must reconfirm her conviction by means of a series of incomplete observations. In the case above, she might inspect the engine, cab, and general design of the car to obtain a more complete impression of it. But, in doing so, she will not be representing to her mind the original details which were previously mentioned.

Nevertheless, it it because of this apparent discrepancy between a representation and the thing represented that an overall mental origin of percepts and extensions is not generally recognized within a mature human sensibility, where the subject/object distinction is already firmly established.

So, consequent upon this predilection of human sensibility for a subject/object distinction, and for convenience in propounding a representationalist, as opposed to an immaterialist, viewpoint, it can be, and generally is, said that objects, and the perceptual images representing them, exist separately in experience.

But again, if consciousness is spirit (as is maintained in this work and as seems reasonable upon critical examination), and if the content of consciousness is composed of percepts, and thoughts are formed of percepts, then thought is in consciousness. But it is not consciousness. So neither is it spirit. Rather, it is a product of spirit acting within the confines of material awareness by means of the intuitions. Thus thought is spiritual in form and material in content.

The material content of both consciousness and thought is finite because it is made up of percepts. These percepts make their debut in the mind through the noumenal precipitate, which employs focus in the delineation of experience. Focus introduces limitations. For that which is focused upon is something in particular as opposed to something else. It is this percept, this association, or this extension as opposed to that one.

Thus, since they are products of focus, the percepts and their associations are experienced as limited, or finite. Otherwise, distinctions could not be made between them. Nor could associations be recognized among them. And it is these percepts and associations of percepts which go into the making of both the mental and spatial extensions of the phenomenal precipitate.

Consequently, due to the finite character of the noumenal precipitate's presentation of percepts and their associations, and due to the retention of this characteristic in the phenomenal precipitate, all the content of a person's awareness, aside from the experience of consciousness itself, is finite. Thus the person concludes that, if everything in material experience is finite, what besides consciousness can be the exception?

She further concludes that consciousness is a mystery. For it can neither be conceptualized nor explained in material terms. Yet she wishes to understand what she is. Therefore she arrives at

The Immaterial Structure of Human Experience

the position that human beings are material. This, at least, can be explained. And it accords with the limitations which experience seems to place upon the exercise of her will.

As a result, she believes herself to be a limited physical extension constrained by contiguous extensions in space, incremental time, and change. Thus she experiences herself as existing within the phenomenal precipitate. So she is a physical body. And, as such, she can be an object of her own perception.

Personal feeling, emotion, thought, and any personal inclination toward a particular course of action become attributes of her body. For she is her body. Yet her thoughts and actions are experienced subjectively, in spite of their seeming to originate objectively within the physical extension of her body.

In other words, her thoughts and actions are experienced as her own human creation and not as an integral part of an external realm. But they are expressed in that realm. So it is in this way that thought, will, and emotion are understood to be separated from the objective realm of physical extension. Yet they are an integral part of it.

If it should be asked why a human sensibility should perceive certain thoughts, actions, and emotions as its own, this answer must be given: it is because these phenomena are so arranged within the sequences of physical change (and therefore incremental time) that a distinction is made between them and the physical extensions.

This distinction, of course, arises in the noumenal precipitate of secondary mind in the order of its initial presentation of associated percepts. It results from the fact that some of these associations can be linked with a continuing sense of self. For they appear to be regulated by, or fall into an accord with, the whims of an individual will.

Moreover, as these particular sequences of phenomena take place within a unified consciousness (i.e., they are all confined to the same knowing awareness), they participate in its unity. This is to say that they do not in any way contradict the unity of their apprehension. They do not appear to belong elsewhere.

The resulting sense of personal continuity is further assisted both by what is understood as will and by what is taken for memory. The sequences of thought, feeling, emotion, and personal action are set before the mind in such a manner as to follow upon one another, as though they were expressions of individual purpose or elements of recall and therefore subject to an individual inclination.

Other sequences of phenomena, on the other hand, may in various circumstances follow upon one another as well. But they cannot be made subject to individual inclination without simultaneously expressing their independence from it. In other words, a kettle of water may be made to boil, but only by following the physical laws of nature. Thus these external laws appear to contradict the perceiving individual's unity of apprehension and cannot be associated with a continuing sense of self.

But, when returning to an immaterialist perspective from these speculations concerning a representational viewpoint, it will once again be found that thought and personal action are included within a more comprehensive phenomenal precipitate. So, from this point of view, it could certainly be said that a homogeneous presentation of all extended phenomena has been created. For, since there is no subject/object distinction in this case, all extended phenomena are rendered subjective and are to be found within spirit, or conscious mind. Thus the more encompassing view clearly attributes a dominant role to spirit.

The Immaterial Structure of Human Experience

Yet, in such a point of view, the role of spirit can be overemphasized, since it can lead to an inference that human beings do not truly effect anything. For then it would appear that the individual human character of thoughts, affections, and acts is merely illusory. They would all seem to be the work of universal spirit, operating independently of the finite limits of an individual person.

So it becomes reasonable to investigate even further into what it is that renders human emotions, thoughts, and actions answerable to an individual human will. Why is it advantageous to view them in this manner? Let something more elaborate than a single emotion or thought, or a series of unrelated images or concepts, be considered. For the meaning and purpose of life does not lie in single emotions or thoughts. Nor does it lie in a series of unrelated images or concepts.

For example, take a complex theoretical construct, such as a scientific theory. The development of the kind of integrated system of concepts belonging to a scientific theory requires personal commitment. Someone creates the theory to fulfill a human purpose. So can it be said that a person creating the theory or some part of it should not consider herself personally responsible for it simply because, from an immaterialist perspective, it can be broadly surmised that it is the general work of spirit? If so, then nothing would be done.

Moreover, this universal perspective would also lead a person to speculate that every living, breathing moment of her life is the same type of work, a work outside her material purview. And, in principle, she would be correct. But can she choose accordingly to forgo devising a plan for her daily sustenance? If so, the "illusion" of hunger will certainly assail her in such a manner as to convince her to assuage it. Thus she will very likely turn back from her initial lack of resolution to embrace a determination to alleviate what for her is a very real cause of personal suffering.

So the limited human outlook provides a practical advantage. And that practical advantage is moral. For it involves individual responsibility. This is precisely what the representational perspective accomplishes. It answers to the design of spirit, which assigns motivation to the individual.

With motivation comes choice, meaning, and commitment. Thus it involves responsibility. And why should this responsibility not be the case, since the will of the individual is anchored deep in the core of spirit? For it is that spiritually embedded will which makes the choices, albeit that it determines them in one instantaneous movement, which is undetected by the drawn-out awareness of a temporal human mind.

It should be recalled that the individual and universal spirit are ultimately one, set apart from one another only as a single wavelength of light is separated in a prism from the full spectrum of light. The white light which inhabits the prism, each color frequency of it passing through the prism along its own unique trajectory, is the equivalent of one will differentiated into many. In other words, reducing this discussion to practical terms, what would be the point of living a life, much less having an ambitious project like a theory and acting upon it, if living, thinking, and acting were merely illusory?

This would be the case if, thinking in human terms, any single wavelength of light were considered to be continually aware of its origin in the full spectrum of light. The attitude might arise: why not let spirit take responsibility for everything, since it has access to all the possibilities of its spectrum? Thus it can be seen that an important function of the role of individual limitation is to confine a person's sense of responsibility to herself.

The Immaterial Structure of Human Experience

Moreover, what distinguishes personal thought and action from the things thought about and acted upon should be more carefully considered. This should be closely scrutinized because it has been asserted that both thoughts and physical objects are given within the noumenal precipitate as associations of percepts.

It has been further asserted that, since the associations of percepts which constitute thoughts and objects are initially presented to human awareness in this way, their common origin constitutes a prior or foundational condition for human sensibility. Thus thoughts would neither occasion nor follow upon, but would coexist with, extensions and events in the physical realm. Such a coexistence would deny any human participation in facilitating causal events between physical objects.

The answer to this is to be found once again in the observation that human awareness does not experience the world in this manner. Only secondary mind and, for a very brief period, the infant mind does so. For the subject/object distinction is soon formed in a child's mind. So, while it is true that both a theory and the data it encompasses (or, in other words, both thought structures and sensory perceptions) occur simultaneously within the noumenal precipitate, they do so only in the mind of spirit and a newborn infant. That is, they occur within primary and secondary mind prior to any development of human experience.

Once human experience develops the subject/object distinction, this distinction screens the work of secondary mind and its noumenal precipitate from human awareness. Thus, for a developing human awareness, the situation is otherwise than indicated above. Due to the phenomenal constraints of space and incremental time, taken as a framework for the objective content experienced within the mind of a human being, a theory (made of thoughts) and its foundational data (made up of physical objects and events) are completely separate from one another. This is because a human being experiences thought and sensory intake, not as simultaneous in occurrence, but rather as sequentially integrated.

Her thoughts and acts (i.e., decisions), are coordinated by secondary mind in such a manner as to precede or follow other thoughts and acts associated with herself. They are thus perceived to be independent of and either prior or consequent to the events with which they are associated. The priority or consequence of the relationship depends upon whether a particular train of thought is understood to effect the event in question or to be brought about by it.

In other words, her thoughts are subjectively located in her person, while their temporal relationship to the physical events which are understood either to be occasioned by them or to occasion them is determined objectively by these events. The physical events are located objectively outside her person.

It is these which become the means of providing an incremental time frame which determines the sequential integration of her thoughts among physical events. So, in this sense, thoughts and physical events, though integrated in occurrence, are otherwise completely independent of one another, as though they took place in different domains.

Berkeley, if he were supplying the terminology used in this work, would call percepts "ideas." And, due to his focus upon the problem of things-in-themselves, he would make no graduated distinction among them, such as has been done here. He would thus shorten the work and reduce its complexity in the interest of a greater focus upon his central concern. But there would be nonetheless a fundamental connection between his philosophical scheme and that of this work.

The Immaterial Structure of Human Experience

For it is the case that his "ideas" belong to the noumenal precipitate, which expresses the full range of sensations within human experience, and which is originally made present to the human mind as a sole source of its ideas, or percepts. But, for advancing human awareness, the formation of the phenomenal precipitate intervenes to determine the character of human experience.

Granted that, even in Berkeley's mind, it is not the case that the subjective origin of ideas must preclude a separation between thought and physical perception. What is true is that Berkeley does not explain this. He does not apparently see or find it necessary to explain that such a separation comes about according to the human experience of the dictates of space, time, and change within what in this work has been called a phenomenal precipitate.

As a result of this separation, those extensions which remain within the objective realm are contiguous physical bodies in space, incremental time, and physical change. Those which do not are the extensions of thought and their changes. It is this distinction in human awareness between the objective and subjective which Berkeley neglects to explain.

Rather, his emphasis is upon the problem of the thing-in-itself and the eradication of the confusion this problem causes. So it remains true in his thinking (and that of this work as well) that, for human awareness, some of these ideas, or percepts, do constitute thoughts. Others constitute what human beings come to recognize as sensory perceptions. However, since Berkeley recognizes sensory perceptions directly as thoughts, and not as representations, no clear distinction is made between thought and perception.

This is the principal difference between Berkeley's thinking and that of the present work. Nevertheless, when considered philosophically, in neither his case nor the one at hand, need the subjective and objective realms of experience be considered to have any origin but the mind. Consequently, sensory perceptions should not be understood philosophically as originating from things-in-themselves. They are composed of percepts, just as thoughts are.

Collectively, Berkeley's ideas are equivalent to the more inclusive phenomenal precipitate already mentioned in this discussion. But, as has also been indicated, a human being develops a subjective sense of self, separating those percepts which belong to the subjective from those which are objective.

This results in a subjective human attempt to map a bewildering multiplicity of mental representations into a recognizable order. In childhood, such a process amounts to the coordination of a sense of reality. In adulthood, it may be the development of a scientific or philosophical system, which, of course, is a further coordination of the sense of reality.

Thus, in the complex, ongoing operation which is this mapping process, those images which were initially experienced as mental associations of sensation replicating physical extensions in varying degree now appear to be altered, rearranged in relation to one another, and generally developed into creations of the mind. As this undertaking begins in early individual development, the child is induced to recognize that it has thoughts.

Consequently, an interrelated set of images (and eventually concepts) is developed, which is of particular interest in regard to human subjectivity. For it is made up of those percepts which begin to be associated strictly with the mind in the earliest period of human development. In infancy, childhood, and finally adult-

The Immaterial Structure of Human Experience

hood, these percepts form the images (and later, concepts) which are experienced subjectively as imaginative creations and personal thoughts.

But they are not completely detached from the objective domain. For their perceptual content is understood to have originated there. Moreover, they become intermingled by the child's inexperienced sensibility with those images which appear to represent external facts of experience.

Interestingly, this is done in the very act of determining what those external facts are. So there is no clear delineation at this period. And much of this intermingling will determine the objectivity of the child's, and later the adult's, world. Some of it will be corrected in later life, but not all.

Because of this early blurring of subjective/objective domains, the activity of the human mind approaches a fundamental apprehension of the phenomenal precipitate in that original inclusive character which precedes its bifurcation into subjective/objective realms. That is, it approaches a recognition of the noumenal foundation of the precipitate as it is presented to human awareness by secondary mind.

However, any such activity of the infantile human mind is intended to provide no more than a foundation for a developing subjective awareness of that portion of the phenomenal precipitate which constitutes the objective domain. So the inclusive phenomenal precipitate and its noumenal origin is soon obscured behind the subjective/objective dichotomy.

Nonetheless, there is a continuation of much feedback between the developing phenomenal precipitate and the noumenal mind. The noumenal precipitate, proceeding directly from secondary mind, is tasked with providing a precise synchronization of input with the phenomenal precipitate, just as the phenomenal precipitate must only replicate in modified form what it receives from the noumenal precipitate.

Thus a synchronization between the noumenal and phenomenal precipitates is fully maintained. For there is nothing which appears in one which does not appear simultaneously in the other. Each must register the same percept input in its individual way. And there is no temporal differentiation in the occurrence of the input in both precipitates. It happens in unison. For they are ultimately one and the same. This is why the translation of impressions from one precipitate to the other is matched percept for percept. And it is immediate.

It is in this reciprocal manner that the feedback from the phenomenal precipitate is immediately expressed in the output of the noumenal precipitate, as though it had originated there. Which in fact it does. Otherwise, it could not exist in the phenomenal precipitate. For everything in the phenomenal precipitate is a reworking of what is in the noumenal precipitate. Yet the human mind believes its accretions to the phenomenal precipitate to have originated with it. Whereas, in truth, these accretions have their origin in the deep heart of spirit.

Because of the initial prominence of both precipitates in this feedback process, a distinction between the immaterialist and representational views is indiscernible in the early awareness of an infant. For the infant child begins life in an entirely subjective state of mind. She knows nothing but the kaleidoscope of impressions which passes before her awareness. As such, she is more spirit than material being.

But later in her development, the older child becomes increasingly aware of a detached reality around her. Insofar as she can determine, it is a reality partially of her own making and partially not. For she can shape her understanding of it. But she can

The Immaterial Structure of Human Experience

only do so inasmuch as the fixed order of her impressions will allow.

Consequently, an adult person's sense of reality, as occurs at the most advanced stages of the still continuing feedback, will include an elaborate intellectual overlay on the inflexible ground of experience. This intellectual overlay will be modified by repeated self-correction in response to further thought and experience, as well as by any amendments which will arise from cultural conditioning by other human beings.

In other words, the more developed person will have a sense of a completely independent physical world around her. And this will lead to a recognition of her own limited independence within it. As a result, her view of that world becomes entirely objective. She understands that she is both free and bound by her material environment.

Thus, since she can only effect a limited influence on her world, she will, as her experience continues to grow, become fully cognizant of an ongoing need for changes in her view of it. She will see them as personal adjustments. Consequently, she will believe that she is directly involved in such changes and is either actively or passively responsible for them. Hence her increasingly embedded sense of exercising an independent, though limited, will within her material circumstances.

Yet, as the immediate synchronization of feedback with input indicates, deep reality is not material. Rather, it is due to the regulating influence of secondary mind that an individual human awareness is kept sufficiently uniform in her development in relation to her world, herself, and other human beings.

One spiritual mind controls all through both the collectivity of individual minds and through each one alone, so as to allow for a general communication, for an individual self-correction in relation to the common experience of all, and for a resulting intellectual progress. All this occurs in spite of personal differences among the original and isolated infantile responses with which each person begins her material life. For such early development remains closeted at the most fundamental levels of each mind.

This is to say that each mind, however much it may find itself in harmony with others, has its own unique foundational makeup, which forms the ground of its unique personality. Hence the complex conviction which arises in each person that she has both an individual will, which is exercised within her material circumstances, and a shared reality with others, which includes an ability to build a common interpretation of that shared world.

Now the principal distinction being worked out within an infant mind is between subject and object. Given such a welter of sensation as greets the newly active mind, this must be settled as soon as possible. What it involves is a positing of a physical reality which is separate from the individual self.

But, since the entire process takes place within the mind, none of it requires the actual existence of anything external to the mind. Consequently, objectivity and the independent existence of a thing-in-itself are not the same. The objectivity is necessary for the individual functioning of a person within her environment. But that environment need not be suspended in an imaginary realm independent of spirit.

Rather, within this developing human frame of mind, the mental impressions both of subjective thought and of the objective data of physical experience originate inside a single framework of space, time, and change, which is the noumenal precipitate. But a physical projection of space, time, and change comes more and more to be objectively conceived. In this way,

The Immaterial Structure of Human Experience

the phenomenal precipitate is developed out of the materials of the noumenal precipitate.

At first, the phenomenal precipitate is developed within the mind in its original inclusive character, like that of the noumenal precipitate. But later it bifurcates and forms a subjective awareness and an objective field of reference for that awareness. Thus what finally appear to be made available to the subjective human mind are objectively apprehended percepts within physical extensions. These extensions, or physical objects, submit themselves to an independent regularity of interaction. The regularity of their interaction allows them to be brought under the cognizance of science, where such relations provide data for research and experimental verification.

All that is required for the inductive reasoning necessary to a systematic apprehension of the physical world is a consistency in the relations of the representational images and concepts which appear before the mind. These relations must express a uniformity within a single objective framework of space and time. Chief among such relations are those of similarity and difference. Regularized proportions among these allow for relations which are causal.

Causal relations occur because certain associations of percepts, understood as physical objects, relate predictably to one another in terms of change in uniform circumstances. It is this predictability, or uniformity of occurrence, which establishes causal relations. They occur in regard to whatever uniform events human beings either may observe to take place independently of their own volition or in accordance with their actions.

What is more, in this matter one need not be tempted to succumb to Hume's denial of an objective necessity in causal relations, since that denial is rendered irrelevant by the immaterial character of the noumenal precipitate, as originally posited by Berkeley—immaterial in the sense that there is no need for a thing-in-itself. So how those things labeled objective appear initially in the mind is how they must be understood to appear in physical reality. For this appearance is in accordance with the order of input of the noumenal precipitate.

A significant portion of the output of the noumenal precipitate is recognized within human experience as objective. Nevertheless, spirit is the origin of all percepts and associations between percepts within the noumenal precipitate. Thus it determines the necessity of objective relations among extensions in the phenomenal precipitate and human awareness. This ordered origin also holds for the subjective realm, so that thought would appear, upon initial consideration, to be no less determined than physical events.

However, this view provides a false sense of determinism, which is obviated by the deep origin of human will. For the human will is not located in phenomenal appearances. Nor is it located in the products of the noumenal precipitate. Rather, in the former case, it is located outside of physical space and incremental time.

In the latter case, it is located beyond non-incremental time as well. It is to be found in the heart of spirit. In other words, the intended order and flow of human events, ultimately being determined by this will, is logically prior both to its experience in the human mind and to the expression of it in the noumenal precipitate.

For, in accordance with this personal will, the entire panorama of an individual human experience unfolding in time is initially constituted by a simultaneous and instantaneous presence of the whole in self-limiting spirit. Since universal spirit and self-

The Immaterial Structure of Human Experience

limiting spirit are one and the same, as primary and secondary mind respectively, what is present to one is of course present to the other.

To restate the above, let it be said that the expressions of secondary mind, where a sequential presentation of percepts in non-incremental time occurs, are put forth within the noumenal precipitate in a manner which is logically (but not temporally) subsequent to their timeless origin. Once put forth, they are, in turn, converted into the extensions of the inclusive phenomenal precipitate. And these are then divided along subject/object distinctions.

Nevertheless, this deep spiritual origin of events does not preclude the practice of science. For science can be and is developed in spite of the spiritual origin of the will and its instantaneous determination of events in an individual life. This is possible because, in a human life, the experience of time alters the simultaneity and instantaneity of what occurs. It puts it into sequence. Yet there remains a necessity to be found in the relations of those events. That necessity allows for a recognition and development of the laws formulated by science.

But, if regarded superficially in material terms, none of this is precisely as it might seem. For the causally determined order of events exhibits a necessity arising from two sources, which two sources are ultimately one: it arises in part from the general character of universal spirit and in part from the individual will of self-limiting spirit, which is the spirit of each individual person.

In this way, the individual wills her life, while the universal expresses the collective whole. Both of these seemingly separate, but ultimately united, currents enter into human experience. The former performs what a personal will can effect. The latter performs what it cannot effect. Again, both of these are illustrated as working together by the example of water, which can be made to boil, but only in accordance with certain laws. The fact that they are both united in a single origin has already been explained in terms of a prism and its refraction of light.

So the principal point to be made here is that the physical necessity encountered in causal relations is located in spirit, not in the apparent physicality of the relations. In other words, it is not enough to say that causal relations appear to human awareness as they do simply because they are laid down in the noumenal precipitate in a specific order of presentation of individual associations of percepts.

They appear as they do because their order is determined by spirit, both in its independent character as provided by universal spirit and in any activation induced among these relations by self-limiting spirit. It is this order which is identified as causal. And it is this order again which holds in its consistency for each individual and for all individuals together.

37. Kant's transcendental categories. The ideas set forth in this book propose to account for human awareness in the simplest terms of *unity* and *division* as expressed under the operation of *mental focus*. Their methods are associative, more akin to the British empiricists—Locke, Berkeley, and Hume—than they are to Immanuel Kant. But, though quite different in its particulars from Kant's system, much of what is contained in this book does broadly parallel his thinking.

So an attempt will be made here to use Kant's twelve transcendental categories to illustrate the parallel. It should be kept in mind, however, that Kant's intuitions of time and space cannot apply. Furthermore, this exercise is intended to demonstrate a reduction of his twelve categories to the first three. For these

The Immaterial Structure of Human Experience

three alone are treated in this work, not as intellectual categories, but as intuitions.

Thus it is the three intuitions—simple unity, plurality, and totality—which are being employed in this discussion of Kant's categories. Clearly, this is not an explication of Kant as he would have understood his own transcendental categories, which he derived from Aristotle. Neither is there any concern as to whether Kant's categories cover the whole of human cognition. Rather, what is being demonstrated is that these categories can be explained using nothing more than the three intuitions presented in this book. To begin, the three intuitions are equivalent to the first three of Kant's categories.

(1) Under the general heading *Quantity* are the three categories, *Unity*, *Plurality*, and *Totality*.

Unity. One, as in one apple. Or one, as in one sensation, or percept. This unity is derived from simple awareness—i.e., the awareness of consciousness *without regard to its content*. Consciousness is here understood as indivisible and unbounded—a simple unity. The example of one apple, however, would not be possible without a pattern of other objects to which it belonged.

For an apple has properties. Thus an apple is known as an apple because *what it is not* is known. It has precisely these properties and not those. Nevertheless, its unity is all that is at issue here. A sensation, or percept, on the other hand, is fundamental. It is indivisible. It is a simple unity.

The example of an apple was given for the sake of an illustration from common experience. An apple is an extended physical object, something frequently encountered and recognized. As such, it is a compound of properties, such as round, red, sweet, etc. This compounding of properties is best understood under the next two categories. For unity, plurality, and totality, which are the first three of twelve transcendental categories in Kant, have been converted into the three fundamental intuitions of the system expounded in this book.

Plurality. Two or more, as in dividing an apple into halves, thirds, or quarters. This intuition results from an awareness of the *content* of consciousness, as opposed to consciousness itself. The content of consciousness is where all the percepts of human awareness are located. Both the objects of sensory awareness and the objects of thought are made present to the human mind by means of percepts, or impressions on the mind. It is these percepts which are combined into properties. So the properties of physical extensions, or objects, are derived from them. So are the properties of the objects of thought.

Thus, since the objects of the sensory realm and the objects of thought are both composed of percepts, they are discovered within an individual consciousness. For that is where percepts are encountered. They are not encountered in any manner which would imply their existence independent of the mind. Or, if it should be the case that they were, it could not be satisfactorily demonstrated.

So these percepts appear associated together as extended entities within two contexts: a context of physical experience and a context of thought. For physical objects are physical extensions. And thoughts are mental extensions. These two realms of extension are distinguished from one another in terms of their differing relationships to human will. What is considered sensory is held not to be subject to human will, though it can in many cases be acted upon. But thoughts are understood to be subject to human will alone.

The Immaterial Structure of Human Experience

Now there is a recognition of a distinction between individual percepts—say between blue and red—at the noumenal level of human awareness. [27] So this constitutes a division between the percepts. Division makes one thing into two or more. Consequently, it is apparent that there is more than one percept.

The recognition of this distinction is where the intuition of plurality makes its debut. For there could not be any distinction between percepts if they were not recognized as individual and therefore multiple in character. Thus the inauguration of an intuition of plurality occurs with its use. As with the intuition of simple unity, it is a function of mental focus. The mind focuses on the experience of blue, then upon the experience of red. These are different experiences. Therefore, they are multiple.

Thus the mind recognizes that there is a plurality of percepts. But such a recognition in a particular case is also a recognition of the possibility of plurality in general. Accordingly, the intuition of plurality is brought into independent practice and may be applied elsewhere. In this way, the mind has advanced beyond the intuition of simple unity. For there is more than one unity, each percept being recognized as an independent unity.

It is the intuition of plurality, then, which is both created by an awareness of the individual character of percepts and which, in turn, firmly delineates them one from another. And it is the intuition of unity which allows them to be combined into properties. Under the influence of these same two intuitions, these properties are again, by the same means, combined into extensions. The extensions are physical objects and parts of physical objects.

---

[27] This level of awareness is called "noumenal," not because it is unknown to the human mind, but because it is unacknowledged by a mature human mind. It is also noumenal because, while it reveals the percepts of human experience, it does not disclose their origin.

They are also mental objects enclosed in thought. All of these together constitute the extensions which make up the inclusive phenomenal precipitate.

Beyond this function of recognizing a multiplicity of limited entities, it is plurality as well which makes possible the distribution of physical extensions in such a manner as to form physical space. For it is the plurality of these extensions which demands separateness. And, as there is naught physical but them, their simultaneity demands contiguity. Thus their separateness and contiguity form the relations of physical space. Similar relations also form the individual mental character of thoughts. But, since they are not encountered as simultaneous, they appear before the mind in sequence.

In addition to this static character of the human awareness of material experience is its dynamic. This material dynamic is a condition in which physical objects change and thoughts are replaced by other thoughts. It is a dynamic because there is always something undergoing a process of change, be it physical or thought or both. As a result, there is a continual flux in human experience.

The flux is regulated by a continuous but varying noumenal flow of percepts. For the percepts appear singly and in both unique and repeated associations. Slight alterations in the repeated associations of percepts become modified extensions in the phenomenal precipitate. It is these which register a dynamic of material change. And it is the physical registry of change which marks the flow of incremental time.

All these phenomena are made manifest in the more inclusive phenomenal precipitate, which includes both physical objects and thought. However, as previously stated, the mind's first development of the intuition of plurality occurs initially in the

The Immaterial Structure of Human Experience

noumenal precipitate. For one percept limits another and must, to form an extension and its properties, be involved in an association. As also previously stated, that association originates in the noumenal precipitate as well.

But the extensions formed from these associations appear in the inclusive phenomenal precipitate. Here plurality distinguishes one extension from another, creating either contiguity or sequence among them. Contiguity results in a development of simultaneity in space, as in simultaneously existent physical objects. Sequence in appearance results in a progression through time, as in the successive extensions manifesting physical changes or in the succession of thought extensions which appear singly before the mind.

There are exceptions to this rule of extension. And these exceptions lie outside the inclusive phenomenal precipitate precisely because they are not extensions. These are feelings and emotions, the latter a compounding through a coalescence of the former. Feelings appear as independent (i.e., unassociated) percepts in the noumenal precipitate, where they may also appear collectively in close succession to one another as emotions.

Because they are not extensions which appear in the phenomenal precipitate, feelings and emotions are neither physical objects nor thoughts about physical objects. For feelings gathered together as emotions are not associated with one another in the fluid, simultaneous manner of the qualities of an extension. Rather, they build upon one another in an independent succession to create the mounting revelation of an emotion.

In addition to the peculiar character of feelings and emotions, it should be noted that to assert that thoughts are extensions is to say that thoughts are understood to be representations of extensions. In other words, thoughts are invariably directly or indirectly about physical objects. Thus a thought, as an image, encloses an extended object and thereby takes on the characteristic of extension itself. But this is a mental, not a physical, extension. The thought is an extension only in its representation of the object.

This is as true of abstract thoughts as it is of representational thoughts. For, in the former case, a thought may be about certain properties of an object or about another thought, the properties of which are ultimately based on physical experience. In thinking, a thought image or concept is rarely completely faithful in its supposed representation of physical experience. So, in this sense, all thoughts may be understood to be in some degree abstract.

For example, to be represented in any detail, the many different circles encountered in experience must be placed one at a time before the mind. Since any one of these circles is meant to represent circles in general, it is thus abstracted in representation because it clearly does not fully represent circles in general.

This abbreviation, or abstraction, in representation is necessary because a characteristic of the many physical circles encountered in experience is the possibility of a variation in the curvature of their circumferences. These variations cannot be represented at once in a multiple image. There are too many of them.

On the other hand, a deliberate abstraction fares no better. For a thought about a perfect circle is a thought about any one of the above particular circles, which has been limited in the curvature of its circumference by the Euclidean definition of a perfect circle. As Euclid states, no point on the circumference of the perfect circle can be at a distance of more or less than one standard radius.[28]

---

[28] *Euclid's Elements,* Book I, Definition 15.

The Immaterial Structure of Human Experience

Such a concept or its supporting image, which is formed from this definition, is therefore a thought about a physical circle in which the possibility of numerous variations in its circumference has been removed, or abstracted. So it is based upon, but not fully representative of, experience. For no such perfect circle can be demonstrated to have been encountered. Other abstract or purely imagined thoughts about such things as angels, unicorns, and spirit are thoughts similarly constructed by definitional limitation, imaginative recombination, or negative representation.

Now there is the problem of the general character of mental focus, which is of course involved in the awareness of plurality. The percepts of extensions, not to mention the extensions themselves, are experienced sequentially through time, as well as contiguously in space. But, in fact, contiguous entities in space, be they percepts or extensions, can also be said to be experienced sequentially, since the mind can only focus upon one of them at a time or upon the point of contiguous contact between two of them. To imagine three entities is to induce the mind to move back and forth between them—i.e., to shift its focus.

It is for this reason that an image of an extension must be imagined crudely to be imagined whole. And space is an intellectual construct, supported by more than one imaginative image. For multiple entities cannot be presented to consciousness distinctly. Thus a representation of an extension is continually altered in the mind, the percepts associated together as its properties coming and going within mental focus.

But not only does differentiation occur within an extension or between two extensions. Sometimes it affects the character of an extension in a manner which relates it in a new way to a preceding condition. This is a different issue from the previous two forms of static differentiation. For it involves change and is thus causal in nature.

Causation is based on the fact that objects come and go. They change their state or their presence. Since change is nonetheless also predicated upon differentiation, it is as much an expression of plurality as is any static differentiation in spatial extension. And change is perceived as incremental time. The word "incremental" indicates that the changes are progressive and do not turn back, undoing themselves in terms of their circumstances. The emphasis here is upon circumstances, not just the object itself.

A theoretical scientist may imagine a reversal in time and find isolated evidence to support it, as he also does in positing a universe of multiple dimensions greater than three. For logic will veer in whatever direction imagination wishes to take it, so long as a chain of reason and an array of evidence supporting it is not violated. And this practice may be beneficial in uniting disparate phenomena in one efficient system of thought. But the common functioning of the human mind is not so. Hence the disparity between "common sense" and an elaborate theoretical construct following the dictates of logic.

This discussion does not by any means suggest an attempt to say the logic is wrong or that its conclusions are in some sense untrue to experimental evidence. Much of the complex structure of present knowledge could not exist without it. Neither would the effectiveness of human efforts in manipulating physical phenomena be as far reaching without it.

But this systematic thought often defies common sense precisely because logical development relies upon exact and therefore unvarying definitions in a world of common experience in which no two things or events are ever exactly alike. Common

The Immaterial Structure of Human Experience

sense responds to the thing, as being most proximate in experience. Whereas science responds to general relations, stripping experience of its inessential, or "accidental," accompaniments.

So, insofar as a strictly human regard is concerned, the concept of time is as follows. Though something in direct human experience can be changed from A to B and then back to A, it cannot reverse its relationship to other changes in terms of their mutual direction of occurrence. For example, a prairie fire may start and then be put out, restoring the prairie to a state of non-conflagration. But the burned grass remains as a unidirectional indicator of what has occurred.

Likewise, there is the fact that one entity in certain circumstances, such as a clock moving at high velocity in relation to another clock, may alter its functioning in comparison to the other clock. It may slow down. But this does not imply a reversal of direction. For the functioning of both the affected and unaffected clocks continues to progress in the same direction.

Why is this? It is because of the subjectivity of the human experience of time. Sequence is a necessary expression of the material self-limitation of mind. To reverse not just one incident, but an environment of sequence, is not to change it, but to undo it. It is to deny order and sense to phenomena. So, for this reason, the noumenal laying down of percepts and associations of percepts occurs in a sequence.

This is to say that the overall process registers the direction taken by mental focus. Incidents within it may be reversed. An A may change to a B and then back to an A. But the general noumenal flow is in one direction. And it is this broader, more inclusive, sequence which is the ground of finite experience.

But the noumenal flow of percepts is non-incremental because its alterations cannot be referenced to a context involving other alterations in an environment of contiguous expression. Nevertheless, it is unidirectional. For non-incremental time unfolds according to the mind's recognition of percepts and associations of percepts.

However, it should be pointed out that an extension in incremental time is unlike an extension in space. For the former is indeterminate, while the latter is not. In other words, how something occurs in incremental time lacks the precise, concrete character of spatial contiguity, since time is recognized indirectly in terms of changes in spatial extensions.

The reason for this is that in any temporal designation a point of reference must be specified. One set of changes must be compared to another, as the progress of a runner is compared to a stopwatch. Yet possible references vary in occurrence. One watch might run faster or slower than another. So which set of changes (which watch) is brought to the comparison matters because it alters the standard of measure. Hence the arbitrary need to set a standard for the measure.

The recognition of time, in this sense, is probably the first science. Its development would have occurred when the cycle of a day was determined according to the regular repeated appearance of the sun. For, by means of such a designated measure, a system of relations was imposed on experience.

Much of the foregoing has taken on the appearance of an elaborate digression. It is important to point this out, lest the reader should lose sight of the intuitions, as these are the principal subject of the present discussion. The digressions in this particular case have been elaborations on the second intuition, plurality.

Now it cannot be said that extension and change are prior to a sense of unity and plurality. For both extension and change, and

The Immaterial Structure of Human Experience

therefore incremental time as well, must be understood by means of these intuitions. Without such intuitions, which appear initially as a function of focus in secondary mind, neither extension nor change could be made present to human awareness.

It is mental focus which transforms the simple unity of consciousness into the finite unities of human experience. And it is mental focus which transforms finite unity into plurality. It does this by the very act of making the unity finite in character. For finitude is limitation. And limitation demands a limiting presence other than the limited entity. It demands another entity.

So only subsequent to the operation of the intuitions of finite unity and plurality do these intuitions create extensions and the properties of extensions, which become an environment for change and incremental time. Thus the intuitions are prior to the phenomenal world of human experience.

They are also coexistent in appearance with the percept output of the noumenal precipitate. For they are necessary for a primal recognition of that output. This is a recognition which fades from human awareness with the maturation of the mind. But it does not desist in its influence in supplying the material of experience to the phenomenal precipitate.

Totality. To continue with the image of an apple as an illustrative example, let it be said that unity and plurality combine to make a totality of two halves of one apple. The whole apple should not be described in this case as being apprehended under the intuition of simple unity alone, as it was when it was initially considered under that intuition. It is now apprehended under the intuition of totality. This third intuition is a combination of the first two working together. It is an awareness of division, or plurality, held within a context of simple unity.

In other words, it is an awareness that each half of the apple is an independent unity and that there is therefore a multiple of unities comprehended within one unity, the whole apple. Thus, by means of a shift in the focus of consciousness, a multiple of finite unities, regarded as a plurality in which each individual unit may be considered in turn, is again united under a single unity of mental focus. This is to say that the focus is broadened to take in the totality of units as a unity of unities.

Under the aegis of focus—i.e., once the mind has fixed its attention in this manner—the undetermined multiplicity of unities becomes a determinate unity. It becomes a specific, finite unity made present to awareness by a fixed attention of the mind. To reiterate, there initially emerges an enlarged but indeterminate focus encompassing a plurality of units, which then settles into an awareness of the same expansive, but now finitely determined, unity which is referred to as a totality.

Now let it be considered why it is that the relationship between the three intuitions, on the one hand, and the phenomena of extension and change, on the other, may appear to be a bit confusing at this point. It should be recalled that it was said that the noumenal precipitate is laid down as a ground for human awareness by secondary mind.

It is laid down in such a way that there is an initial awareness of percepts appearing in sequence, each exhibiting an individual character. Some are unassociated. But others are apprehended associatively as they appear in the sequence. Some of the latter, when their patterns of association are repeated in slight variations, are supportive of the phenomenon of ongoing change.[29]

---

[29] The variations are slight and progressive. But, if they are exhibited rapidly at the phenomenal level and are individually very slight, a more extensive

The Immaterial Structure of Human Experience

In other words, for change to occur, an association of percepts will appear in the noumenal precipitate. Then, in the next appearance of an otherwise identical association, some percepts must be missing from it. That is, either the percepts are simply missing or they are missing and other percepts have been added in their place. Moreover, this subsequent association of percepts will be identical to the first in location as that location would appear in the phenomenal precipitate. This is the process for change without a change in place, as it is exhibited in the phenomenal precipitate.

For change in place, or motion, to be registered, the alterations occur between the associations of percepts, rather than within them. Thus an association of percepts is altered in its spatial relation to other associations of percepts. In other words, the association of percepts of concern appears in the noumenal stream in a new order involving different associations of percepts. The new order is reflected in terms of spatial location in the phenomenal precipitate. Thus what results in the phenomenal precipitate is an object shifting in place. This is observed as a change in its background. Within a single motion, the change is continuous.

It should also be pointed out that change within an association of percepts, as in water becoming ice or wood disintegrating into fire and smoke, is itself a more subtle form of motion. For in such a case percepts are either moved about or replaced by different percepts. Thus it can be seen that all change involves motion.

So far as this goes, it is well and good. But note must be taken of the fact that it is a change in the noumenal stream which determines any change in the phenomenal stream. Thus a compli-

---

change, incorporating many steps at once, will be observed, as in the changes in number display on a digital clock or in an explosion.

cation arises from the fact that it would seem reasonable to suppose that the phenomenal extensions and changes to them, observable in a mature human awareness, are not immediately amenable to any activity of the three intuitions, since these extensions and changes have already assumed their character among the associated percepts in the noumenal precipitate.

This would imply that the operation of the intuitions of finite unity, plurality, and totality in determining associations of percepts, and thus their character as extensions, takes place only at the noumenal level of mind. For the noumenal determination of these associations of percepts is prior to their phenomenal spatial organization as extensions.

The same would be true of the experience of change, since a recognition of physical change depends upon these extensions. And the character of the extensions depends upon associations of percepts in the noumenal presentation. Consequently, insofar as human participation is concerned, the everyday physical realm, which is the realm of extension and physical change, would appear to be little more than an independent display unaffected by human action.

The problem arises from the fact that one must not confuse logical precedence with temporal occurrence. So, to clarify the matter, it must be made clear that secondary mind and human awareness are considered to be separate faculties only for the sake of discussion. Thus it is that any order of precedence between them—i.e., between the noumenal and the phenomenal—is merely logical and not temporal. The events of the one do not precede those of the other.

They are not only concurrent but coextensive. For it is evident that there is only one mind. In other words, what occurs in the human awareness of the phenomenal precipitate *does not fol-*

The Immaterial Structure of Human Experience

low upon what occurs in the noumenal precipitate. They are one operation, one complex interrelationship between intuitions and percepts at both levels.

In other words, by means of focus, secondary mind limits both the noumenal and phenomenal precipitates to percepts and the configurations of change. That is the preliminary self-limiting step of secondary mind in converting itself as universal spirit into a limited human awareness. Its use of focus is the source of the three intuitions which express the limitations. For the three intuitions are forms of focus.

It is these intuitions, then, which create individual percept recognition, an identification of the percept associations and their modifications in the noumenal precipitate, and, concurrently, the extensions and changes which appear in the phenomenal precipitate. The point being made is that the extensions and changes which appear in the phenomenal precipitate *are* the associations of percepts and their modifications in the noumenal precipitate.

This is the manner in which focus operates upon the material of the two precipitates. Both may be understood to occur simultaneously. For they are one and the same. The phenomenal precipitate is a reconfiguration of the noumenal output in terms of space. But it is not a separate thing. It is the manner in which a mature human sensibility recognizes experience.

Thus the specific applications of the intuitions which are employed by human awareness to recognize extension and change in the phenomenal precipitate are the same as those which present and recognize the material of the noumenal precipitate. The presentation is somewhat altered, but not the single activity of the intuitions, both subliminal (in the noumenal) and superficial (in the phenomenal), which acknowledges the same percepts in the same associations.

Accordingly, to recognize something in terms of the phenomenal is, as it were, to recognize it in the noumenal as through a lens. For example, a magnifying glass does not make something bigger. It makes it appear bigger. But, rather than the intermediary of a refraction of light, what occurs here is a refraction of mind. It is a refraction which may be said to occur at a far greater speed than light. For it is immediate.

So these two operations do not represent separate functions of mind, as though there were two minds or two independent compartments in the mind. They occur as one indivisible, complexly interrelated (as though porously layered) function. But when the process is viewed from a mature human perspective, only the structure of the phenomenal precipitate is observed.

This eventual omission of the noumenal perspective can be understood as the increased effect of the "lens," as the phenomenal precipitate grows in complexity due to human intellectual development. The lens becomes the human mind's means of losing sight of the original character of its perceptions.

But even this intellectual development, though registered to human awareness as exhibiting a growth in complexity of the phenomenal precipitate, is reflected in the original flow of percepts in the noumenal precipitate. That flow and what occurs at the phenomenal level always mirror one another.

The fact that this is all one operation is why the intuitions may best be said to be not only prior to the presentation of the phenomenal precipitate. They are prior to the noumenal as well. For they are involved in recognizing and manifesting both as one development. This is because the human mind in its limited awareness *is* secondary mind in its final condition of self-limitation.

The Immaterial Structure of Human Experience

(2) Under the general heading *Quality* are the three categories, *Reality, Negation,* and *Limitation*.

Reality. Something exists within the context of awareness. This involves the application of mental focus to a specific content within mental awareness. The mind acknowledges that specific mental content by focusing upon it. In doing so, the mind acknowledges that content in relation to something else, a context, even if the particular context in question is not made immediately present to the mind. Thus it is the content of the mind which determines reality for that mind. And it is focus and reference which determine the specific character of that reality.

The character of the reality requires only that the content be true within a context, as in the case of a unicorn being true within an imaginative context or a horse being true within a sensory context. The mental representation of a unicorn is thus as real in its subjective context as is the mental representation of a horse within its objective context.

However, once again it should be remembered that thoughts, and thus imaginative representations, participate in the inclusive phenomenal precipitate. For, since percepts are made present to human awareness only within the mind, the percepts enclosed within a thought image share an equal validity with those enclosed within the extensions of physical objects. For the extensions of physical objects are also revealed as thought images. Both must be represented in the mind to be known. So their only distinction from one another is their subjective or objective relationship to the will.

Negation. A sensory percept or object under contemplation may be removed from focus. This is the point at which the percept or object of awareness is put outside the mind's center of attention. But for something to be out of the mind's focus may yet mean that it is at the periphery of awareness, causing its presence in the mind to be faintly registered without the attention of the mind being upon it.

This is a situation in which mental focus occasionally shifts toward whatever is not in focus, but does not dwell upon it. It would be represented in the noumenal precipitate perhaps by isolated single appearances of a percept or by isolated single appearances of an association of percepts. Thus it is still present for the mind. But, if it is not within awareness at all, it is not in existence for that mind. It does not exist for that awareness.

Now, by means of an imaginative or conceptual context, it may be understood that something exists, as when one departs a room and the table in the room is said to continue to exist. But when not thought about in this way—i.e., when not thought about by means of an imaginative or conceptual context—the table does not exist for awareness when the person possessing that mind is out of the room. The same is true of any recall from memory. Prior to recall, the thing does not exist in the mind.

Though these phenomena would not appear to express logical negation, in which something is held not to exist at all, they are the grounds for it. For when it is said that an object *is not*, what is meant is that it does not exist within any context. If the above table were held not to exist in the room, either in terms of a sensory image, an imaginative image, or conceptually, it would appear in the mind only in a sense of negation, where it would be represented as not being present in the room. So, if it were held not to be included in any other context as well, except this negative representation in the mind, it would be understood not to exist at all.

For example, take either the image or the concept of a unicorn. If this image or concept is considered within the context of

The Immaterial Structure of Human Experience

what is presumed to be the sensory world, it is said not to exist. For it is held to be imaginary. So, applying the law of the excluded middle, it could be asserted that a unicorn must either exist or not exist in a sensory context. No evidence of the presence of the unicorn within such a context is found within the mind. So the latter is declared: it does not exist.

Logically, what is being stated is that the unicorn is not included among the mind's representations within a certain context. This determination of existence or negation would be the case, regardless of whether the context under consideration should be sensory, imaginative, or conceptual.

For example, in 1900 in Sigmund Freud's book, *The Interpretation of Dreams*, the idea of the unconscious was introduced. He demonstrated—insofar as something which is not itself evident can be said to be the cause of evident events—that there is a subconscious mechanism working within the mind.

Since this mechanism was not a representation of sensory experience, but since it did explain certain events which were held in the mind as representations of sensory experience, it was assumed to exist within a conceptual context. It was part of a system of explanation. It could only be held to exist in this way: as a theory. Any assertion beyond that is purely conjectural. For the evidence supporting its material existence is not to be found. That is to say, it has no objective, sensory expression, or at least what is assumed to be such by a material mind. So it does not exist in a material context.

Limitation. A particular thing is limited. It is not the whole of existence. Awareness of limitation is a product of the first and second intuitions, the intuitions of simple unity and plurality. It is finite unity. It is the awareness that division implies limitation, or more than one finite unity. Thus, if something determinate must share its simultaneous appearance in awareness with something else, then they cannot either of them be coterminous with awareness.

For, if they were the only two percepts or objects made present to the mind, or if many percepts or objects were presented to the mind as being concurrent (i.e., brought before the mind in a close sequence understood as a contiguity), they would altogether in either case seem to be coterminous with awareness.

Furthermore, if the mind's focus is entirely on one object, which is thus made present to the mind, while it should be held that something else exists but is not present to the mind, it is being maintained that both are present to awareness. So awareness implies more than focus. It implies context.

So, inasmuch as each percept or object is, the other is not. But no further. Accordingly, two percepts or two objects exist. For each excludes the other only insofar as pertains to its individual existence. Thus each negates the other insofar as is necessary for the existence of each and no more. In other words, it does not negate itself. Nor does it negate the other, except inasmuch as is necessary to manifest itself.

Hence the roles of reality and negation are both involved in the concept of limitation. Hence also, insofar as objects are concerned (as opposed to individual percepts), the mutual exclusion of two concurrent objects (or physical extensions) by one another determines not only their mutual limitation and multiplicity, but the phenomenon of space as well.

(3) Under the general heading *Relation* are the three categories, *Inherence and Subsistence, Causality and Dependence,* and *Community*.

The Immaterial Structure of Human Experience

Inherence and Subsistence. An inherent thing is a thing conceived to be necessarily within another thing. It is a universal attribute (a property, as understood in this work). Thus, since there may be multiple universal attributes, it can be conceived definitionally as a part of a thing. But this is not as is the case with a physical piece of a pie, in which a part might be taken away from the whole. That is to say, this subdivision of a thing is inherent, distinguished from other such subdivisions, but pertaining to the whole and cannot be removed from it.

Any such subordinate unit, as well as the unit to which it is subordinate, may nevertheless be focused upon in terms of itself alone—i.e., as subsistent in itself. Thus an equilateral triangle may have three equal angles which together are inherent within it as an attribute. Considered as such, the triangle is subsistent. And the three equal angles are inherent.

The equilateral triangle, though it is subsistent, may yet be said to be dependent upon the equality of the angles. For this reason, these angles are understood to pertain to the triangle *necessarily*, just as three equal sides pertain to it necessarily. Both the three equal angles and the three equal sides are attributes of the equilateral triangle. For the equilateral triangle could not exist without them. But if one of the angles should be considered in itself, or even if all three together should be considered apart from the triangle, it or they would be independently subsistent.

The emphasis behind this discussion is again upon mental focus and the variation in limitations it can produce in predicating one classification of another. The inherent classification, involving three equal angles, is predicated of the subsistent classification, which is the equilateral triangle. Its inherence, which implies that it is a necessary attribute, indicates that it is universally predicated of the equilateral triangle.

The mental process for producing the universal predication is this: Wherever mental attention is placed, the focus of that attention becomes the limitation of greatest interest for the mind. It becomes the principal focus. In the case at hand, this principal focus will be upon whatever is considered subsistent, say the triangle. Thus its three equal angles are inherent to it.

However, if the focus is transferred to the three equal angles, which were the attribute previously understood to be inherent to the triangle, then that attribute is now considered to be subsistent. For such a transferal of focus removes primary consideration from the triangle and places it upon the three equal angles alone.

It is in this way that relative limitation is created by mental focus. When this mental process is illustrated in terms of Euler's circles, the related limitations, the inherent part and the subsistent whole, may be considered to be classifications which are nested, the lesser classification within the greater.

Causality and Dependence. Something causes something else, or something is caused by something else. Causality and dependence can be illustrated by the concept of efficient cause in which there is a cause and an effect. The effect is dependent upon the cause. If in a game of pool, a five ball is struck by a cue ball, the result, or effect, is that the motion of the cue ball will appear to have been proportionally transferred to the five ball.

Thus the five ball is said to have been caused to move by the motion of the cue ball. In other words, one pool ball is seen as having a proximate effect upon the other. So what the mind observes is a change of pattern. It is a change within some type of previously recognized relationship.

Accordingly, lacking some other factor which might appear to influence the outcome, the change is experienced by the mind as a direct interaction of the two phenomena within its field of

The Immaterial Structure of Human Experience

attention. In other words, the change is observed to take place as a result of that particular relationship between two phenomena which is under focused consideration.

There is nothing present to the mind's range of attention but its field of awareness. This field of awareness involves more than one focus on content. It relates two forms of content. Where there is a relation, there is a pattern. So a pattern is produced within the awareness. It is the interaction of the two pool balls. Thus the relative motion of these objects is what is being associated in causal terms.

The contact between the two pool balls is the only thing which would explain the sudden, simultaneous change in their relationship. Initially, the cue ball is in a state of motion and the five ball is not. They make contact. Then it immediately follows that the five ball is in a state of motion and the cue ball is not. Or, at least, the cue ball is in a state of reduced motion.

What this indicates is that the mind has grouped two objects lying within its purview into a relationship. When the state of each of these objects changes simultaneously upon the contact of one with the other, the relationship between them changes. Due to the occurrence of this contact at the precise moment of their changes in state, and due to there being no other observable influence upon them, the change in their relationship is recognized as occurring between them alone.

Consequently, each object is understood to cause a change in the other. The cue ball causes the five ball to move. And the five ball stops or diverts the motion of the cue ball. In this way, motion is seen to be lost to the one and gained by the other. Thus it is the energy of motion (theoretically coupled with the role of mass) which is understood to be the mutual cause of both changes. Accordingly, a single cause may be assigned to a single effect.

That effect is observed in two simultaneous phenomena. Together, these phenomena are the change in relative motion of the pool balls.

Community. The two intuitions, unity and plurality, comprise the intuition of totality. For a totality is a unity which is a plurality of unities. Now, when a definitional part expresses a universal aspect of a definitional whole, it exists in a relationship of mutual reciprocity of the part to the whole. It is thus inherent to the whole. This is the form of totality which expresses community.

It is in this way that the category of community combines the previous two categories which fall under Kant's general heading of Relation. For the category of causality and dependence (i.e., cause and effect) combines with the category of inherence and subsistence to create the category of community. As a result of this combination, the category of community is enabled to exhibit a reciprocity between a community and the members of that community.

So, in consonance with this reciprocity, an interdependence is expressed. An effect arising from a cause, and a cause leading to a specific effect, are logically bound up within the single concept which is causation. Thus the concept, cause-and-effect, denotes a community of two concepts: the whole, causation, on the one hand, and the parts, a cause leading to an effect and an effect proceeding from a cause, on the other—the unity of which expresses a necessary relation of whole to parts and parts to the whole.

For the whole—causation—cannot exist without either part—both cause-to-effect and effect-from-cause. In other words, the cause-to-effect and the effect-from-cause are attributes of causation. For all expressions of causation exhibit both cause-to-

The Immaterial Structure of Human Experience

effect and effect-from-cause. Thus cause-to-effect and effect-from-cause are inherent to causation. Causation and its attributes, cause-to-effect and effect-from-cause, are a community.

Moreover, the assertion that that which is inherent is necessary to a particular subsistent, and vice versa, arises from a universal predicate exhibiting a relation of causation to the character of its subject, as in "all equilateral triangles are triangles characterized by three equal angles," and in "all equilateral triangles are triangles characterized by three equal sides." For the subject could not be what it is without either of these predicates.

These universal predicates are attributes of the subject. They cause the subject to be what it is. The subject is therefore determined by each of the predicates. Thus to say that "all equilateral triangles are triangles characterized by three equal angles *and* three equal sides" is to state a tautology.

For nothing else is needed to characterize an equilateral triangle than these combined attributes (assuming prior definitions and common notions concerning straight lines, angles, and equality). And nothing more is required to characterize the combined attributes than to state that they are an equilateral triangle. Nothing can be more intrinsically causal than to assert that it causes something to be what it is.

Likewise, in consideration of such a universal proposition alone, the character of the subject, being what it is, determines the predicate in the sense that, for the subject to be what it is, the predicate could not be other than it is. In this way, subject and predicate form a reciprocal proposition, which is a community of concepts. In other words, the subject and predicate define each other.

Moreover, together they are what is necessary to the character of the proposition. For the proposition is the subject and predicate together. So there is a community within the proposition. And that community *is* the proposition. And the proposition is that community. And there is a community between the proposition as a type of statement and its subject and predicate as the necessary terms of that statement. Thus the subject and predicate in relation to each other, on the one hand, and the proposition in relation to the subject and predicate together, on the other hand, are both reciprocal communities.

(4) Under the general heading *Modality* are the three categories, *Possibility–Impossibility, Existence–Nonexistence,* and *Necessity–Contingence.*

Possibility–Impossibility. It can be the case; it cannot be the case. Once pattern is recognized—as in contiguity in space or sequence in thought—then it establishes conditions of possibility and impossibility. Something may be held to be an integral part of the pattern. Or it may be held not to be. The pattern referred to may be the entirety of experience. Or it may be a portion of it.

Again, the issue is determined by the character of focus. If the mind's focus is on the entire range of experience—past, present, and future—then something may *be* or not *be* in general. It is either possible or impossible. If the focus is less than the entire range of experience, say the physical realm and not the realm designated as thought, then the range of possibility/impossibility is reduced accordingly.

A strict materialist would maintain that unicorns are not physically possible. He would say they are mere figments of imagination and cannot be encountered in physical experience. However, from a materialist's perspective, human beings have only a probable grasp of physical circumstances. For induction is understood to be the means by which a person becomes cogni-

The Immaterial Structure of Human Experience

tively familiar with the physical realm. And induction is generally understood to be selective in its details.

If there is this division between the subjective and the objective in the materialist's view, then the objective must be presumed to be more than the mind can encompass in any detail. However acute the scrutiny, observations will be missed. Therefore, human beings never have a certain grasp of circumstances in matters of induction and experience.

So if the physical possibility of unicorns is allowed to be considered in a broader context of meaning—that which extends beyond any recorded human experience—it cannot be said that unicorns are thus impossible. Rather, given the facts of experience as heretofore determined, a sudden appearance of unicorns in the physical realm is deemed to be highly improbable.

Existence–Nonexistence. Existence indicates that which either does or does not have reality. It exists; it does not exist. As already mentioned in the discussions of both reality and possibility, pattern establishes conditions of existence. Something exists, or has reality, because it is found within a context. For it to be related meaningfully to that context, the context must have a recognizable pattern. Only then is something understood to exist within that context.

When it is not found within an established context, and that context is considered to be the full possible range of experience, it does not exist. The matter is no different when applied to lesser or greater contexts. For any context considered solely in terms of itself, existence and nonexistence are applicable. For instance, a field of mental focus can be narrowed. It may be said that, unaided by artificial means, horses do not exist in viable form at great ocean depths.

Such focus may also be expanded beyond what is understood to be the full possible range of experience. It may be postulated that in an alternate universe horses do exist at great ocean depths. Thus, once it should be conceded that there are limits to human awareness, what in effect is being asserted is the possibility that something may exist beyond such limits.

Necessity–Contingence. Necessity is certainty. It must be the case. Contingency is uncertainty. It is dependent upon chance or the fulfillment of a condition. In human experience, things are often logically necessary because the human mind can strip down and control the meaning of its concepts. But things are never physically necessary.

If it is asserted that $2 + 2 = 4$, pre-established conceptual circumstances demanding a specific outcome have been set. An equivalency is here established. And it determines the relationship. In other words, the relationship is constructed in such a way that there is an identical quantity of arithmetical units before and after the expression of the equivalence: $x\,x + x\,x = x\,x\,x\,x$.

The individual arithmetical units are held to be uniform, and thus identical to one another, precisely because they are not encountered in physical experience. They are imaginatively conceptual and thus can be made uniform. Their one-to-one identity further implies an identity in the aggregate when the aggregates are the same in quantity. For mathematical quantities are held to be uniform in terms of arithmetical units: a 2 has two units, a 4 has four units, etc. Thus the two sets of two x's above are the same in quantity as the one set of four x's.

All these identities are determined in the mind independently of physical experience. Whereas, in the realm of physical experience, such identities cannot be established beyond human doubt. For, in spite of appearances, and insofar as can be definitively

The Immaterial Structure of Human Experience

determined by observation, neither two rocks nor two manufactured glass marbles are ever exactly the same. Neither is the sun which is seen today necessarily the sun which was seen yesterday. Nor is it that which will be seen tomorrow. In fact, it is generally understood that these appearances of the sun are not exactly the same.

Nevertheless, in the realm of physical experience circumstances are often said to be in a necessary state of equilibrium or disequilibrium when, as several things are observed in an isolated spatial pattern, their precise position relative to one another is established and recognized in terms of a proportion or disproportion.

Thus the fact that two objects positioned on a lever on either side of a fulcrum appear to be either in equilibrium or not in equilibrium in terms of the weights of their masses at the respective distances of those masses on either side of the fulcrum. What they exhibit is a proportion in weight/distance on one side to weight/distance on the other side.

This expectation of a proportional regularity results from three things. First, the order of presentation of percepts in the noumenal precipitate maintains a regularity and thus establishes an expectation. Second, the phenomenal precipitate arranges the regularity in a manner which renders proportional relations possible. Third, the human mind, in its development of a practical and intellectual understanding of experience, organizes that experience in proportional terms for the sake of analysis.

Thus, in the example given above, the noumenal precipitate contributes a regularized and repeated input of certain associations of percepts. In the phenomenal precipitate, extension distributes distances and the property of weight. And, in its intellectual overlay on the phenomenal precipitate, the human mind provides concepts like mass and gravitation to create a proportional integration of the distances and weights.

So altogether these three things establish proportional relations which submit to an anticipation. In other words, such experience can be relied upon for its understandable integration and predictability. As a result, when a physical disproportion occurs under observation, it suggests a necessary return to proportion. That return will either be supplied by the noumenal precipitate or delayed by the same.

Finally, it is in the following way that the third category under this fourth general heading of modality, this category being *necessity–contingence*, may be recognized as a product of the first two: *possibility–impossibility* and *existence–nonexistence*. If something is necessary, it is both possible and existent, either potentially or actually.

If it is necessarily not so, it is neither possible nor existent. If it is neither necessarily so nor necessarily not so, it is contingent. If it is contingent, its existence within a particular set of circumstances remains in question. That is to say, it is possible. Yet it may not exist within the context under consideration.

38. *The first three Kantian categories as intuitions explained further: from these the development and limitations of human awareness.* As previously stated, there are two fundamental intuitions of the human mind and a third drawn from these two. There are no others. The first of these intuitions is derived from universal spirit, which is experienced as pure consciousness. That intuition is simple unity, a reflection of the character of pure consciousness, which is a simple unity.

The second intuition, derived from the character of the input of the content of consciousness, is a recognition of plurality. This

The Immaterial Structure of Human Experience

intuition of plurality renders the experience of limitation, or finitude, for human awareness. For where there is multiplicity there must be a mutual boundedness of one by the other, which is the character of limitation and finitude.

When the second intuition is brought under the influence of the first, it becomes the intuition of totality. Under this third intuition, unities are more definitively recognized as multiple and mutually exclusive of one another. For together they form a greater unity: a totality. Thus the intuition of totality is a recognition of the bounds of limited individuality which is more definitive than is achieved under the intuition of plurality alone.

In a totality, moreover, individuals are not only bounded by one another within a determined group. They are subject to inclusion in these totalities in such a way that together they are in turn capable of being included in ever greater totalities. For there are totalities of totalities. So the totalities are limited by one another—the greater encompassing the lesser. Thus units, groups of units, and groups of groups of units are always brought together in such a way as to be further grouped in other ways. So it is that, by means of this third intuition, a sense of universal limitation is brought about.

How is this? It is that, the intuition of unity having been applied to the intuition of plurality, the limitation, or finitude, of individual things is not the only thing determined. Rather, the limitation, or finitude, of any combined whole is established. It may be that the greatest combined whole cannot be reached in imagination or thought. For the process of inclusion of one by another is unlimited. But it is nonetheless understood that, if a final totality could be reached, it would itself be limited, or finite, like all other totalities.

Thus the intuition of totality establishes a recognition of the possibility of an indeterminate, yet finite, realm of finite things. An example of this is the indeterminate count of whole numbers, which count at any point is finite. For human experience, revealing its character through ongoing change, creates an open-ended and indeterminate expression of possibility. However, the possibility, though indeterminate, remains finite at all points—finite in its individual content and finite in its inclusiveness. Thus, at all points, this possibility renders only a recognition of finite groupings of finite things.

Each of the three intuitions is exercised by means of one operation of the mind, which may be called its focus. Focus is initially an expression of secondary mind. For it is secondary mind which presents both the individual percepts and the unextended associations of percepts of the noumenal precipitate to human awareness. These are presented and clarified through mental focus.

But, increasingly, the human mind comes to regard this presentation in terms of a phenomenal precipitate, where a coexistence and ongoing change of extended phenomena occur. And it is mental focus which continues to operate within the phenomenal precipitate in the imaginative formation of its contiguous relations of extensions and in the formation of a interpretive conceptual overlay of the same.

Thus focus also functions in what would appear to be an independent manner at the human level of awareness. It is with increasing maturity that this human level of awareness becomes a fully fleshed out phenomenal precipitate, obscuring the noumenal origins of its content. So here mental focus may sometimes be referred to as the faculty of attention.

The Immaterial Structure of Human Experience

It may be referred to in this manner because it is experienced at this point as a shifting of the mind from one thought to another. Thus, at the level of secondary mind, focus determines the material which is to be enclosed within the phenomenal precipitate. At the level of human awareness, it works interpretively within the phenomenal precipitate.

In order to restate the activity of focus in greater detail, let the three intuitions be considered as foundational agents of its operation. For they are the instruments of focus. To begin, it can be seen that the three intuitions are initially derived from the alternate turning of focus inward upon human consciousness itself and then subsequently and more practically upon the perceptual input of the noumenal precipitate.

Both of these areas of principal interest, conscious awareness and the noumenal precipitate, are direct expressions of secondary mind and are brought about by means of self-limiting spirit. That is why they are the initial points of attraction for focus. So, in the first activity, focus turns back, as it were, to attend to the pure consciousness whence it originates.

That pure consciousness is viewed as though it were an entity. Thus it is experienced as a simple unity. Focus takes up this experience of simple unity as an instrument of its activity. Employing this, it can then move its attention to the percepts of experience, where it regards them in terms of their individual unity. This is the origin of the first intuition.

In this way, under the influence of the first intuition, mental focus attends to the noumenal precipitate. In other words, focus begins to exercise its function of recognizing limited unity. The manner in which this occurs is that the noumenal precipitate initially exhibits the content of consciousness, which content is composed of individual percepts, in an unclearly distinguished form. For each nascent percept appears as though it would fill the whole mind and admit of no other experience.

But there is more than one percept of sensation. For there is more than one kind of sensation. So it is in this operation of recognizing that each unit of perception is limited by a prior and a subsequent perception that the mind apprehends the individuality of the percepts, thus acknowledging a plurality among them. By focusing on one individual percept then another, it isolates each under the intuition of unity.

Thus it clarifies the individual uniqueness of any one percept in contradistinction to any other. And, of equal importance, it has discovered in itself the means of making such a distinction. This is the origin of the second intuition, plurality. Moreover, because plurality definitively expresses limitation, it brings about a sense of finitude. In consideration of the universal involvement of the intuitions in human mental life, this sense of finitude conditions the whole of experience.

Finally, in attending to the first and second intuitions and interpreting experience through them both—that is, in considering the latter intuition in terms of the former—the mind creates a third intuition. This is totality. Totality makes possible the organization of experience. It recognizes repeated groupings of percepts in the noumenal precipitate as associations. And it facilitates the transformation of those associations into extensions, or objects.

Furthermore, the third intuition allows for a construction of space by means of complexly ordered extensions. It also renders the experience of physical change into an ordered sequence occurring within a contiguity of relations. It is this sequence which is understood as incremental. And it is this which renders possible the measure of time. In addition, the third intuition is the

The Immaterial Structure of Human Experience

source of the mental power of classification, where it brings diverse properties under individual headings.

As a child matures, the power of classification receives greater attention and acknowledgement. Increasingly, it becomes a source of organized thought. By means of an expanded role for focus within the phenomenal precipitate, organized thought arranges classifications, which are concepts, into hierarchical logical structures. These are the building material for theories, also a product of enlarged focus.

In this way, human awareness builds upon and within the phenomenal precipitate, interpreting it and restructuring it with each increasingly sophisticated interpretation. For many interpretations, both practical and abstract, do gradually become fully integrated into the phenomenal precipitate of the person concerned. They are a part of what she understands herself to have experienced.

The phenomenal precipitate was, of course, initially presented to her awareness by means of the noumenal input of secondary mind, secondary mind being self-limiting spirit. The presentation of the noumenal precipitate to the mind is prior to the articulation which is found in the phenomenal precipitate.

The noumenal precipitate is the ground for that articulation. The articulation exhibits two forms. It is the initial imaginative structuring of the phenomenal precipitate. And it is also the layering of interpretation and meaning which both imagination and the human intellect build upon the initial imaginative structure of the phenomenal precipitate.

Now, the phenomenal precipitate is articulated in this way because it must be in order to be recognized in a practical manner by human awareness. For it is the phenomenal precipitate which constitutes recognizable human experience. And it is within that experience that human beings are enabled to live and function.

Or at least it is by means of the limitations of the phenomenal precipitate that they become convinced that they exist as material beings and are obliged to function in this way. As the phenomenal precipitate arises from a final limiting of human awareness to the finite, a belief in the phenomenal is what grounds that human awareness in the representational viewpoint. In other words, it is when the maturing human mind loses its awareness of all but the phenomenal precipitate that it becomes imprisoned in the material and its representational viewpoint.

In the phenomenal precipitate, the content of consciousness is expressed in terms of the limitations of a multiplicity of physical and thought extensions. But, prior to the articulation which renders it such, a variety of sensations is initially encountered in the noumenal precipitate. Here it takes the form of changes in the flow of individual and associated percepts.

At this level, limitations and multiplicities only concern an articulation of percepts and their associations. They do not concern physical extensions or objects of thought. In other words, as the noumenal precipitate is presented to human awareness by secondary mind, the changes which constitute alterations within and between extensions in the phenomenal precipitate take place among the associations of percepts which compose the noumenal precipitate.

For example, one association may differ slightly from the next—say by a few percepts. Thus the two similar associations of percepts may represent a slight alteration in the same thing. But this is contingent upon an identity of location being preserved in the phenomenal precipitate. Such an identity of location, or an absence thereof, is determined by the underlying complexity of

The Immaterial Structure of Human Experience

the phenomenal structure. And this, in turn, is dependent upon what occurs in the noumenal precipitate.

This is to say that the underlying (pre-imaginative and pre-intellectual) complexity of the phenomenal precipitate is reflective of both close and broad relations between associations of percepts in the noumenal flow of percepts. If there are repeated appearances of similar associations of percepts in a close sequence with other associations of percepts which remain the same, the result will be an identity of location for the similar associations of percepts. Thus the similar associations of percepts may represent slight alterations in the same thing.

But, if there are appearances of similar associations of percepts which are interspersed among other associations of percepts which differ significantly from one another, the situation will translate into a change of location. In this case, the similar associations of percepts are not the same thing.

It is this change, either within an object or involving a change in its location, which lends a sequential character to both physical and mental experience. In the case of the physical, the sequences are experienced as incremental. Those changing associations of percepts and changing relations between associations of percepts at the noumenal level, which are destined to be physical changes at the phenomenal level, become the physical objects which undergo either internal change or displacement.

A similar relation characterizes the extensions which become the objects of thought. For they too are sequential, though not incremental, except by reference to the physical. It must, of course, be remembered that, in considering a broad, immaterialist point of view, all objects, both mental and physical, are images of the mind.

It is through the experience of change that human beings learn to differentiate between an internal and outer sense. As an example, think of a child learning how to negotiate her experience. When a toddler sees a vase grow larger in proportion to herself as she approaches it, or smaller as she withdraws from it, this establishes a recognition of the separateness of the vase from her person. For circumstances cannot be willed otherwise.

It might at first appear to her as if the vase were under her control. But, as she approaches or withdraws from it, she simultaneously experiences sensations which will, with increasing maturity, be associated with the working of her muscles. These she cannot dissociate from the particular regularity of the observed changes in the size of the vase.

So, by repeated trial, she learns that the sensations of the working of her muscles relate regular changes in the vase to her in a different way from any varying images of the vase which might appear randomly in her mind. In contrast with this, and prior to the repeated trial, all her experience, being registered in her mind, would have seemed to have been conditioned by her mind alone.

In sum, what she learns is that she can exercise a willed control over those sensations directly connected to her bodily movement. But she cannot do so with the changing character of the vase associated with that movement. She can decide to stop producing the muscle sensations. And, yes, this will put a halt to the changes in the vase, but only as a result of the cessation of the muscle action. She cannot continue her muscle action in the accustomed manner and prevent the vase from changing size.

So she cannot keep the vase from becoming larger as she approaches it, or smaller as she withdraws from it. When she wills her muscles to move her forward, the enlargement of the vase

The Immaterial Structure of Human Experience

inevitably follows. When she wills her muscles to move away from it, the diminution of the vase inevitably follows.

Her will cannot detach these changes in the dimensions of the vase from the particular actions of her muscles which are associated with them. Consequently, though the changes in dimensions of the vase do accord with her muscular movements, it would seem that they cannot be effected without them.

Of course, they can be effected in her imagination. But it is not the same. For then there is no accompaniment of the muscle sensations which closely regulate the changes in a prescribed manner and allow of no other. So it is the muscular sensations, which she can directly control, which come to be associated with her sense of internal being, or personal subjectivity. And the vase becomes associated with an external reality.

It is this awareness which establishes the limits of her physical person for her. She associates these limits with her consciousness and will. They are herself. For, when considered together, her body, consciousness, and will become her subjective person. The vase, the enlargement or diminution of which she cannot directly control, comes to be recognized by her as objectively separate from her person.

As a result, she sees herself as inhabiting two worlds, the one subjective, the other objective, her physical body being the nexus, or transition point, between them. For physical events correlate with and appear to cause sensations in her body. Fire burns it. Hence the personal sensation of pain. Water drowns it. Hence the appearance of a loss of all sensation in others.

This establishes an objective correlation between the physical body and the physical realm of experience. She believes that her body is a part of that realm. Yet, the pain of being burnt and the sensations of drowning are registered in her mind. And her mind seems to function independently of the physical realm.

Thus it is in her mind alone that her definitive subjectivity lies. But the appearance within her mind of both the visual images of the vase and the felt working of her muscles raises an issue: both kinds of these percepts are apprehended only within her consciousness. They are therefore in one phenomenal precipitate, which is made present to her awareness.

This is so regardless of the subjective or objective roles they have been assigned. For they are the mutual content of consciousness. Yet they are not consciousness itself. Rather they, the percepts of both the noumenal and phenomenal precipitates, are a ground for the sense of material limitation.

Initially, as newborn infants, human beings do not begin with a sense of physical space and incremental time. The child's individual percepts must become differentiated in consciousness and compounded into objects, as the infant learns in the earliest stage of life to distinguish the incremental character of change and frame her perceptions accordingly.

Change is a reference to the altered succession of associations of percepts presented to consciousness in the noumenal precipitate, where they appear in the flow of non-incremental time. But even these associations of percepts must come to be recognized as associations and not as individual percepts. And, as the mind matures, change is increasingly accepted by human awareness as occurring directly in the phenomenal precipitate, the realm of extensions and incremental time. For time in either case, the noumenal or the phenomenal precipitate, is nothing more than change.

Now, were it not for the demands of an awareness limited to expressions of finitude, the percepts would present themselves to

The Immaterial Structure of Human Experience

the mind without succession, differentiated only into the general types of sensation that they are. But, for the sake of a more discrete discrimination one from another, and for the sake of a recognition of one association of them from another, particularly when those associations are closely similar, percepts are impressed sequentially upon human consciousness.

The sequence is exercised for the sake of a clarity of perception by a mental faculty which cannot hold multiple percepts simultaneously together in a state of discrete individual discrimination. The acute apprehension of such distinctions and separations as is demanded by a finite awareness can only be achieved in this way.

Most importantly, the need for sequence also arises from the fact that the entities involved in relations can only be held in the human mind in pairs. Consequently, the development of sequence does not reach its final form as a work of distinction and separation alone. It supports a discrimination of relations. And it is relations which underlie a recognition of physical change.

So a distinction between any two percepts constitutes an awareness of limitation and division. An apprehension of the relationship between two associations of percepts is supported by the same awareness. Both require the exercise of a faculty which is inherently oriented toward finitude. For otherwise how can such distinctions be discerned?

Thus the two precipitates, the noumenal, and especially the phenomenal, become the finite world of human awareness, as opposed to the *in*finite (*not* finite) character of universal consciousness, or spirit. The awareness of limitation is most fully developed in the phenomenal precipitate.

It is the limiting faculty of mental focus in both secondary mind and human awareness which creates this finitude by means of the sequential nature of its operations. Thus it is focus, moving from one association of percepts to another related but altered association of percepts, which underlies the expression of physical change. The altered associations of percepts are registered in human awareness as changes among the extensions of the phenomenal precipitate. For the extensions are the phenomenal expression of the noumenal associations.

Closely related to the phenomenon of change is causation. Cause-and-effect relations are derived from a recognized orderliness in change. The orderliness occurs as a consistency of internal alteration in the character of physical objects. Or it occurs as a consistency in the alteration of their relation to other physical objects. The latter case involves a change of location.

But spirit is that which is without limitation. Therefore, as regards itself in its exclusively internal workings, it is without change or causal relations, insofar as these might be understood in a material sense. For how can such a change or causal relationship be known but in the manner of a finite awareness?

The observation that something should be the consistent forerunner of a specific alteration in itself, or that it should register a change in its location in relation to other things, requires its individual isolation and submission to a temporal comparison. In other words, it demands an expression of finitude.

Conversely, in regard to the internal relations of spirit, though the things which are involved in such relations may be varied, they cannot be held to undergo change in any material sense of the meaning of change. For they do not give place to one another. One thing or situation does not arise as another departs from awareness. All persist together in spirit.

In spirit, all is existent at once. Thus, so long as a thing is considered as being in spirit, there can be no means of a temporal

The Immaterial Structure of Human Experience

comparison between it and anything else. For this reason, the same thing cannot be a forerunner of itself in an altered condition. In other words, it cannot be an object which was formerly water but is now ice, nor formerly at one location but which is now in another. For there is no sequence, no time. Rather, the two conditions must exist simultaneously as representing two objects or situations, each expressing its own unique condition.

So spirit may be described as a dynamic of unlimited but unspecified change. In other words, in spirit a thing may seem as though it undergoes a change in itself or its situation. But where the former state of the thing coexists with the latter and there is no possibility of its removal, as is the case in spirit, there can only be a noted proximity and difference between the one and the other.

There can be no clear indication of a dependency of one state of existence upon another. For there is no possibility of one condition being replaced by the appearance of another previously unidentified condition. Thus, a bruised apple cannot be substituted after a fall for an unblemished version of itself. For both exist simultaneously in spirit and cannot therefore be identified as the same apple having undergone an alteration in its character. That is, they cannot be understood to represent a material dynamic of change, where one state of a thing is replaced by another.

In addition, should a person take universal spirit as a whole under consideration, she would have to concede that it cannot stand apart from what is engendered by it. Nor can it be engendered. For, as an expression of the infinite, it does not admit of limitation, a requirement for determining the distinctions of a causal relationship.

So, when it is said that spirit is the cause of all things, what is meant is simply that all things are expressed *within* spirit. In other words, spirit *is* all things. It is not a first cause setting other things in motion. To assert this would be to assert that spirit exists apart from that which it has caused. If it exists apart from something, then it is limited by what it is not. Therefore, as a limited, or finite, thing, it must itself be caused. For the definition of a finite entity is an entity whose limitation is brought about by another.

To avoid this problem, a regressive definition—i.e., "self-caused"—would have to be applied to the existence of spirit. But, if something is caused by itself, the self acting as a cause must also be caused, a regression without termination. For these reasons, universal spirit can neither, in its generative character, submit to a causal law of temporal relations, nor can it be limited by a cause. Rather, it is that within which all things express what they are, as they partake of the fact that it is what it is.

These observations make it clear that whatever is known must be known by means of spirit. For all is in spirit. And spirit is the all. But let it not be forgotten that the present discussion is principally concerned with the character of human awareness as it is exhibited through thought. And thought seems to have the peculiar characteristic of being that which is not physical. Does this mean it is not material? It does not.

It can readily be seen that the content of human thought is composed of percepts and is therefore an integral part of material experience. Material experience is the experience of the finite. So, given this finite content, can a thought be understood as material in part—i.e., finite in its content, but not in its form? It cannot. For an entity cannot be finite unless it is limited in all aspects.

So both the content of a thought and its form must be finite. Otherwise, if the content of a thought were not finite, nothing fi-

The Immaterial Structure of Human Experience

nite could be represented in it. And the thought would have no object. Neither, if the form of a thought were not finite, could one thought succeed another. For each thought is cut off by a preceding and succeeding thought.

For these reasons, a human thought is an integral part of the phenomenal precipitate, which is the definitive but ever-changing representation of the finite realm for human awareness. The limitations of the noumenal precipitate are imposed by secondary mind, and the additional characteristics of the phenomenal precipitate by human awareness. The phenomenon which is specifically recognized as a thought occurs within the phenomenal precipitate.

The phenomenal precipitate exhibits extensions for human awareness. Thought is a mental extension, just as a physical object is a spatial extension. Both originate in the percept associations of the noumenal precipitate and are converted into the extensions of the phenomenal precipitate.

Like percepts, extensions exhibit limitations. The limitations of all extensions in the phenomenal precipitate, including thoughts, are a product of mental focus. They are delineated by and made apparent to human awareness under the aegis of mental focus. For all things are known only to the mind.

So, for any physical object to be made present to human awareness, it must itself be enclosed in a thought image, though it is distinguished in that awareness from any thought which is not understood to be a direct representation of a physical object. It is in this way that a physical object is made present to human awareness.

To reiterate in greater detail: A physical object is a spatial extension. Objects of thought are mental extensions. Both originate from associations of percepts in the noumenal mind. These associations of percepts will all constitute objects of thought in the phenomenal precipitate. But some of these may be recognized by a mature human awareness as physical objects extended in space. And others may be recognized as objects of thought.

In other words, any noumenal association of percepts must become a phenomenal representation within the mind. That phenomenal representation is a thought image. But, due to the distinguishing of the subjective from the objective, some of these representations in the mind are, in fact, recognized as perceptions belonging to the physical realm. Others are recognized as thoughts.

Now, to compound matters further, any thought involving, but not limited to, an image representation of a single physical object will encompass the image of the physical object and more. Thus a thought about household pets, may encompass a series of images of dogs, cats, and cage birds. As the thought (or train of images, to be more precise) is directly representational and includes varying imagery, the imagery maintains an immediate presence in the thought. And the thought shifts between the images.

But such a thought may be a concept. If so, its imagery will be strictly ordered by a definition. A concept is, of course, a classification composed of images which are delimited by a definition. In a concept, the images may be somewhat obscured by the language symbol of the thought—i.e., by the word or words signifying the representation. This is particularly the case when the language symbol has been much used and is quite familiar, as in the case of the informal classification, "household pets."

It is all the more the case when a formal classification is employed. Thus the word canine is supported by a plethora of images: fox, dog, wolf, etc. These fade somewhat from direct mental

The Immaterial Structure of Human Experience

representation, as they cannot all be entertained at once and the word signifying them is intended to represent them all without any special significance being applied to any one of them.

Nevertheless, the point to be made is that, in either case, image or concept, images form the groundwork of the thought. And their percept content can ultimately be referenced to what is considered to be the objective realm. For the percepts involved in what is understood to be sensory perception are the groundwork of material awareness.

In contradistinction to perception, a nonrepresentational thought, rather than being recognized as a direct representation of a physical object—i.e., a perception—is recognized as a thought *about* that physical object. So it is understood to be a thought and not an object, while the direct representation of the object is understood to be a perception of a physical object.

Examining the matter further, it can be seen that the human mind, still operating within the phenomenal precipitate under the aegis of focus, involves itself ever more exclusively in the increasing complexity of the phenomenal precipitate. It moves well beyond its initial role in recognizing associations of percepts in the noumenal precipitate and reorienting them into extensions. It creates a subject/object division.

This arises from the fact that those extensions which are to be designated as thoughts are found to be more closely linked to bodily sensations than those which are destined to be recognized as physical objects. That is to say, thoughts appear to have a more direct influence over bodily sensations than they do over physical extensions.

But a spatial arrangement alone cannot produce a progression of events. Therefore, no motivation for human activity would arise, not to mention a recognition of thoughts as more closely linked to bodily sensations. Something more is needed. And that something is the variation in the presentation of associated percepts which occurs in the noumenal precipitate independently of the human mind's activity.

The variation arises from two principal factors. A segmentation into individual percepts and associations of percepts is required by the limitations of mental focus. This results in their presentation to the mind as a flow. In addition, the particular character of each percept or association of percepts is determined by secondary mind.

This can result in a variegated flow, which may be presented in a progression of minute differences. The progression of minute differences is experienced as a flow of alterations in the presentation of one particular association of percepts. In this way, change is registered in the phenomenal precipitate. Such change occurs both among thought extensions and physical objects.

In contrast, a sustaining of an association of percepts, as representing one particular extension not undergoing change, would require a progressively repeated presentation of the association without differences in the character of each presentation. Thus, as this generally occurs in the physical realm, the object would remain in a condition of stasis.

In either case, change or stasis, it is this process which accounts for the associations of percepts being converted into both thought extensions and physical objects which exhibit either a sustained character or a character of change. The appearance of change amidst stasis in the physical realm invites human activity. For, where there is change and stability together, the change may be focused upon.

Where change may be effected by human effort, there will be a sequential concentration of thought leading to action. The pro-

The Immaterial Structure of Human Experience

gression of this thought signifies a motivation of the will. And, where change in the physical realm can be effected by such thought, it provides an environment for an exercise of the will. [30]

It also follows from the presence of change amidst the contiguity of physical extensions, that human awareness should develop an articulated sense of time. Since that time can be measured in terms of comparative changes in the physical extensions among which it occurs, it is apprehended as incremental time. It is this incremental time which constitutes the normal human experience of past, present, and future.

So, as the activity of mental focus is transferred from the noumenal precipitate to the phenomenal precipitate, it increasingly appears to human awareness to operate within what is, at least in part, a humanly structured environment. For this environment is partially responsive to what comes to be understood as personal will. Thus the mind experiences something more than static spatial relations.

There is such an acute awareness of this personal will that it brings about a perceived separateness of thought from physical experience. The general flow of events, the individual's sense of being immersed in these events in terms of past, present, and future, and her apparent influence over some of the events—all these contribute to this perceived separateness of thought from physical experience.

Thus thought is freed from the relations of the objective realm and enabled to act independently of and within it. As a result, the mind is felt to be responsible for its own behavior. In this

---

[30] This is, of course, an expression of the representational viewpoint. For an immaterialist perspective supports the thesis that true will is buried deep in spirit.

way, a distinction between "me" and "not me" is created. This is the "I" of the material self.

But the means by which such a distinction is brought into final form involves a mental structuring at the maturing level of human awareness, which has hitherto been referred to as an articulation. That articulation is a product of focus working exclusively at the phenomenal level, where it gradually becomes the instrument of an increasingly self-conscious, intellectual mind.

Thus the intellectualization takes place at the level of human awareness. And the original character of the noumenal input is overlooked. For human awareness is transformed into the phenomenal precipitate, an ever-growing and continually modified reflection of the experiencing self and its circumstances.

But the self is understood by the human mind to be subjective. As such, it becomes the center of its experience. So the phenomenal precipitate is a reflection of a greater unity of selfhood which includes not only the self, but also the experience of objective circumstances involving the self. Thus it is grounded in universal spirit. For spirit encompasses both the subjective and objective elements of human experience, the former subject to human will, the latter not directly, and in certain respects not at all.

So it is that the articulation which occurs at the level of human awareness cordons off the mental representations which are experienced as belonging to independent thought processes and places them within a broader context of "objective" perceptions. In the sequence of the presentation of percepts and associations of percepts in the noumenal precipitate, this is done in such a manner as to make thought appear to both influence and be influenced by physical events.

The Immaterial Structure of Human Experience

Thus it can be seen that there is a rearrangement in the order of associated percepts, differing in the phenomenal precipitate from that which originates in the noumenal precipitate. It is a rearrangement which determines the contiguity of spatial relations, as well as the particular sequential character of change peculiar to those relations. It involves a conversion from the non-incremental time of the noumenal precipitate to the incremental time of the phenomenal precipitate. In the midst of this is the sequence of thought, measured by but not productive of the sense of incremental time.

So the transition from the noumenal to the phenomenal is somewhat like the bending of a pencil observed through a glass of water. It is the same pencil but distorted to the viewer's eye. Thus the flow of various associations of percepts in the noumenal precipitate is undifferentiated between subjective and objective. But in the phenomenal precipitate that changes. For a human being sees her own thoughts as though they were on a different track from the extensions of physical space.

Now let the reader's attention be directed to the fact that, as a human being matures, there is a growing sense of the awareness of finitude in her mind. For, on the one hand, observing pure consciousness alone can induce a sense of spiritual oneness, as a result of the removal of any reference to limitation. But, on the other, observing the *content* of consciousness, specifically noting the relationship between two or more percepts or objects (compounds of percepts), renders emphatic a sense of limitation.

Thus it is that two seemingly incompatible realities may be conceived to exist: the spiritual and the material. For they subsist simultaneously yet separately in human awareness. Experience may be interpreted in terms of one or the other. But, though concurrent, they are not equal. For spirit encompasses the material realm in the way that consciousness envelops its material content.

If the mind's attention focuses on consciousness alone, it experiences simple unity. If it focuses on the content of consciousness, especially its interrelations, it experiences plurality. If, furthermore, it should focus on that plurality in light of simple unity, there is a sense of totality. From these, and only these, three intuitions, it can be seen that the fundamental experience of space is initially derived from an intuitional awareness of consciousness as pure, unlimited, indivisible unity. Thus space may be imagined to be unlimited and divided indefinitely, just as a person's consciousness may be imagined to be unbounded and have an indeterminately extended content. Though in practice, due to the role of focus, this does not occur in either case.

Consequently, space must be understood to be a construct of the extensions within it, never superseding the sum total of them in extent. Whereas consciousness is not the sum of its content. It cannot be constructed. Neither can a human conceptual understanding of consciousness be established.

It is rather the case that the constructs of space follow upon the content of consciousness, when the human mind focuses upon relations between associations of percepts and converts them into the mutually limiting extensions in space. It is this development of contiguous extensions which is the origin and justification for a sense of space. For even apparent empty spaces are a result of the particular configuration of contiguous extensions in their vicinity.

For this reason, what has just been said does not imply that space itself is an intuition. In its simplest origin in an intuition derived from the unity of consciousness, it is nothing more than a reflection of the unbounded unity of that consciousness. But it

The Immaterial Structure of Human Experience

cannot be experienced as determinate space until a recognition of distinct individual percepts and the structuring of extensions begins.

This is the reason that neither physical nor mental space are intuited by human awareness. They are constructed by the mind. In particular, what is spoken of here is secondary mind, which is mind prior to the construction of the phenomenal precipitate. The noumenal precipitate's expression of associations of percepts foreshadows the spatial relations of the phenomenal precipitate. After the construction of the latter has commenced and progressed a certain distance, the mind's operations are limited to the phenomenal precipitate alone, insofar as human awareness is concerned.

So the cognitive experience of time may be understood to be built up with that of space. For it is derived from it. It is in this way that a sense of incremental time is developed. It is developed from changes in spatial relations. However, though the experience of incremental time does appear to be derived from an awareness of these changes, there is a more fundamental form of time which is prior to the experience of space and incremental time. This is non-incremental time.

Incremental time must presuppose non-incremental time because nothing can be "built up" without a prior capacity for progression, or unfolding. Consequently, an elemental, non-incremental sense of time is revealed. It is a form of time which cannot be understood in terms of commensurate units of progression. Hence it is non-incremental.

The reason for this is that a sequential flow of percepts in the noumenal precipitate is all that is fundamentally determined by secondary mind's focus. This involves an identification of percepts and their associations, the recognition of associations being determined through close repetitions in the appearance of those associations.

But this strictly linear progression of percepts is substantially prior to the development of extensions of the phenomenal precipitate. In other words, it supports the latter. Thus it "precedes" (logically, not temporally) a means of commensurate measure, which depends upon comparative extensions.

In other words, the noumenal presentation of percepts becomes a progression because of the mind's limitation to focus. It is that focus which creates both non-incremental and incremental time. But in the noumenal flow time is not measurable. For there are no commensurate extensions, the sequential variations of which would provide a standard of temporal measurement. Thus such time is not incremental.

Incremental time is derived from a more complex progression which unfolds the phenomenal precipitate to human awareness. As a result of this latter progression, which occurs in terms of changes in extensions, those changes are experienced incrementally. Thus time is also experienced incrementally.

But this latter progression should not be understood as *following upon* the mind's recognition of the content of the noumenal precipitate. It is not an independent operation of mind. Rather, it results from the same progression of mental focus as that which unfolds the noumenal precipitate. For it is the movement of the mind's attention across the range of noumenal input, converting it to a sequential flow, which simultaneously results in an unfolding of temporal and spatial relations in the phenomenal precipitate.

Now to move to a different issue. It may seem a bit odd to suggest such a thing as mental space when referring to the extensions of thought. But do not objects held in imagination produce

The Immaterial Structure of Human Experience

a spatial extension? For example, the image of an apple is extended. It is extended in the mind. Moreover, a plurality of apples can be imagined together, though the greater the plurality, the less the detail. It could not be visualized as a plurality without extension. For each apple must exclude the other. So this thought is also extended.

As just suggested, this brings up another issue, which has been discussed previously in less detail than will be presented here. In fact, much of this essay is a modified discussion of what has come before. But the development is somewhat different. And this has been deemed necessary to fill out previously missing elements in the discussion.

When contained in one thought, a delineation of two apples will not be as distinct as in a representation of one. For the mind's focus is limited as to detail. This is because focus must hone in on detail. Which is to say that the object under consideration must be enlarged to cover the entire field of that thought. Thus, in a single thought, the emboldened details of one apple would encompass the same span of representation as the two apples, whose details would be less notable.

Think of a plate of fruit in a Cézanne painting. When viewing the whole, does a viewer see each piece of fruit distinctly? Or is it that, in an attempt to increase its observation of detail, the focus of the viewer's mind passes momentarily over each piece of fruit in turn? Under such consideration it is clear that, when it comes to mental images, the greater the field of inclusion, the less the distinction in terms of detail.

This is due to the peculiar character of mental focus, where no exact comparison is ever made between more than two things at once. Thus, as a field of comparison is expanded—say beyond two proximate sides of two apples—more detail must be included in the comparison, which is always a comparison of two. So a comparison of two entities of few details is more exact than a comparison of two entities of many details. For an examination of the details requires multiple subordinate comparisons. And, as the number of details increases, some of them are likely to be passed over.

Accordingly, if details are to be observed, any compounding of impressions on the mind must be progressive in character. It will therefore be sequential in consideration, however rapid the transition from one mental object to the other. The overall effect is cumulative. Thus, in any deepening recognition of detail, a viewer observes a bowl of fruit horizontally from one side to the other, or vertically by degrees, then all together in a built-up impression.

One might object that this includes the efforts of memory. And memory is a separate compartment of mind. Therefore, it is physical. But in answer to such an objection, it must be reasserted that the input of memory is also fed to human awareness through the noumenal stream of percepts. Thus its direct origin is spirit.

A more complicated problem lies in the nature of abstraction. For example, let the mathematical concept of a perfect circle be considered in terms of its supporting imagery. This can and should be done because all concepts are grounded in imagery. Considering its supporting imagery, can it be maintained that the circle is apprehended *a priori* as a whole, as some have thought?

No, it cannot, since there is a compounding of imagery: a plane surface, a curved line, straight lines, etc. But, if its origin is not within a simple *a priori* unity, nonetheless the overall circle can be said to originate from a transcendent foundation. For it arises from the three fundamental intuitions of the mind: unity, plurality, totality.

The Immaterial Structure of Human Experience

A circle, or any other complex single image set forth in the mind, must be composed of first one simple unity then another: the unity of a plane surface, the individual unities of straight lines, of a single curved line, etc. Then a recognition that there is a plurality of these unities follows. Finally, there is a totality of the unities, which comprises the final united image. This compounding of multiple images into a single image might be referred to as layering.

A geometrically perfect circle is composed of a plane area enclosed by a single, continuous, unvaryingly curved line, referred to as its circumference. Such a line will meet itself, producing a line without discernible origin or termination. Furthermore, the circle contains innumerable equal straight lines having a common origin within the enclosed plane. These are referred to as its radii. The radii terminate at different points on the curved line. Since the straight lines referred to as radii are all equal and have a common point of origin, that common origin must lie at the center of the circle.

So far, this has only been imagined visually, with the possible exception of the logic which assisted the construction by convincing the intellect of a center point. It is as though these imagined features were piled one on top the other to compose the figure of the circle. However, they are not three-dimensional. Rather, they are fused into one plane, thus becoming a single plane figure.

So this final plane figure is a unity of individual image units. The individual images, which were destined to be unified, are each figures of a geometrical orientation and description within a plane, such as the circumference, radii, and center point. Each image has been descriptively identified—once again with the exception of the logic of the center point, which is descriptively imagined only subsequently to its logical determination. They are then united together in a single plane figure, which figure is the final unity. That figure is the image of a circle—a *perfect* circle, to be exact.

Now, when the approach is altered and the circle is considered strictly in terms of its verbal definition, that one figure, the circle, is once again created only by virtue of a combination of definitional features. The lines are defined as straight or curved, the straight ones having equal lengths, etc. The final definition is a combination of these prior definitions. They become its properties.

Thus the fact that the circle is introduced by Euclid as a complete definition does not alter the situation. He makes no logical transitions between the prior definitions and his definition of a circle, which includes the prior definitions. Such prior definitions are those of a point, a line, a straight line, a plane surface, a boundary, and a figure. They just happen to appear together in this definition of a circle. An acceptance of their combination is expected.[31]

In spite of this expected acceptance, the final verbalization, which is the definition of a circle, is still a compounding of those several independent concepts into one concept, that of the circle. Each supporting concept is grounded by an image. And the circle is a unification of those images into one image.

Note the peculiar fact that Euclid identifies the center point *following* the definition of the circle.[32] And the logical connection is implied rather than stated. His method differs in no way from the imaginative representation which has been presented

---

[31] *Euclid's Elements*, Book 1, Definitions.
[32] Ibid., Definition 16. This definition follows definition 15, which is the definition of the circle.

The Immaterial Structure of Human Experience

above, other than by its abstraction into concepts rather than images.

To get a handle on the mental process of abstraction, let an inventor of the concept of the circle be posited. How would she do this? Perhaps she has encountered apples and oranges, the moon and the sun, and other such "round" things. She has formed a general image of roundness as experienced in these objects.

To arrive at a generalization of the characteristic of roundness, she has focused mentally on the one property, roundness, which has caught her notice and is of interest to her. She has put aside consideration of other properties in these objects, since these other characteristics do not resemble each other in the different objects—i.e., color, texture, etc.

So how did she do this? How did she isolate roundness? First, she examined each of the objects as a materially limited unity. Then she considered the separate and differing properties of each object. She saw that together these properties constituted the totality, or material unity, of the object in question. But, as they are properties, they are not parts. Thus the object in this sense is a plurality of properties.

A totality, unlike a simple unity, is a unity which must be understood as being built up either from parts or from properties, depending on the point of view. For it is a unity of both parts and properties. Thus, if it can be built up from its properties, it may be intellectually disassembled into its properties.

From each disassembled object, the inventor retained only the property of roundness. In this way she created a useful, albeit indefinite, abstraction. For she has not defined roundness. Of course, this process takes place rapidly in the mind by means of association and is not labored over in the manner presently suggested.

The problem is one of inexactness. The inventor has isolated the property of roundness in a number of objects which appear to possess that property. Then she gathered the like instances together as one characteristic and proceeded to consider them as a new totality of one property, which she calls "roundness." It is a rough image in her mind. That is, it is not yet a concept. For it is not defined.

Roundness is now considered to be a general attribute of certain types of objects which possess it as a characteristic. The inventor has gotten this far by shifting her mental attention, or focus, between simple unity, plurality, and totality. She has sifted out different instances of a property and classified them together. But she does not have a clear sense of what roundness is. So she wants to define roundness.

Roundness might be imagined as a continuously curved line without a discernible beginning or end (i.e., the two ends join) and without the appearance of angles—that is, without the appearance of any discernible point delineating an abrupt change in direction of the continuous curving of the line. This is what was roughly observed in the various objects from which the characteristic of roundness was abstracted.

Every part of the circumference of a perfect circle, however small, exhibits a uniform curvature. And the number of such parts that the circumference can be divided into is indeterminate. So no discernible part can be designated as that which determines a change in curvature. This provides the general attribute, "roundness." But it is still not a carefully delineated definition of what roundness is.

After all, such an imaginary representation of roundness as the inventor now has may come in an indeterminate variety in actual experience. For, however carefully something is measured,

The Immaterial Structure of Human Experience

there may yet be undetected points at which there *is* a change of direction. As an obvious example, the apple was not perfectly round. So is the sun perfectly round? This inconsistency accords well with the physical world of experience, where no two round objects appear to be exactly the same, or exactly round, for that matter.

What this leaves the inventor with is a sense of uncertainty as to exactly what she means by the term, roundness. She needs a precise definition, a definition which can only be interpreted one way. Such a definition could then be relied upon for exact thinking, though the thing thought about might exist nowhere in the physical world. What she wants is an ideal, an idea, a concept that generally represents what she means. It can then be matched up with things which roughly resemble it—that is to say, things which resemble it within certain tolerances for slight deviation.

Perhaps she has had in mind some general attributes regarding plane figures, such as the number and length of sides in various triangles, rectangles, squares, etc. None of these is exact in her physical experience. But she does know what she means when she thinks of them—or more precisely, when she imagines them. And she knows that roundness is not any of these.

These figures involve angles, or clearly demarcated linear changes of direction that she can visualize. And roundness does not have any clearly demarcated linear changes of direction. That is, it does not have any angles. So, since it is different from the above polygonal figures, she decides to call her definition of it the designation of a circle. A circle will not only be a roundness. It will be a roundness which is exact. The exactness means that only one such roundness can be imagined.

To reach this final goal, the question she must ask is, what is *not* roundness? This was how she got to the general characteristic of roundness in the first place, when she extracted the characteristic of roundness from the sun, the moon, an apple, an orange, etc. She decided roundness was not red, orange, texture, and so forth. That left her with roundness as a general type of spatial extension—a particular figure, or shape. Now she wants to be more specific. She wants an exact type of spatial extension. Nothing else will be like it.

She starts thinking: It is not a polygon. Why not? Because it does not have any angles. But the absence of angles alone does not get her very far. When she eliminates all angles, at least all angles she can see, she still has only a rough idea of what she means by roundness. So she must ask herself: what is it that changes when an angle is perceived?

Looking closely at any number of mental representations, she observes that if she chooses a rectangle, what changes is the direction of the perimeter line at certain points. How can she know the line changes direction? She can observe each change from a specific reference point. So she decides to place this reference point inside the rectangle. She chooses the point at which the two diagonals of the rectangle bisect each other.

She then picks another point on one of the rectangle's sides. Let it be assumed that, of any point on the perimeter of the rectangle, it is the shortest distance from the reference point. Thus it bisects one of the long sides. Since there are two long sides of equal length and two short sides of equal length alternately joined at right angles, there will be two such points on the perimeter. They bisect each of the long sides.

So she observes the side of the rectangle which has the designated point, and notices that, as the perimeter extends either to the right or the left away from the point on its long side (say it extends to the right), it grows incrementally more distant from

The Immaterial Structure of Human Experience

the reference point. But the perimeter of the rectangle eventually takes a sharp turn. In fact, it does so four times.

In the first instance, it becomes one of the short sides. At this change of linear orientation, the uniformly increasing distance of the perimeter from the reference point is abruptly altered. The distance now begins to grow shorter. It continues to grow shorter until the perimeter's shortest distance from the reference point (on the short side of the rectangle) is reached at the bisection of the short side.

After that, the distance begins to lengthen again. When the opposite long side is reached, and another 90° degree turn is made, the distance from the reference point begins to shorten once again until the midpoint of that side. Then, past that, it lengthens. Then it shortens and lengthens again on the opposite short side. Finally it shortens again the rest of the way to the starting point on the first long side.

So the observer's most pressing clue is that the perimeter of a rectangle is a number of alternating distances from the point of reference. And these distances vary abruptly in places, growing alternately longer and shorter as one follows the perimeter around the rectangle to its initial point of departure. The places of abrupt change are where there are 90° turns in the perimeter and at the midpoints on each side. Overall, this signals an inward and outward oscillation of the perimeter in relation to the central reference point.

So she thinks, what about a square? This appears to hold true for a square as well. What about a many-sided regular polygon, the perimeter of which has so many abrupt changes in direction, it might be described as a uniformly jagged line? Here the differences in distance from the reference point are less. And the turn angles of the perimeter are more numerous and greater than 90°, if they are measured from within the polygon.

Then what about a much less jagged perimeter enclosing such a polygon, one with perimeter turns that are so small, and also so frequent, they might be described as indeterminate in both size and number? The case of a differing range of distances from the reference point is the same here as in the previous cases. But the distances are much less varied. Between any one point and another, there is almost no change in distance to the point of reference.

Now it occurs to her that through this process of elimination, she might, at least ideally, arrive at a perimeter in which all points on that perimeter can be described as equally distant from the point of reference.[33] So she decides to call the perimeter a circumference. And since all points on it are equally distant from the point of reference, she designates that point of reference as the center of a circle. Thus a circle is that which has all points on its circumference equally distant from its center.[34]

But the problem is that she has never seen one of these. However, that does not matter. What matters is that she always knows exactly (in terms of her definition and her figurative experiments) what it is that she is talking about when she refers to a circle. And she knows that no other form of extension fits this definition.

She knows this because in her thought experiment she systematically eliminated all other forms of extension. The perfect circle is by definition unique, one of a kind. By definition, it is

---

[33] See Archimedes, "Measurement of a Circle," Proposition 3. This is what Archimedes attempted to approximate in his effort to calculate pi.
[34] *Euclid's Elements*, Book I, Definitions 15 and 16.

The Immaterial Structure of Human Experience

always what it is and not anything else. Thus it possesses a certainty which is a certainty she has given it.

It seems to have been born in her mind without any connection to the external world. This is because she cannot demonstrate that it exists anywhere in the world, just as she cannot demonstrate that there is such a thing as a line without width (a breadthless line being exactly like itself and nothing else). Neither can she demonstrate the physical existence of any of the precise concepts concerning extension which are called geometrical figures. There are no demonstrably perfect triangles, squares, rectangles, etc.

The physical world does not seem to contain two or more things which are exactly alike, at least not so far as anyone can demonstrate. It is true that the noumenal precipitate creates identity in terms of repeated associations of percepts. But this identity can be ascertained in the phenomenal mind only in terms of a recognition of the same object when it is not subject to change.

The human imagination and intellect, on the other hand, recognize or create identity in two or more entities by means of a sleight of hand. That is to say, they do so through a deliberate process of elimination. This is what gives mathematics its aura of certainty, its *a priori* feel. For the same process of eliminative reasoning just employed on the circle also creates concepts like the line without width and the abstract arithmetical unit one.

The arithmetical unit, however, is a special case. For it is made to somewhat resemble the intuition of unity itself. And, since arithmetical units are multiple, the intuition of plurality is also employed. Thus, the first two intuitions of the mind are being exercised in an elemental and immediate way. Consequently, a person can better see how they work in creating an identity.

The arithmetical unit is a finite unity—i.e., a simple unity delimited by a plurality of other unities identical to itself. However, the precise extension, and thus inclusion of other unities within its finitude, is undetermined. It is, in effect, an empty unit. This means it has no attributes other than unity and limitation. It does not express extension.

In what may seem at first glance to be a contradiction of this statement, the unit one in the number 1.0001 clearly exhibits different relative extensions registering different levels of inclusion. The 1 to the left of the decimal is inclusive of ten thousand of the 1 four places to the right of the decimal.

But that does not matter, so long as it is understood that all such units are the same within a particular context. That context is determined arithmetically by a mathematical operation or series of operations. In other words, the appearance of a property of extension is not inherent to the arithmetical unit. Rather, it is a function of the operation.

For a more closely examined example, take the similar number 2.0002. The positive integer 2 to the left of the decimal contains two identical unit ones. These are units such as the unit which is found to the left of the decimal in the number 1.0001. And the number 2 four places to the right of the decimal in 2.0002 contains two identical unit ones, such as the unit which is found four places to the right of the decimal in the number 1.0001.

Now examine the intuitions. Under the aegis of mental focus, pure consciousness provides the intuition of simple unity—i.e., a unity devoid of any consideration of a possibility of its division. For the source of the intuition is pure consciousness, which is an indivisible unity. This intuition allows the mind to recognize a

The Immaterial Structure of Human Experience

unity in its content. That is to say, in its most fundamental employment, it recognizes unity in a percept.

Were it not for this operation of the mind, each different percept would fill the mind in such a manner as to be unique yet remain indistinct from the other percepts. For example, though blue and red are perceived in quite individual ways, the two percepts would be blended imperceptibly into one another.

So there could be no clear sense of demarcation as to where one ends and the other begins. Thus they would remain individually unclear. As a result, they could not form a distinct relation to one another in the mind of the perceiver. For there can be no relation where there is no clear distinction.

It is mental focus which isolates a percept and brings it under the intuition of unity. For mental focus, as an operation within consciousness, *is* that intuition. It is a limitation brought about as an expression of where the mind places its attention. Following upon the placement of this attention, a different placement of attention may be observed in contradistinction to it.

So there is a plurality in objects of attention. Each delimits the other. Accordingly, as the content of consciousness may be observed to be divided into a plurality of mutually delimiting unities (the multiple percepts), the intuition of plurality is awakened. The mind recognizes plurality and limitation.

Thus each of the unities within the content of consciousness is recognized as finite. At this point, the special act of creating an arithmetical unit may take place. However, rather than creating the arithmetical unit at such a fundamental level of awareness as is involved in the initial recognition of percepts, the mind creates it at the imaginative and conceptual level of the phenomenal precipitate.

In regard to any finite unit which is encountered within consciousness and held under mental attention, or focus, all attributes but unity may be imaginatively removed from it. Fingers or toes might well have served as models for the abstraction. Hence the common speculation that the Western decimal-based system arose from the ten fingers and ten toes on the hands and feet. With all attributes but unity and limitation removed, these digits presumably could have become arithmetical units. Similar events would have occurred in other number systems.

Now unity and limitation alone, recognized as the principal (and in this case, only) attributes of a finite unit, may once again be set in reference to pure consciousness. Pure conscious is empty, since it is consciousness experienced without its content. This is true as well of the finite unit, after it has been stripped of all material attributes other than unity and limitation. The finite unit is empty.

That is why it appears to resemble the first intuition. For it is as though it were prior to any specified content, like the intuition. But in this case, it is held in the mind as a concept without content, as if the intuition might have been suspended in mid-delineation of an object. Also, in the manner of pure consciousness, the unit is indivisible. In this way, the unit drawn from the content of consciousness, then stripped of all but its unity and finitude, may be considered specifically in terms of its *emptiness and indivisibility*.

The characteristic of emptiness holds firm, with the single added stipulation that, as a unity, the arithmetical unit also continues to be considered finite. In other words, it is understood to be finite without consideration of any specific material attribute, such as extension, color, shape, etc. Nothing can be predicated of

The Immaterial Structure of Human Experience

it but unity and finitude. Thus it is a unit which is both empty and finite.

Yet this peculiarity pertains: due to its finite nature, the empty unit can be limited by other such identical units, since being limited in such a manner is what it means for it to be finite. Finitude is always a reference to external delimiting factors. Thus, if all such units are emptied of anything other than unity and limitation as attributes, they may be deemed identical units and may be added one to another as discrete units in numerically precise totalities. This is the origin of the natural numbers.

Totality is, of course, the third intuition. Numbers are various totalities of arithmetical units. This includes fractions, where the operational context of the unit changes. The units of the numerator are held within the context of the units of the denominator. Thus 1/6 and 1/4 represent different contexts.

A numerical totality also includes irrational numbers, in which the operational compounding of units of increasingly diminutive reference remains indeterminate. All numerical operations, whatever the type of operation, are in essence a nesting of totalities, whether they be determinate or indeterminate. In this way, arithmetic is born.

Most importantly, the fact that an arithmetical unit can be operationally positioned in such a manner as to appear to contain other units of lesser inclusion, as in the case of 1.0001 or 2.0002, does not imply that any such unit has become a physical extension. For the inclusion is operational and not physical.

The termination of this essay is at hand. So, once again, the only mental traits which are irrevocably present in the human mind, and thus truly innate within it, are those of focus and the intuitions of unity, plurality, and totality. Focus is the attention the mind pays to its experience. It is the means by which it recognizes and organizes the material world. And it may extend over a large or smaller field. Thus it is enabled to shape that experience in terms of its interaction with it.

The mind may focus upon a percept, or upon combinations of percepts, such as constitute an object, which is a spatial extension. Or it may extend to more than one object, though one must always remember that focus considers only two entities in comparison. Greater fields of comparison are compilations of focus, a layering of separate instances of focus into a single observation.

The intuitions are derived from (1) the experience of pure consciousness, (2) the experience of discrete percepts discovered amongst the input of noumenal awareness, and (3) a working together of these two sources of intuition into a third intuition embracing extension, or finite inclusiveness. The extension may be physical, or it may be merely operational, as in the above discussion. In short, all mental functions of a perceptual or conceptual nature, including a sense of space, incremental time, and the system of mathematics, are built up from the three intuitions.

39. The spiritual dynamic. The spiritual dynamic is another term for universal spirit, or universal consciousness. Thus, since it is defined simply as spirit, this dynamic partakes of that which is the ground of being. For consciousness is a necessary condition for awareness. And "the ground of being" is what is meant by universal spirit, or universal consciousness. What is being asserted here is that that ground can be understood as dynamic, as opposed to inert. So, having employed the term "dynamic" in this sense, in contradistinction to the material dynamic, let it be imagined as something which is set into violent motion.

But it cannot be that it *is* motion. For the concept of motion is very specific, involving change of condition or place. Change of condition or place suggests finitude. And that would imply a

The Immaterial Structure of Human Experience

material character. When mechanically understood, one thing cannot change its condition without a rearrangement of its parts, which must be limited in character to be in such a relationship with one another. Change of place is no different. Thus motion would involve a reference to the finite.

However, in referring to the spiritual dynamic, what is being referred to is spirit, which, as universal consciousness, is unbounded and indivisible. Nothing pertaining to it is finite. For finitude is not only limitation, but complete limitation, an isolation, a closing off of one thing from another.

Thus spirit is precisely that in which the characteristics of material entities cannot be considered. So it must be said that the spiritual dynamic resembles motion in its essential character of change. But, as there is no complete closing off of one thing from another in spirit, it does so in an indeterminate sense.

In fact, when examined closely, even the precise character of material motion is difficult to determine. For, when compared to a state of rest, it is always motion and never a state of rest, no matter how minute the segments of time by which one presumes to isolate its increments.

Moreover, incremental time is itself a measure of motion. And motion involves distance. Thus incremental time is change in distance measuring change in distance, as when the hands of a stopwatch are compared to the movements of a sprinter.[35] And the experience of change, in turn, is a result of the limiting character of focus in parceling out differing associations of percepts to human awareness.

---

[35] A digital clock, or any other experiential form of measure, would still involve displacement, which is a form of motion, or change in distance. This is so in the case of an atomic clock as well. For it undergoes particle exchange, though this is, of course, theoretical.

Thus an understanding of incremental time resolves into a matter of relating distances. This is the problem with the argumentative thrust of Zeno's paradoxes, which mistakenly treat time as an entity independent of comparative changes in distance between material components.

But when a person is willing to look at time as a function of material change, she sees that physical motion reflects the indeterminate character of the spiritual dynamic in this one sense: it cannot be pinned down to a precise analysis. It can only be observed that it occurs at differing rates, which rates are varying distance relations.

To insist that these occur in the same time frame would be to involve a third distance relation, which would act as an independent measure. How else could the "time frame" be known? However, all this having been noted, human beings are rarely confronted with this indeterminacy which lies at the heart of the concept of motion. For such a confrontation is the result of a careful delineation which would appear to serve no useful purpose.

Human beings are generally more practical than contemplative. In practical matters, motion can be quantified with great accuracy, so long as it need not be a definitive quantification. Any discrepancy in calculation at a level approaching zero is more than sufficiently excusable for most purposes. Thus motion is generally understood in quantitative terms, which places it fully within the classification of material phenomena.

However, if a person were to define the spiritual dynamic, she would not want to define it in terms of motion. This is because matters in the realm of spirit have nothing to do with practicality. So, since human beings are limited in the resources of their thinking, and are thus required to describe spiritual things in

The Immaterial Structure of Human Experience

material terms, there must be a compromise. It must be said that the spiritual dynamic is a state of indeterminate flux which is quite apart from what people normally think of as motion. It is paradoxically a state of continuous change or motion without a measurable sense of either change or motion.

How can this be? It is possible to assert this because the motion of the spiritual dynamic is not actual. Material change and motion, on the other hand, take place in the midst of the actual. They are realized within the limits of human awareness. But, rather than being actual, the spiritual dynamic is potential. For it is spirit. So it must be characterized as belonging to the realm of possibility, rather than to what is.

That is to say, by "what is" is meant what is for human awareness. This is a limited reference. For the realm of possibility is *being* in a more fundamental sense than the realm of the actual, since the actual proceeds from the potential and has its being in its origin. All this discussion of spirit and the spiritual dynamic is opposed to matter and human thought, which are those things which are called actual in human experience.

Now human beings participate in the spiritual dynamic in a manner which is limited by their precipitate-bound minds. Thus for a human sensibility the world is not a spiritual dynamic. It is a precipitate of the dynamic. It is actual, which actuality constitutes the world both for human perception and for human thought. Thus the human mind is only aware of the potential through its experience of change, which change is always actual—always realized and thus determined—except insofar as matters of anticipation are considered.[36]

---

[36] Note that anticipation implies memory. And memory has been accounted for by means of what is fed by secondary mind (self-limiting spirit) into the noumenal flow of percepts. Thus to remember is to know in terms of thought

Furthermore, in dealing conceptually with this materialized, actual world, human awareness can isolate certain phenomena. It can determine limits and classify. This process of classification, when functioning at its best, is equivalent to the scientific method—the scientific method being essentially a rigorous focus of human mental activity, where the data of the phenomenal precipitate is brought under conceptual organization. [37]

By this method the human mind discovers causal relations. That is to say, it creates a particular pattern of causal relations as a consequence of its structuring of conceptual classifications and as a consequence of the order of realized events. Let the classifications be changed. And the causal relations will be altered. But only within the bounds of order and proportion, proportion being an inherent characteristic of the relations which both secondary mind and human awareness have sewn into the structure of the phenomenal precipitate.

If human thinkers are rigorous in their approach, relying upon a careful measurement of observed phenomena, certain relations, such as extension and change, may be expressed in quantitative terms. For quantification is a product of the classification of the proportions inherent in the phenomenal precipitate. Or more precisely, it is a product of the application of a number system to the classification of those proportions.

So what now? Shall it be said that the conceptual activities of humanity have killed spirit? Shall it be assumed that they have stopped the spiritual dynamic in its tracks by bringing the phenomenal precipitate under the abstract relations of classification?

---

what has previously occurred in material experience. And to anticipate is to apply this knowledge to a recognized consistency in patterns of experience.

[37] Where contemporary scientific reasoning may be said to fall short is in its omission of a full consideration of the active role of consciousness in human experience.

The Immaterial Structure of Human Experience

This precipitate is, after all, a product of the indeterminate flux of the spiritual dynamic. To tie it down with classifications and causal relations would presumably be to nail down the spiritual dynamic as well, even though the spiritual dynamic should be one step removed from the process.

So has the flux been pinned down? By no means! The human intellect has simply taken a photograph of ongoing change in the precipitate. It has stopped the action, so to speak, and observed its order of appearance. For the phenomenal precipitate is no more than the shadow of a complex dynamic. In arranging classifications and their subsequent causal relations in dealing with the order of events in the phenomenal precipitate, human beings have created an illusion of intelligibility.

The illusion of intelligibility is something which allows human beings to determine those relationships which are both classificational and quantitative. It is what establishes experimental results in the macrophysical world and supports their theoretical context. Isaac Newton's systematic world, for instance, is just such a photograph.

In general, practical human knowledge of the everyday world human beings live and act in is also such a photograph or, shall it be said, a series of such photographs which may be only loosely linked together. For the thinker, the hunter, and the artist do not classify in exactly the same way. Moreover, one person may be all three of these.

But now let the microphysical world be entered. For it presents problems largely overlooked in the macrophysical. To represent this subtler view of the phenomenal precipitate, let the macrophysical photograph be more closely examined, say with a magnifying glass. The image is grainy, unclear. It is also lumpy, less smooth appearing in its relations, with sudden apparent shifts in those relations. It looks as if the macro view has not, in fact, captured the whole of reality. It has only approximated it.

To bring such a close up view under scrutiny, humanity must begin to describe micro reality in less specific, more probabilistic terms to account for the uncertainty of its relations. Thus it turns out that the ghost of spirit—i.e., the ghost of the spiritual dynamic—is always present in the midst of the phenomenal precipitate. Material reality, which was apparently causally linked and neatly determinate in the macro realm, now in the micro realm begins to dissolve into indeterminateness, into the realm of possibility.

But the spiritual dynamic, it should be recalled, is a realm of unspecified and unlimited possibility. It is not truly in motion. Any motion previously associated with it was simply an illustrative model. For no better tools are available to describe it. The spiritual dynamic is, insofar as humanity's limited comprehension is concerned, simply a realm of possibility.

Human beings can in no way assert its relations. But neither can they justly define its nature as a realm of no relations because, if they could, they would be converting it into something determinate. It would be *determinately* indeterminate, a kind of reverse precipitate—what is generally referred to as chaos.

Of course, to get a better sense of what the indeterminate character of spirit is, or at least what it is not, a brief thought experiment is in order. Let the reader momentarily transform herself into something equally indeterminate. She can imagine herself as spiritual in a spiritual realm. But if she does, she will quickly discover that she can no longer be in a determinate relationship with her former material existence.

There will be no common ground for discussion between her and a person bound by the two precipitates. This is, of course, the problem of the mystic, insofar as her mystical experience is con-

The Immaterial Structure of Human Experience

cerned. She cannot effectively communicate her ecstatic experience to those who have had no such experience. Neither can human beings discuss general matters of spirit in mortal terms.

Those precipitate relationships which human beings perceive as material existence and contemplate as determinate, are initially created by finite limitation and change. The character of mental focus and material finitude is a product of secondary mind. And the phenomena of change are also initially presented to human awareness by secondary mind.

This occurs in the noumenal precipitate. But, insofar as they also appear to be structured in human experience of the phenomenal precipitate by means of a pre-conceptual imaginative awareness and later by thought, they are created by the three primary intuitions: unity, plurality, and totality.

Thought is not only conceptual thinking. It is also imaginative association. So it includes those early childhood processes of the mind by which human beings learn to combine associations of percepts into a comprehensible world of extensions without conceptualizing it. This is what is meant by pre-conceptual. It is a world in which the perceiver is already rendered capable of distinguishing her subjective self from the objectively perceived.

The laying down of the noumenal precipitate through variation in associations of percepts is the principal characteristic of secondary mind. Its order of presentation determines non-incremental time. Change in the phenomenal precipitate (and, accordingly, a recognition of incremental time) is derived from this variation.

But time in the phenomenal precipitate is also somewhat modified as a result of the contiguities and sequences of spatial extensions. Thus it differs from non-incremental time in more than a capacity for measurement. As a result, it is something which is thoroughly distinct from the unity of being, or spirit, which is primary mind. That is, it is so in the sense in which "distinct" is meant. For the term distinct, as used here, means distinct for human awareness.

Secondary mind is, of course, self-limiting spirit. So change acts as a conveyer belt, unveiling the indeterminate dynamic of spirit in a determinate flow of percepts directed to the limitations of the human mind. Or at least it conveys that portion of the percepts of spirit which falls within the perspective of the unique individuality of each person. These percepts are not all the percepts available within spiritual being, but are those percepts which are revealed uniquely to each individual human sensibility by means of their flow within her consciousness.

Non-incremental time, which is a product of the apparent consecutive character of presentation of associations of percepts in the noumenal precipitate, may be said to possess an illusory character because human beings are unable to settle upon a precise and indisputable measurement of its increments. It is also something which arises from the limitations of mental focus. There is no linear sense of time in spirit.

There is so much differentiation in the presentation of change to human consciousness in the phenomenal precipitate, that choosing any exemplar of it as a measure is entirely arbitrary. Not only that, but the very nature of the change is in question. For example, if a particular motion is fastened upon as a stationary reference, another relative state of rest may appear to be in motion. Such is the case when the sun is thought to rise and set in relation to the earth. But, were no motion (or change) to be chosen as a reference, how then would time be measured?

Moreover, human beings find themselves capable of indefinitely dividing time into smaller and smaller units and thus never

The Immaterial Structure of Human Experience

arriving at a definitive measure. In doing this, they encounter nothing determinate but the general character of change. Yet the sequential character of change demands a measure.

Associations of percepts and their alterations are much interpreted in human experience as changes in extensions—i.e., changes in objects. This is true both of collective human experience and of individual human experience. Science is an example of collective human experience, where the interpretation of phenomena has been standardized. Individual human understanding is largely forced to conform to this, but not entirely. Occasionally, a Maxwell expands the interpretation in an unexpected way. Or an Einstein modifies the received model.

So, like material change itself, its instrument of measure, time, can be said to be illusory, since its origin in the spiritual dynamic is not change as human beings know it. It is a general flux, the indescribable realm of potential. Out of this potential comes the presentation of change through both secondary mind and human awareness. Nevertheless, when experienced at the human level, change is the author of what human beings imagine not to be illusory. That is the unfolding of the phenomenal precipitate.

It is from this phenomenal precipitate that the impressive edifice of science has risen. And it remains unquestioned, so long as human beings do not enquire too closely into the systematic structure which they have bestowed upon it. This they do periodically, but only at long intervals. So, in short, science may be described as a convenient map which works well in practical situations. It gets the human race where it wants to go. Nonetheless, knowing they themselves drew the map in the first place, they remain uncertain of its fidelity to the terrain.

40. The priority of spirit. The spiritual dynamic is beyond any human reckoning. It is what is referred to simply as universal spirit, implying that it is a universal consciousness, which is that which is not material or finite. However, if spirit were to convert itself into a material phenomenal precipitate comprehensive enough to correspond entirely to its full dynamic, and if this precipitate was such that a human mind could at least imagine itself understanding it, it could be imagined to take the form of a universal material domain.

What is spoken of here is not the more restricted phenomenal precipitate which is presented to human awareness by secondary mind. It is a precipitate which would directly reflect the character of the spiritual dynamic. For in this universal state there is no linear progression of time. All events, all changes would be revealed at once, somewhat in the manner of presenting all the frames of a film at once. Thus there is not a development of events. All stages of change would appear together. This is primary mind.

Yet individual human consciousness is also spirit. Thus the human spirit is likened to universal spirit, or primary mind. However, a human consciousness has gone through the process of the self-limitation of spirit, which self-limiting of spirit is secondary mind. Therefore, a human consciousness is, as it were, but an isolated frequency of light projected from the prism of secondary mind.

Thus, when humankind is spoken of, it is asserted that universal spiritual being is focused upon a particular perspective. And that perspective is an individual human awareness. It is as though universal spirit were concentrating on projecting itself through only one frequency of the full spectrum of light which is its being.

The Immaterial Structure of Human Experience

For this reason, human awareness is more limited than universal spirit. In other words, it is more limited because it is focused by secondary mind. That is to say, it is self-limited spirit. But it is not only this. It is also spirit bound up *within* material existence. What does that mean? It means that in the human dynamic, as opposed to the universal dynamic of spirit, human awareness is limited by more than perspective. It is limited by time. Its experience is progressive, rather than universal.

Conscious material beings are both awareness itself and the world of which they are aware. As awareness, they are spirit. But they cannot precipitate their entire world at once, as universal spirit can be imagined to do. Only portions of their world are made available to their awareness as those portions are revealed in the unfolding of time. This is the work of secondary mind. Secondary mind is the author of the quotidian realm of human awareness.

Human consciousness is thus bound up in material limitation. Yet, while this may be the case, human beings remain aware of the unlimited spiritual core of their being. This is pure consciousness, which human beings regard as their essential selves, when they regard that consciousness without consideration of its content. The content they regard as their world. This world is the source of their sense of personal limitation.

How does human consciousness obtain its content? It does so through a precipitate, a limited projection of the spiritual dynamic. This projection is laid out in a discernible order for human awareness. For, since human consciousness is limited by time and thus unable to grasp any portion of the spiritual dynamic whole, the human mind must operate within what it is given. The human precipitate must therefore have an order subordinate to change, or time.

That precipitate must either be given by secondary mind in a discernible order. Or it must be organized in a discernible order by human awareness. Or it may be both, which it is. Out of spirit, then, is spun the web of the material. Of course, this implies that perception is entirely and exclusively within the mind. Thus it would suggest an immaterialist view of the world. And so it does.

But, given the limitations of human awareness, human beings can and generally do reverse the order of this relation. By overlooking the transcendent origin of the material, they attribute absolute validity to the phenomenal precipitate alone. And consciousness occupies a small space within it. For to human experience, the precipitate is seen as something apart from conscious awareness. It becomes a world in its own right.

It is in this way that human beings begin their speculations. They begin with a sense of the limited and the physical. They take the material world as their point of reference and infer from it an order which is independent, consistent, and reliable. From this they derive a sense of their own separate material existence, apart from other material manifestations. Thus a person's individual consciousness is understood to be centered in only a small portion of material existence.

Also, building up from such a metaphysical structure composed of the human precipitate alone—i.e., the material realm—they discover relations, devise natural laws to account for those relations, make predictions based on those laws, and construct bodies of knowledge which are called sciences.

Evolution is one of these sciences. And from the observed relations of this science one can see how the human mind might have been formed by natural selection. That is, the mind's rational properties can be accounted for in material terms. For instance, the indicator-response conditioning of other animals can be ob-

The Immaterial Structure of Human Experience

served. This leads to an accounting of the emergence of various levels of cause-and-effect reasoning in humans and other animals.

But in following a chain of induction from the material perspective, one finds oneself unable to account for spirit. For there is no way to deduce consciousness from the material. To be sure, consciousness may be paralleled in material explanation—mind state as to brain state—but not deduced from it. In other words, a person can adduce complex synapse mechanisms in such a manner as to imply consciousness. But he will not be able to demonstrate the implication.

It is convenient to speak of synapses and networks of neural integration and interaction. Brain function may even be chemically or surgically deranged. Thus the content of consciousness will be affected. But this does not establish a definitive causal link between the material brain and consciousness. Again, it only indicates a parallel.

Moreover, it may strongly suggest that certain elements within consciousness can appear to be affected in conjunction with alterations in the brain state. But it does not demonstrate that consciousness itself is affected. This is because only a consciousness can know itself. What is sleep or a coma or even death to an observer may not be so to the consciousness concerned.

But such a connection between consciousness and the material realm cannot be ignored altogether. For without the active role of consciousness through its intuition of simple unity, how is one to account for the faculty of intellectual abstraction which is needed to make sense of the material realm? Any thought, be it a concept or an image, is after all a unity. More significant than this is the fact that a recognition of physical unity, as in a unity of parts or properties in one object, also implies a previously existent sense of unity in the mind.

So both the mind's reasoning and perceptive capacities demand a prior condition of unity. For both a thought and a perceived object are formed in the mind as unities. This is a condition which expresses itself in a conundrum. The mystery is that there is a human capacity to reason uninterruptedly from spirit to matter. But there is not a parallel faculty linking matter to spirit.

Nevertheless, this largely unexplored and inconvenient difficulty does not invalidate material reality as experience. It simply indicates the common origin both of human awareness and of the content of that awareness. Awareness is spirit, or consciousness. Spirit, in turn, is the author of the phenomenal precipitate, or the human material realm.

The human material realm is more limited than the universal material dynamic which has been suggested as a hypothetical reflection of universal spirit. But, while conceding a radical disparity in encompassment between the two, it can be observed that the human material realm is not altogether different from the proposed material dynamic of spirit, insofar as it is a dynamic. Thus the dynamic of the human material realm clearly bears some relation to the dynamic of spirit.

However, if the character of spirit is truly that of a dynamic, by virtue of its being spirit it cannot be clearly brought into focus by either human imagination or reason. Thus the universal material characterization of spirit is at best a crude representation of it. For a spiritual dynamic must be differently understood. In itself, it is not material. Nonetheless, the point remains that it is from the dynamic of spirit that the dynamic of the phenomenal precipitate follows as a restricted expression.

The Immaterial Structure of Human Experience

Now the phenomenal precipitate, as representing a single human perspective, shrivels in comparison to the plenitude of universal spirit, as representing unlimited awareness. It is equivalent to comparing one photograph of a sunset to an unspecified number of such photographs taken from multiple perspectives, not to mention a mélange of other photographs included in the set. These altogether would form a composite of human perspectives and a good deal more.

Spiritually, a human being is universal spirit under focused circumstances: a unified, unidirectional mind as opposed to a unified, multidirectional mind. But from a material perspective, a human being cannot apprehend himself as spirit—that is, as a spiritual dynamic. He knows his being only as a material dynamic. Material being thus becomes for him an independent reality. For he fails to comprehend that his material being is an expression of universal spirit.

From this limited perspective, he is simply an individual awareness set adrift in incomprehensible loneliness—a tiny aperture of consciousness amongst a few others in a sea of largely insensate being. He is conscious. But what is he conscious of? He is conscious of a precipitate realm, accepted by him as substantially real—that is, as subsisting in itself. This precipitate realm, the material world, is held to exist in contradistinction to the ground of his personal awareness: his consciousness, which he finds inexplicable.

Thus he sees his consciousness as limited, while the content of that consciousness is experienced by him as a separate material world. This is due to the impressive importunity of the percepts in his mind, including impressions of pain and emotion, which cause him to imagine that his consciousness is subordinate to and, in fact, somehow itself a product of the material world.

On the other hand, just as an individual human consciousness must be understood in terms of universal spirit—for it is also indivisible and unbounded—so the material realm as a whole (not just one person's experience of it) is an expression of universal spirit. As is the case in George Berkeley's philosophy of immaterialism, percepts (which Berkeley calls ideas) are not only understood as being expressed in the individual mind of a person, but must have their origin in a universal mind. [38]

Universal spirit, or primary mind, is the source both of the individual's awareness of the material world and of that world itself. Thus an imagined universal phenomenal precipitate great enough to reflect the whole of spirit may be regarded tentatively (and with grave reservation) as the equivalent of the dynamic of spirit, though that equivalence must include what is withheld from each individual human awareness and even from the totality of all human awareness.

In other words, what remains beyond the collective human phenomenal precipitate includes both what is possible for human experience but not made actual and what is not possible for human experience. It is the unactuated potential and that which is not potential. It is this unactuated potential and non-potential which must be placed together in a scale with the collective human phenomenal precipitate to counterbalance the spiritual dynamic as an equivalent.

So the spiritual dynamic (disregarding any hypothetical material expression of it) relates to human experience in three ways. It is a potential which is being converted to the actual that is realized in the human precipitate. It is a potential which exhibits the

---

[38] George Berkeley, *The Principles of Human Knowledge* and *Three Dialogues Between Hylas and Philonous.*

possibility of doing so, though it may never be actualized. And it is that which bears no relation to human experience.

41. The limited human mind. When the dynamic of primary mind is considered as a universal material domain, it should be understood as nothing more than an imaginary precipitate of the dynamic of spirit. It is a way of understanding spirit as mind—spirit itself being a dynamic which human understanding is unable to penetrate. Thus the reason human beings do not experience this material precipitate of primary mind is that it is a purely conjectural notion.

Secondary mind is what is experienced. That is, what is experienced is the world as a precipitate of secondary mind. This is a world which is experienced under a condition of finitude undergoing change. It is initially introduced in non-incremental time. For this reason, such a precipitate—the noumenal precipitate—is helpful in forming an understanding of human limitation as that limitation is ultimately experienced through the phenomenal precipitate.

Primary mind corresponds to a necessary existence which is independent of any cause. It simply is. It corresponds as well to the possession of self-knowledge, which is inherent within it. This is what the philosopher Benedict de Spinoza would have referred to as the one and only substance, the ground of being.[39]

However, the system being presented here does not concur with him in other matters, such as his deterministic interpretation of human will. For primary mind cannot be directly known. Therefore, its expression in a more limited human character cannot be said to be as tightly fitted to it as one gear to another in a gearbox.

---

[39] Benedict de Spinoza, *Ethics*.

Moreover, what the self-knowledge of spirit is comprised of remains inaccessible and thus incomprehensible to a human understanding. It is simply understood as necessary because human awareness, possessing a form of self-knowledge, must be an expression (though not a reflection) of that which has made general awareness and self-knowledge possible.

The time-bound precipitate of secondary mind can be described as necessary existence, or being, without a universal self-knowledge. For the self-limitation of spirit has eschewed universal awareness. In this way, secondary mind represents a transition point between primary mind and the human mind. So it is only in its contribution to human awareness that the precipitate of secondary mind must be understood.

This definition of secondary mind does not violate the one-substance definition of Spinoza. For secondary mind is in fact primary mind under self-limitation. So these two modes of spirit—primary and secondary mind—accord respectively to the dynamic of spirit and to the dynamic of human awareness. The latter dynamic is grounded in a consciousness of limited content.

Unlike universal spirit, human consciousness must be conscious *of* something prior to its expression of self-knowledge. For human consciousness is not only conscious of itself. It is conscious of the phenomenal precipitate, which it comes increasingly to regard as other than itself. Thus the phenomenal precipitate is understood to limit human experience and therefore human consciousness. So it must know the precipitate to form a concept of itself. Accordingly, human self-knowledge is conceptual. It is acquired. Whereas that of universal spirit is immediate.

It can be said that human beings are bound by the precipitate of secondary mind. This means they experience the universal dynamic of spirit (or primary mind) through the dynamic of second-

The Immaterial Structure of Human Experience

ary mind. This amounts to an individual human perspective within spirit. It is human awareness, or consciousness.

But within human consciousness there is both the knower and the known, an interaction between secondary mind as an expression of universal spirit (pure consciousness as such, or the knower) and the limited precipitate produced by the spiritual dynamic. The limited precipitate is the material world, a stratum of percepts laid down by secondary mind for human awareness.

This precipitate, the noumenal precipitate, is known through the stream of non-incremental time. The limitation of mental focus makes it so. Moreover, the phenomenal precipitate is organized from the noumenal precipitate by the human mind (which is in fact secondary mind in its phenomenal mode). Initially, imagination contributes to this process without intellect. But intellect eventually takes increasing hold and proceeds in such a manner that the order of change created in the phenomenal precipitate becomes a foundation for an incremental sense of time.

Thus the human sense of time is as much a product of the phenomenal structure as it is of the initial laying down of percepts by secondary mind. For the percepts are given foundational order by secondary mind functioning in its fundamental capacity. But the order is also modified by secondary mind's reflection upon its own activity, as it acts in its human capacity. It is in this way that secondary mind becomes human awareness. Thus it can be seen that human awareness is secondary mind in a final material mode, a mode twice limited by a simultaneous formation of the two precipitates, the one being transformed into the other.

As a result of the transformation from the noumenal to the phenomenal precipitate, it can be understood that the phenomenon of change in the latter precipitate is a creation of human awareness. Change, originally presented as alterations in associations of percepts in non-incremental time, becomes a sequential appearance of extensions expressive of incremental time. This sequential appearance of extensions is the domain of human awareness, particularly as that awareness matures.

But both the laying down of the noumenal precipitate and the early formation of the phenomenal precipitate are primal acts, which are prior to any self-awareness of the human mind. Human awareness is what seals the human mind within a sense of its own limitation. But this is not self-awareness.

To return to the beginning of the process, it is prior to a recognition of non-incremental time that the noumenal presentation of percepts lies in a state of unarticulated distinction of one percept from another. Thus there is disorder in the mind. But due to the activity of mental focus, which functions in the earliest days of infancy, percepts are articulated. They are articulated in such a manner that this disorder is followed by the recognition of a flow of both single and associated percepts in non-incremental time.

Some of these associations of percepts differ but slightly from one another. Others more significantly. In either case, this leads to a recognition of differences among associations of percepts. For there are sequential relations among both the similar and dissimilar associations of percepts.

The more notably different associations of percepts with consistent sequential relations in the noumenal precipitate are organized in the phenomenal precipitate as individual extensions exhibiting contiguous relations with other extensions. Where the sequence of these associations of percepts is altered, there is a phenomenal change in the form of motion. But, where there are subtle differences among them as they appear in close sequence,

The Immaterial Structure of Human Experience

there may be a recognition of change within a single extension of the phenomenal precipitate.

This environment of contiguity and change is the phenomenal precipitate. Its manifestations include extension, space, change, and incremental time. Due to the fact that the phenomenal precipitate exhibits a more complex set of relations than the noumenal precipitate, its incremental time differs significantly from the original non-incremental time. But it is not independent of it.

In this transition of mental awareness from one precipitate to another, the latter increasingly screens the former from human awareness. Yet both exist and function as one, developing together as a combined operation. Thus it can be seen that the recognition of the phenomenon of change in the phenomenal precipitate is a concurrent product both of secondary mind in its initial phase and of human awareness.

But human awareness as such is not self-awareness. For self-awareness is a function of intellect. And intellect involves concept formation. When that occurs, the human mind has become fully absorbed in the phenomenal precipitate. It can no longer conceive itself apart from this precipitate. Thus its self-awareness is achieved in terms of this precipitate.

It is due to the confinement of the mind to the precipitates in general that human consciousness appears empty when deprived of its percepts. For its entire world is confined to its content. And its content is perceptual in the sense that it is made up of percepts, which are individually limited impressions upon the mind. In final form, this content is organized as the phenomenal precipitate. It is in this way that the human mind is limited to the contemplation of its own precipitate.

So intellect is also confined to this limited awareness. For it develops in the more advanced stages of the laying down of the phenomenal precipitate. Since intellect is laid down at an advanced stage of human awareness, human awareness must be understood a being more inclusive than intellect. Thus it is not equivalent to intellect. Rather, intellect is a faculty of human awareness. Neither is human awareness self-awareness. Self-awareness requires intellect. Thus, both intellect and self-awareness develop at a later stage in human awareness.

Intellect is consciousness developing a conceptual understanding through its ongoing interaction with the material world, the realm of percepts, which has been, and is being, configured in its final form as the phenomenal precipitate. The phenomenal precipitate, often referred to here as human awareness, is secondary mind acting upon its own original projection and ordering of percepts in the noumenal precipitate.

Significantly, it is doing so in a manner which affects what that projection is. This results in what is for human understanding the incomprehensible simultaneity of the two precipitates, the phenomenal feeding back to the noumenal in such a manner that the noumenal may anticipate it. Thus a concept or an image which appears to originate in the phenomenal precipitate is paired with matching associations of percepts in the noumenal precipitate. Neither precedes the other in this process.

But the intellectualization of experience in the phenomenal precipitate is experienced within human awareness as an act which is independent of that experience. Therefore, it is productive of a separate sense of self: a self which is the thinker who produced this interpretation. And this separate sense of self is self-awareness.

The Immaterial Structure of Human Experience

Images have been included with concepts in this process of building up an understanding of the phenomenal precipitate within human awareness. They have been included because thought in general is both imaginative and conceptual. For human awareness maps the percepts of its experience by organizing them imaginatively and conceptually. This is done both at pre-conceptual and conceptual levels. Thus it is done prior to understanding, as well in conjunction with it.

The pre-conceptual level is purely imaginative. Whereas the conceptual level is intellectual. But in the conceptual working of intellect, imagination is nevertheless still at work. For concepts are supported by images. And the ongoing structure of chains of reason, or logic, alone produces nothing but an increasingly complex thought organization. Thought origination, even when conceptual, begins in imagination.

The achievement of both imagination and concept formation working together in reasoning is the development of understanding. And understanding is the development of an articulated self-awareness. This is a self-awareness which can reason about the self and project the self forward and backward in time. It can acknowledge and contemplate the self's relationship to things and their relationship to the self. Thus this development is the foundation of wisdom. Prior to it, human awareness can only see itself as part of a world by which it is conditioned.

Complete understanding, were it possible under the limitations of secondary mind (which is not possible), would be the full self-awareness of primary mind, or universal spirit. It would be transcendent self-knowledge and universal wisdom. However, if this is conceived as taking the form of an understanding, it would be spirit understanding itself as spirit under the limitations of time and space, which is the universal material precipitate. This is a contradiction. For the universal precipitate is a product of human imagination. It is not spirit as such.

Consequently, when the human mind does direct itself toward a knowledge of spirit, only an imaginatively projected understanding is attained. This is true even though the imaginatively projected construct may go so far as to be conceptualized and organized in logical terms. Such metaphysical speculation is the language with which human beings attempt to understand the whole of reality. That is, it is the means through which human awareness attempts to plumb the nature of being.

Now logic is often thought to be the one thing within human intellectual grasp which is infallible, even if the material to which it is applied is subject to scrutiny and verification. So the question should be asked, are logical relations unassailable? The answer is that the limitation in understanding described above applies not only to the concepts bound up within logical relationships, but to those relationships as well.

So, for the following discussion, universal relationships involving the quantifier "all" will be considered. But the principle discussed does, with slight modification, also apply to the existential quantifier "some." For, though a restricted classification may be indicated under existential quantification, it is, as it were, universally applied in that case. Thus "some dogs are intelligent" means that it is universally the case that some dogs are intelligent. This emphasis on the universal will be made more clear in what follows.

In logical relations (specifically, in this case, those of the universal quantifier "all") concepts will be brought under the aegis of universality, though as components of the relation they are not themselves universal. In other words, universal propositions are thought to form a universally valid relationship between sub-

The Immaterial Structure of Human Experience

ject and predicate, though the specific terms of the subject and predicate remain subject to question.

An example would be the statement, "All people are tall," which asserts that tallness should be considered a characteristic of every person. Yet, upon reflection, it becomes evident that this is empirically untrue because it can be demonstrated that, unless someone shorter than the shortest person is taken as the standard of height, not all people are tall. But how can there be someone shorter than the shortest person?

The problem is empirical. It has to do with the subject and predicate, which can be investigated to determine the validity of their proposed relationship. But what is important is that it is not the form of the statement which is understood to be the problem. It is the wrongful attribution of a characteristic, in this case, tallness.

Replace "tall" with an empirically valid characteristic like "human" and the problem goes away. The statement, "All people are human," is experientially verifiable. The form of the statement is thus enabled to demonstrate the validity of its function. For is it not understood to be true that *all* people are human?

Another universal statement similar to the above would be "Socrates is mortal." This one is believed to be true because the appropriate relationship of its terms, *as expressed in the logical relations of previous statements*, can be verified. The previous statements, forming a syllogism concluding in the above statement, are "All humans are mortal" and "Socrates is human." It is the relations proposed between subject and predicate in these two statements which must be justified to make the relations in the concluding statement true. If the first two propositions are true, the statement, "Socrates is mortal," is justified.

The three statements under consideration form the universal syllogism

> All humans are mortal.
> Socrates is human.
> (therefore) Socrates is mortal.

So the form of the final statement, as the conclusion of the syllogism, is understood to be true if the truth of both the statements containing its referential terms—Socrates and mortal—is verified as universally applicable and if there is a means of transition between the first two statements which results in the third.

The verification is established by determining the truth of the first two statements in which the terms initially occur. And the transition to the concluding statement is facilitated by both statements possessing another term "human" in common between them. "Human" (or humans) is the subject of the first statement and the predicate of the second.

Withdraw these (as they are alike) and one is left with the subject, Socrates, and the predicate, mortal. So the connection made by a repetition of the term "human" brings the terms "Socrates" and "mortal" into a common relationship. The universality of the relationship is indicated by the quantifier "all," which is either stated or implied in all three statements.

Why does this work? Why does the consistent universality of all three statements hold with such seeming rigor, such that the universality of the third statement is understood to follow invariably from the first two? First, it should be noted that it works in spite of the fact that the initial two statements concerning Socrates and mortality are only general statements. They are not inherently universal in character.

The Immaterial Structure of Human Experience

In other words, they only appear to apply generally in experience. There is only one Socrates of interest. And that Socrates appears to share human traits with other human beings. So it is assumed he is human. Moreover, "all" human beings seem to share the common trait of mortality. At least, there are no known exceptions.

But it is not an unassailable truth that there are no exceptions to these observations. Thus, when something is spoken of as being universal, as when it is stated that "*all* somethings are such-and-such," which is the case in each of the three statements of the syllogism, the supposed universality is not immediately evident. For, if it is being spoken of from the perspective of the limitations of human understanding, its universality cannot be certain. Rather, it is assumed. So how is it that such a condition of universality comes about?

Human understanding is shaped by the two precipitates of consciousness, which engender a realm both of limited thought and finite objective experience. But the understanding is also shaped by a recognition of consciousness itself as experience. That consciousness is experienced as unlimited, or infinite (i.e., not-finite). It is by this means that universality enters into logical relations. For it arises from an attribution of an unlimited condition to such relations.

Concepts proceed from a sense of limitation. But a concept can be understood as general in extent. This is simply a matter of its being widely pluralized so as to include every experience of it. Such is the case with the concept, *all humans insofar as they have been experienced*. Such is also the case regarding a specific application applied to a single individual. Thus Socrates the philosopher can be taken as *the only Socrates of interest*.

However, it is possible that both of these concepts can be further enlarged to the point of universality in the mind, though such an enlargement will be unsupported by any mental imagery. For what is universal is unimaginable. It does not come from the precipitates. Rather, this final enlargement comes about when a concept is universally quantified in a statement through the use of either an expressed or implied word "all."

Given that it is unsupported by material experience, and thus unsupported by mental imagery, "all" turns out to be an extraordinary assumption. For in a finite world it can only imply the unlimited and unifying character of consciousness, or spirit. Here alone is the experience of such a universal application of meaning. Universal is what pure consciousness is, when its content is left out of consideration. This is spirit. And spirit is universality. Thus a thought at this point takes on the character of consciousness itself, or spirit.

For this reason, any two limited concepts so united may come to be understood as universally connected, provided there is no contradiction in material experience concerning their *general* application. Thus human and mortal are universally connected in the statement, "*All* humans are mortal." And Socrates and human are universally connected in the statement, "(All) Socrates is human."

Finally, through a transference of the universal application of predicate to subject, by means of the repeated concept, human, which is included in both the prior statements (the premises of the syllogism), the subject term "Socrates" of the second statement and the predicate term "mortal" of the first statement can be universally united in the conclusion as subject and predicate. It is in this way that, since both the premises are universally quanti-

The Immaterial Structure of Human Experience

fied, they can be followed by the universal assertion that "Socrates is mortal."

To press the point a little further, it can be noted that the concept, universality, is arrived at in the same way. What is universal is considered to be without exception. What is without exception is considered to be everywhere the same. But something that is without exception is not known with incontrovertible certainty in material experience.

This is because everywhere cannot be searched to determine if a circumstance is always the same. There is always a slight probability of an undetected exception. Consequently, universality is known only in consciousness, or spirit. So, only when brought under the aegis of consciousness, or spirit, does a statement take on an unassailable universality, or does the very concept, universality, have any meaning.

42. A review of the mapping of the precipitate. It can be asserted that secondary mind *is* the two precipitates. In other words, all that is truly known about secondary mind is the work it performs. And that work is the precipitates. But it cannot be said that secondary mind is known as the work of pure consciousness.

This is because, though the mental impressions which are the substance of the precipitates are experienced within consciousness, it cannot be laid down as a certainty that they are produced by consciousness. Or, to be more exact, it cannot be laid down as a certainty that secondary mind is an expression of primary mind. For it is not known in this sense. It is known only as the content of consciousness. It is not known in the character of consciousness.

It is the same with pure human consciousness—that is, human consciousness considered without its content. Human beings experience consciousness without any understanding of its origin. To say it originates in universal spirit is speculation, however useful it may be to characterize it in this way.

Thus, for the sake of such convenience of characterization, it can only be asserted that pure consciousness resembles universal spirit in its spiritual character. Human consciousness is observed to be unbounded and indivisible. So universal spirit is identified as this unbounded and indivisible consciousness understood in its full nature without reference to anything but itself.

This universal designation arises from the fact that it is known that pure consciousness is not experienced as originating within the precipitates. It does not share the finite character of the precipitates. In fact, its character is *in*finite, or *not* finite, since it must be seen as not having a finite character. In the realm of the infinite, there is no division, boundedness, multiplicity, or opposition of one thing to another. So there is but one consciousness. That consciousness is infinite spirit.

The designation of human consciousness as universal and infinite spirit is in opposition to the finite content of that consciousness. Yet, if the grounding of human consciousness in universal spirit is thus assumed, the finite content of consciousness must be held to originate in spirit as well. For the content of consciousness is known only in consciousness. And consciousness is spirit.

But since, unlike consciousness itself, the finite content of consciousness is an expression of limitation, it must be attributed to the self-limitation of spirit. Thus it can be seen that the concept of self-limitation is introduced as a means by which the gulf between the infinite and the finite may be bridged. For, since both the not finite and the finite are integral parts of human experi-

The Immaterial Structure of Human Experience

ence, it is reasonable to assume some sort of connection, or transition, between them.

Consciousness is logically prior to its content, since its content cannot be experienced without it. Whereas it can be experienced without its content. It is the content alone which is understood to be limited in character. Consciousness, or spirit, is unlimited. Therefore, the priority of consciousness (or spirit) is assumed as an indication of its universality. For the limitations expressed by its content cannot be imposed upon consciousness.

Moreover, it has been said that consciousness is indivisible and unbounded. Indivisibility and unboundedness are attributes of the infinite. So consciousness is the infinite, as opposed to the limited material which is its content. The material being finite, the infinite is greater than the finite. By this is meant that consciousness, or spirit, is the container and not the contained.

Such an assumption is a fundamental thesis of this book. It is of great utility in facilitating an understanding of the workings of the human mind. However, it must be confessed that it is at best an assumption. Nevertheless, this assumption having been made for the reasons given, let the discussion continue.

As previously discussed, there are three operations working together which contribute to the noumenal precipitate of secondary mind. First, there is the focusing of universal spirit, limiting its content in general. This is secondary mind in its initial mode, when as yet unarticulated percepts of varying character are introduced to the mind.

Second, due to the continued activity of focus within secondary mind, there is a recognition of the fact that percepts individually possess a distinct character and are therefore distinguished from one another. As the percepts are distinguished from one another, they are recognized as individual. And, as they are individual and exhibit distinct characters, they are delineated one by the other, which means that they are finite and multiple.

They appear before the mind in two ways: individually and in associated groups. That some percepts are associated together and some not arises from the manner of their original presentation to the conscious mind. For some percepts repeatedly appear together. Some do not. Thus the percepts inaugurate human awareness. For they provide it both with independent sensations and with the sensory composition of objects.

Third, there is a recognition of sequence as the diverse character of percepts passes through the limited sphere of attention which is focus. This sequence establishes the stream of non-incremental time. For non-incremental time is a flow of individual percepts and groups of associated percepts undergoing the narrow focus of attention.

But the fact that there is an "arrow of time" [40] going from past to future is a bit more difficult to explain. Why should the order of percepts be one way and not another? Why should it be that spirit is said to possess a potential which is revealed in a certain manner in the actual? The answer can only lie in secondary mind, which directs the manner in which focus behaves, just as it supplies particular percepts and their interrelations of appearance (some associated, some not) to an individual consciousness.

Thus time, though it is not expressed in universal spirit (primary mind), is given its character by self-limiting spirit (second-

---

[40] This phrase indicates that in subjective awareness time moves in only one direction: from past to future. It differs in this way from objective time, since the objective view brings time back full circle to no time. It does so because the relations of the space-time continuum place time within a geometrical structure, which can be viewed in static terms. This is the reason that in a previous essay of this work a universal phenomenal precipitate was imaginatively posited. It is a view that is external to individual human awareness.

The Immaterial Structure of Human Experience

ary mind). It is this order, laid down in the noumenal precipitate by the manner in which focus operates, which influences what the structure of the phenomenal precipitate will be. For it determines the sequence of events.

So the three operations above are the work of self-limiting spirit. And they may be understood to exercise the previously mentioned intuitions of simple unity, plurality, and totality. For the intuition of simple unity arises from the exercise of focus. The intuition of plurality arises from a recognition of the distinct individual character of percepts. And the intuition of totality arises from focus as it is applied to associations of percepts.

All this is the work of secondary mind in presenting the noumenal precipitate to human awareness. Human awareness is human consciousness. It is initially limited to the noumenal precipitate. The noumenal precipitate thus supplies a groundwork for the construction of a phenomenal precipitate by human awareness.

But prior to any of this is the raw and unworked material of the dynamic of universal spirit, or primary mind. This greater dynamic is not only the source of the noumenal world of each individual person, but of all persons collectively. However, it is immediately present to each person as a more limited and focused content to which his consciousness is constrained to submit.

Yet in its fullness, that of universal spirit, it is beyond human comprehension. Nonetheless, there is a comprehensive form which falls short of this fullness. It is this which supplies a means of general explanation and agreement that is accessible to individual human understanding. For it is a view which is projected by common human effort, or by an effort of some individuals which is accepted by the many. Such a view is what provides a practical, a philosophical, or a scientific theory of physical reality, among other things.

The phenomenal world is the human mind's mapping of the noumenal precipitate. It is the mind's fundamental template of that precipitate. So, on the one hand, this human template is a creation of human sensibility. It is how human beings see and develop themselves and their view of experience.

But, on the other hand, a question arises: what is human sensibility, if not only objects and sensations, but thoughts as well, are founded upon what is provided to the mind in the noumenal flow of percepts? Given that not only experience, but the human view of experience, is expressed in the noumenal precipitate, it is clear that the noumenal precipitate determines what the thought process can be in its creation of the phenomenal precipitate. So does this mean that the phenomenal precipitate is not a free human creation?

Given these two opposing explanations for the human mind's activity, one seemingly independent and free, the other not, it must be concluded that either one or the other is not the case. Or, if a compromise is needed, then there must be a feedback loop to coordinate them. There is. And it is instantaneous.

Any human structuring of the phenomenal precipitate is accompanied by its immediate reflection in the original flow of percepts in the noumenal precipitate. For the structure of the noumenal precipitate underlies that of the phenomenal precipitate, percept to percept. This includes thoughts as well as things. It is what accounts for the earlier insistence at various points in this book that the structure of the phenomenal precipitate is completely and consistently founded upon that of the noumenal precipitate.

The Immaterial Structure of Human Experience

It is also why the apparent opposition, yet absolute compatibility, between noumena and phenomena must be considered to be one and the same. Of course, the absolute compatibility implies an absence of free will at the material level. And, as a consequence, a difficulty arises which becomes particularly notable when the structuring of the phenomenal precipitate takes on an intellectual character. For what can seem more independent to a thinker than the work of his own intelligence?

As it turns out, even such an apparently independent operation as this work of intelligence is ultimately presented to human awareness by spirit. For it appears in the noumenal precipitate, upon which the phenomenal precipitate must always be understood to be based. Not only objects, but thoughts, are registered in the noumenal flow of percepts.

Consequently, though the human will must, for practical, if not for other, reasons be held to be truly free, it can be so only in the spirit. But this should not be surprising. For it is due to the fact, as already stated, that the human mind is spirit in its self-limited form. Each human being is spirit. Accordingly, though unrecognized in his temporal mind with its sequential revelation of experience, the full range of a person's acts is, in fact, determined by him at once, where there is no expression of time.

In other words, an individual human being's will may be referred to as the coloring of his life, when the whole of that life is viewed contextually. For the expression of will gives his life its unique overall character. Thus each life expresses a harmony, like that of color and line in a good painting.

But this harmony, this hue of personality, can only be understood when the whole of a life is taken under consideration. When the whole is considered, it represents a spiritual view.

Whereas the apparent sequential acting out of an individual life arises from the limited material view within which it is lived.

Now, following the initial establishment of the phenomenal template, which is the pre-conceptual phenomenal world, the conceptual world comes into being. The conceptual world is the mind's deliberative mapping of parts of the phenomenal world. This conceptual mapping is carried out by means of abstraction and classification. In other words, by reasoning, though imagination is always an integral component in any creative reasoning process.

Like so much else, the construction of the rational portion of the phenomenal precipitate is carried out through the agency of the three primary intuitions: simple unity, plurality, and totality. Initially, the conceptual world is held in the mind apart from the phenomenal world. For it is theory. That is how it differs from the pre-conceptual working up of the phenomenal precipitate. But, through long exposure to habitual ways of thinking, it becomes increasingly difficult to distinguish between the conceptual and the pre-conceptual.

A wonderful example of this process lies in an understanding of the development of the concept of energy, which concept is nothing more than an accounting of consistencies in the proportions of the phenomena of physical change. But who today among the multitude of mankind is accustomed to thinking of light behavior as not being an interconnected system? Who would consider that it is no more than a number of independent changes in percepts which appear to be coordinated in effect? Few indeed will allow this interpretation. For this has been veiled from human view.

In the first place, the work of secondary mind has coordinated the various appearances of light with specific phenomenal

The Immaterial Structure of Human Experience

sources of that light. For instance, it has located the sun and its supposed effects in non-incremental time. It has done so in such a manner that, in the phenomenal world, the appearance of the sun at the horizon appears to presage the light of morning. Subsequent to a number of early experiences of this relationship, the pre-conceptual working of a child's mind affirms their regularity. For it is what he consistently experiences.

The child notes the morning sunrise and the appearance of light in his bedroom. He sees the declining sun and the failure of natural light. He imaginatively associates these phenomena. This is pre-conceptual. As he becomes a little older, he deduces a causal relationship. This is conceptual. And he continues to grow older, more experienced. As he does so, he becomes increasingly inclined to embellish imaginative associations with rational deductions.

So, following this personal development through childhood, he approaches and enters adulthood. Here he encounters a conceptual body of knowledge which is to be acquired from what for him is a ready-made cultural environment. Thus science has an opportunity to teach him that light behaves in certain ways as a wave, in other ways as a particle. The mature adult soon finds it difficult to think of light in any other way.

That is why it is so difficult to accept the phenomenal truth that the concept of energy is no more than an accounting of consistencies in the proportions of change. And this unacceptance remains in spite of the fact that it is never energy that is measured. It is the relations of change which are quantified.[41]

---

[41] As an aside, note that the treatment of energy in this work is not far from contemporary practice. Einstein's $E = mc^2$ provides an example. Take the right side of the equation: mass times the speed of light squared. What is mass but matter? And what is the speed of light squared but velocity, or motion? Motion

How then, with such persistence in attitude, can a person look back through the myriads of accumulated and subsequently quantified details of experience to detect the subtle beginnings of so simple an explanation of phenomena as just described? Such an effort would require a careful dissecting of experience, which few are inclined to undertake.

The three intuitions are what make both pre-conceptual and conceptual awareness possible. Thus they are fundamental attributes of human sensibility. Without them, there is no human sensibility, and no workup of reality in the mind. That is why they are called intuitions. By an intuition is meant an inherent faculty.

For these three intuitions are functions of the finite mind which are necessary to perception, imagination, and thought. They are instruments of a person's knowledge of his and his world's finitude. So fundamental are they, that they are initially derived from the direct experience of consciousness and from the initial encounter of consciousness with its content.

Thus one arrives at the observation that discerning a distinction between pure consciousness and its content is characteristic of finite sensibility. It arises from the self-limiting focus of secondary mind, which introduces a limited array of percepts from within its own unlimited sphere of awareness. As a result, the unlimited sphere of awareness comes to be understood by the human mind in terms of the limitations of the latter's content. For

---

is change of place. And all forms of change, including physical and chemical change, are forms of motion. Therefore, what constitutes the right side of the equation is a general statement regarding *matter undergoing change*. The left side of the equation is energy. So energy is made equivalent to matter undergoing change. It is a different term for it, involving a different quantitative measure. Nevertheless, it is an equivalent means of describing it. It is no more than this.

The Immaterial Structure of Human Experience

the human mind can understand the unlimited sphere in no other way.

As previously discussed, simple unity, the first intuition, is derived from universal spirit, which is the unlimited and undivided character of pure consciousness. For here is an indisputable unity. It needs only the activity of focus to render its apprehension a faculty of finitude. In this way, focus cordons off awareness into a finitude. There is a unity of this or a unity of that, wherever focus settles its attention.

Since the content of consciousness provides an experience of differentiated percepts, as in the percept red and the percept blue, it is the origin of the mind's awareness of limitation and plurality, which together are the foundation for the second intuition: plurality. From these two—the first intuition applied to the second—proceeds the third intuition, totality, which is the awareness of a unity among discrete limitations.

It should be noted once again that these three primary intuitions do not only play a role in conceptual mapping. They are initially involved in a pre-conceptual, non-deliberative, imaginative role in developing the compounded and relational experiences of the mind. These are the extensions which form the phenomenal world.

The extensions are objects: physical objects and objects of thought. There is a compounding (one might say a *blending*) of percepts into properties and of properties into these objects. And a relationship is formed between the objects. It consists of contiguous relations between physical objects and sequential relations between objects of thought. Of course, where change is involved, the contiguous relations between physical objects do also undergo sequential appearances, like the objects of thought.

It could be said that the intuitions not only form these extensions. They flesh them out in imagination, supplying an awareness of properties prior to any conceptualization of those properties. Thus, without understanding why it is so, a child knows that a snowball is cold and that it is a compressible solid.

So, underlying any intellectualization of experience, the work of the intuitions has already commenced, where it is employed in the perceptual and imaginative construction of the phenomenal world for human awareness. This is done initially without any conceptual accompaniment. Then, at a latter stage of the child's development, the intuitions are again brought into play, this time in a subsequent conceptualization of that same world for human understanding.

Take another example. An infant sees a plastic rattle. He picks it up and, in doing so, hears it rattle. In his hand he feels its shape, texture, and the difference in temperature between it and his hand. These sensations are at first recognized as independent percepts in the flow of non-incremental time.

They are interesting to the child because, with repeated experience, there is a recognition of a frequent association between them. They appear together. But when the rattle is unseen, unheard, and not felt, these independent percepts are, in their collectivity, absent from his awareness. So they are imaginatively organized into the child's perception of his world. They become an object, distinct from other objects.

In time, and with more experience, the child broadens his outlook. In a more loosely linked association (for these sensations are less often repeated together), he combines the rattle with percepts of the sound of his own cries and of the agency of his mother in bringing it to him. But, though these sensations appear together less commonly, if they do so frequently enough, he finds

The Immaterial Structure of Human Experience

himself in possession of the rudiments of an exhilarating control of his world. For he can summon the rattle at will. This thinking is causal in character. He causes the rattle to be brought to him. But it involves a recognition of causation without the logical aid of reason. He has not formed the general idea in his mind that there are causes and effects.

Thus the world develops as a picture in his mind. The picture involves an organization of percepts into extensions by means of their initial association. The simultaneous delineation of extensions results in a contiguity between them, which leads to an awareness of spatial relations. This is followed by a conversion of non-incremental time into a recognition of a general sequence of changes in the perception of objects.

So now the picture becomes a moving picture. And, when affected by desire, it takes on greater meaning. For the child believes that he has a will which can in some cases effect physical changes: the retrieval of the rattle, his milk bottle, food, personal petting, etc. But his sense of time continues to remain inarticulate because it is not yet configured in terms of incremental transitions in the character or location of objects. There is merely a recognition of sequence in appearance. There is no comparative measure of extensions regarding that sequence.

Learning that things can be moved about in his world, the child discovers that they not only appear and disappear, and in some cases can be made to appear or disappear, they do so in close relation to other things which do not change. This enhances his sense of space. For it causes him to believe that space might be something other than the objects which delineate it.

Space appears to him to be something independent of objects, something within which objects are displaced. Furthermore, the not-yet-appearing, the appearance, and the disappearance of objects enhances his expectation of sequence. Events follow upon one another. And they do not appear to reverse themselves.

In all cases, whether physical objects remain in contiguity or succumb to sequence, the circumstance of one extension delimiting another is always involved. In other words, an extension can be proximate to neighboring extensions. Or it can no longer be proximate to them, since it may take up a proximity to other extensions. Or it may pass completely out of perception. But, whatever it does, as long as it continues to exhibit a presence, it delimits its neighbors. And they delimit it.

Not all events occur in the same way in the child's perception. When mud dries to brick, the water is no longer present in the clay, though it remains elsewhere in the greater community of extensions which constitute space. It may be reduced to multiple small extensions of vapor and take up existence in a cloud.

Yet to the child it seems to disappear. It is no more. For he does not understand the concept of evaporation, of change from one physical state to another. But, when water is squeezed out of a sponge, it does not disappear because it retains its former state. It is still water and not vapor. Nonetheless, it is no longer in the sponge. It is either in a basin or on the ground. So the child more readily understands what has occurred.

However, if a brick is fired, a chemist would say that the bonding is altered. But at first the child would see no change. Nevertheless, it is the case that some percepts have been replaced by others within the brick. Touch, for example, registers a greater pressure of resistance. For the substance of the brick is much harder and more cohesive. Also, the texture and coloring of the brick are altered. So foreign qualities have taken the place of some of the original qualities of the brick.

The Immaterial Structure of Human Experience

But this naive isolation of mind does not remain, however faithful to immediate experience it may be. As a child matures and enters the realm of culture in which he is reared, reason develops. Not only reason, but communal reason. Personal perceptions are compounded by theoretical relations.

Unseen relations are imagined that account for relations which are seen. A world is built up that is not the world of perception. Though it is intended to explain perception, by providing a coordinated explanation of experience. This extends the mind's reach by suggesting manipulative means for effecting material change.

It does appear to effect material change. For power over certain aspects of physical experience is achieved. But its theoretical affirmations are nevertheless indirect. The theory of light is an example of such work. This theory is an intellectual construct which overlays the perceptual and pre-conceptual phenomenal precipitate. And in time it comes to be accepted as true, as equivalent to direct experience.

Now, at an advanced, but still relatively early, stage in its development, the human mind begins to intellectually recognize sequence in the phenomenal precipitate as not just change, but as systematic causal change, whether it be changes in objects or changes in thoughts. One object causes another to move. Or a sensation of heat and presence of flame [42] appear consistently to

---

[42] To understand "flame" in terms of this philosophy, it is important to confine one's thinking to what is actually observed. There are the visual brightness and colors of the flame. There are the appearance of the effects of "light" and sensations of warmth in its vicinity, in proportion to their distance from the flame, insofar as they seem to be unimpeded by obstacles. There are the smoke and particles of the changing extension, say a burning log. All these have long since been put together according to material properties and causal relations between them. In other words, the material properties are repeatedly observed

cause an object to change within itself. Given the ubiquity and multitude of these phenomena, the mind begins to conceive of a principle of causation. This occurs as the mind becomes self-conscious.

In fact, the rise of self-consciousness is best understood as follows. Self-consciousness is produced in the mind when it learns to distinguish its conscious being from the activity of the material impressions being made upon it, involving both internal and external extensions (thoughts and physical objects).

Independent changes in the physical extensions, and apparently willed changes in mental extensions (thoughts) which are yet separate from the will, for they do not appear to be entirely willed—these push an individual's sense of himself into a corner of his awareness. Outside the corner are the changing phenomena. The greater the recognized distinction between them and himself, the more sophisticated the development of his self-consciousness.

This makes it clear that self-consciousness is to be distinguished from self-awareness. Self-awareness is an imaginative state in which an individual unreflectively recognizes himself as an independent agent in the midst of his experiences. Self-consciousness is intellectual. The individual in this state does have a reflective understanding of his position in the midst of a changing world. Psychologically he is in it. But he is not of it.

So there is a relationship between self-consciousness and causal thinking, just as there is a relationship between self-

---

to behave in certain ways when accompanied by the appearance of certain causal agents. But these explanations belong to material theory. What is actually experienced is a consistency of sequential appearances of individual sensations and composite images in the mind. The regularity of these appearances is what lends itself to the adoption of those material relations familiar in varying degrees to both practical and theoretical minds.

The Immaterial Structure of Human Experience

consciousness and the activity of will. For will is called into play by causal recognition. It is heightened to self-consciousness when the cause is understood as cause. For, where there is an intellectually recognized causal relationship, the person, and therefore what is believed to be his will, may be tempted to intervene not just in this case, but systematically. He thus views himself as a free, thinking agent.

Thoughts may be looked upon as objects extended in inner space. That is, there are objects of thought which constitute the material substance of the thought. If a person thinks about a white house, the white house is the object of his thought. And this object of the thought, this image, *is* the thought.

Freely imagined images, like unicorns, also rest upon associations of percepts, or qualities, which make up the objects of a thought. So do abstract concepts. Thus, if a person thinks about the concept, contemplation, he may imagine someone contemplating. He may even imagine a unicorn contemplating something. Or he may imagine a focused train of thought passing through his own mind.

In addition to having content, thoughts are extended. Those thoughts not assumed to be perceptions of physical phenomena are experienced as extended within the mind alone. They are extended in terms of the images they entertain. These images are the objects of the thought. For, however abstract the thought, the images which constitute or support the thought are concrete and physical in character.

This occurs whether or not there is understood to be a corresponding physical object which the thought might represent. For, though some thought images not assumed to be immediate perceptions of physical phenomena are nevertheless closely representative of physical objects, some are not. They are imaginative reconstructions from the properties of physical objects. A thought about a horse and a thought about a unicorn represent these two types of image.

Feelings are also understood as being experienced in the mind. They are single, spatially unextended percepts. Nevertheless, though feelings are not extended in either mental or physical space, they exhibit duration. For they are differentiated by change. Thus they are extended in time. But, since they are unextended in either mental or physical space, feelings cannot be objects.

They are subjects of human attention, subjects which cannot be visualized. That is, they cannot be represented in a thought image because they cannot be objects of thought. Nevertheless, though feelings cannot come together to constitute an extension, or object, they can coalesce into an emotion.

But, in doing so, they remain individual and do not combine in the way the percepts of an extension do. Percepts of feeling in emotions and percepts of properties in extensions are of a different order. Yet they are both percepts. The difference lies in the manner in which they come together.

For the most part, it will be seen that this book espouses a sight-oriented philosophy. This is because most human beings think primarily in visual terms. Though extensions in physical space may be ascertained by touch, the visual sense is the predominant form of human representation. So the principles discussed in this book are being visually illustrated in some way. Those which apply to phenomena that cannot be illustrated, because they are not extensions, are referred to as feelings.

When percepts are combined into physical or mental extensions, they are objects. When they stand alone, they are feelings. When they coalesce without extension, they are emotions. A per-

The Immaterial Structure of Human Experience

son may be said to feel light. But this generally refers to a felt pressure on the eye, which involves a different set of percepts from the recognition of light. Referring to a perception as a feeling ignores the behavior of the percept.

Light does not stand alone in its perception. Nor does it coalesce with other sensations which can stand alone, as does a feeling in an emotion. Rather, a visual quality of perception, which light is, is always inseparably associated with other percepts in an extension. It is associated with other percepts as a quality of the extension.

The extension may be a physical object or an object of thought. The light is a quality of that extension, no matter how frequently it may vary as a quality. Perceptually, light is no more than a brightened hue on the side of a box or a brightened mote in the air. Brightness and dullness are qualities of the object, as are variations in hue. For they are physical perceptions.

There is no distinction between primary and secondary qualities [43] in immaterialist philosophy. Thus texture and shape are no less subjective in origin than colors and their variations. And to hold that light is not a quality (or set of qualities) of an object, that it is not one or several percepts of that object, but that it is independently reflected from it, is a theoretical construct. It is a product of intellect, not sensation.

In other words, insofar as perception is concerned, light is simply encountered as a particular type of variation in the hue of an object: a variation in the type of hue, such as red or blue, and a variation towards brightness or its opposite. The hue of the object

---

[43] For a clarification of the distinction between these two terms, see John Locke, *An Essay Concerning Human Understanding*, bk. II, ch. VIII, sec. 9 & 10. For greater convenience, brief definitions for these terms can be found in an unabridged dictionary.

is a quality of the object. So is the brightness, though either or both of these may change from moment to moment.

The hue and brightness contribute to the overall character of an object. Its designation as a particular object is made without regard as to whether or not these qualities are considered to be accidental or inherent. Thus a panel painted red of a high luminosity becomes simply a bright red panel. The object to which these qualities belong is what is identified as a specific extension. Without these qualities—say, if the paint is removed—it is a different or altered extension. It is no different than if the panel were crushed into powder.

This, of course, does not apply to feelings. For they do not contribute to extensions. They are only extended in time. They have a duration in the mind which begins and ends. Because they are extended in time, they can be subjects of human attention. This is what makes them available for human awareness.

The fact that feelings have duration points up the observation that, to be a part of human experience, they must be finite. They must be finite in all respects which define them. Duration and degree of intensity are the characteristics which define them. These characteristics express limitation and thus give them their finitude.

Their duration is determined by a close repetition of the same percept in the noumenal input, such that it seems all one in experience. Intensity is determined by the degree of uninterruptedness in the repetition of the percept, such that its impression upon the mind seems relatively unrelieved. Though there is a limit to this. For it must be brought within finite bounds. The fact that feelings are subjects of attention emphasizes the role of focus in establishing these factors of finitude.

The Immaterial Structure of Human Experience

Following the division of human awareness into subjective and objective realms, thoughts and feelings are experienced as subjective. That subjectivity is what differentiates them from physical objects. All percepts are presented to human awareness as individual, individually coalesced, or compound. Yet they do not all appear within the phenomenal precipitate. Thoughts and physical objects do appear within the phenomenal precipitate. Feelings and emotions do not.

The differentiation between thoughts and feelings is not their subjectivity, but their extension or lack of it. Thoughts are extended and therefore experienced as jostling each other for space in the mind, one replacing the other. Unlike thoughts, several different feelings apprehended in close proximity to one another can be recognized as coalesced. If coalesced, they become an emotion. Yet, even within the coalescence of an emotion, the individual feelings act separately upon the mind. For the mind's focus shifts alternately between them in a repeated manner.

On the contrary, though the mind can also shift its attention between two thoughts, or among the qualities of the object of a thought, it does so less nimbly and without sustained repetition. For it principally seeks to acknowledge a multiplicity (more than one percept) within each thought, while grasping the multiplicity as a whole and passing it on to the next multiplicity.

Thus the multiplicity is compound. It is this compounding of percepts into properties inseparable from the whole which provides a sense of extension. It is also what separates one mental extension from another. For they are compounded separately, as originating in different associations of percepts.

But there is no extension in regard to feelings, each being a single type of percept. Thus there is no multiplicity of qualities in one feeling. Consequently, the mind easily shifts its attention between feelings, sometimes so regularly back and forth as to appear to combine them, as in an emotion. This loose combination of feelings in an emotion is what is referred to as a coalescence. It is differentiated from a thought or physical object in that the latter represents an inseparable combination of percepts.

The effect of musical sound upon a person is an example of the character both of feeling and emotion. For a musical sound, or a coalescence of musical sounds, exhibits no extensions which can be directly represented in visual terms. The combined notes of a musical score are an *indirect* visual representation. Thus music manifests only a temporal character in its direct impression upon the mind. For example, the recognition of a chord, like that of a melody, is a discernment of distinct but closely associated sounds.

In both cases the sounds are discerned in sequence, though in a chord, which is presumed to combine three or more simultaneous tones, there is indeed a very rapid sequence in the movement of the mind's attention, precluding any recognizable temporal distinctions. In other words, the three tones are heard individually. The mind makes a subtle distinction between them, however closely associated they may be. This preservation of the characteristic of sequence is why musical sounds are registered in the mind as feelings and not extensions.

It is also why the coalesced sounds are enabled to conjure up emotions. Were they combined into extensions, like colored images, instead of following one another individually as coalescences, the emotional effects would have to be derived from a relationship between the images, or at least between extended areas of color, and not from the individual percepts of color. It is for this reason that one must stand back from an impressionist or divisionist painting to appreciate it. Though the color is applied

The Immaterial Structure of Human Experience

in individual units, the units must be combined by the eye to be appreciated.

Paintings are appreciated in direct terms of thought images, even should the images be no more than blocks of color. For the objects of thoughts are characteristically compounds of sensation. They are extended and thus represented as images. In other words, they are subjective objects of human attention.

Inasmuch as they are objects, they are comparable to objects in the physical realm. Thus in the general phenomenal precipitate both forms of extension, subjective and objective, have equal status as extensions. For prior to the subject/object distinction made by human awareness, there are no physical and mental realms. Thoughts stand beside physical objects simply as extensions.

Physical pleasure and physical pain each express a feeling of varying intensity. The feeling is held in the mind in conjunction with an emotion which is associated with it, but which is also independent of it. Thus the physical pain or pleasure is not a part of the coalescence of feelings in the accompanying emotion.

It is rather the case that physical pleasure and physical pain originate in a single independent sensation or feeling. As such, the feeling is a solitary percept, though it may be repeated for intensity. Accordingly, instead of coalescing with other feelings into an emotion, it stands alone and is accompanied by a separate emotion.

Take the percept of physical pain. The emotion associated with it is a coalescence of feelings of revulsion, distaste, and fear. In certain cases, such as purely mental pain, the emotion can appear alone, without being accompanied by a free standing sensation of physical pain. Rather, the emotion is accompanied by a mental image which evokes the emotional reaction of withdrawal from whatever the image represents. Generally, the image may suggest the possibility of physical pain. Or it may threaten an undesirable psychological situation, such as would suggest diminishment or annihilation of the person or ego.

Physical pleasure and pain display the same fundamental characteristics: they are solitary sensations accompanied by emotion. But the free-standing sensation of pleasure, together with its accompanying emotion, is a polar opposite of pain. Nor should it be overlooked that pleasure and pain can appear together. This is to say that they may occur alternately in close succession to one another. This is particularly the case with mental (i.e., purely emotional) pleasure and pain, which do not have the accompanying physical sensation of pleasure or pain.

Now one can have a thought of a thought. But one cannot have a feeling of a feeling. This is because feelings are not extended composites of sensation, as thoughts are. So one feeling, not being extended, cannot be inclusive of another. Nor can a feeling be brought before the mind as an image of thought. For an image is an extension made up of multiple percepts. And a feeling is a solitary percept.

In fact, an illustration of the limitations of such a representation would be an attempt to form an imaginative image of a physically painful sensation. A painful sensation may appear independently in the mind. But it cannot be deliberately called to mind. For a physically painful sensation is a single percept. In other words, a feeling cannot be a representation of itself. Neither can an emotion. For an emotion is composed of independent feelings.

So it is neither the physical pain nor its accompanying emotion which is represented, but only that which is associated with it. Thus a recall of physical pain must be represented by an image

The Immaterial Structure of Human Experience

which does not express the physical pain, but only the accompanying circumstances in which it might have occurred.

For example, a person cannot remember the morning's leg cramps. He cannot directly represent them to himself. He can only remember how unpleasant they were, which he does by recalling the behavioral expression of the accompanying emotion, but not by recalling the emotion itself.

This behavioral expression may have involved grimacing, groaning, or hopping around on the other leg. But in recalling it, the actual pain is not felt. Neither is the accompanying emotion. It is understood what the emotion was. But the emotion is not felt. Thus only imaginative images of his physical reaction to the pain may be recalled to his mind. It is these which represent the pain and its emotion to him.

43. Free-form imagination. Human beings know everything they know through the human mind. Once the phenomenal precipitate has been developed in maturity, they cannot know anything but through the human mind. This is the material human mind, the mind which takes a human being through her daily course of living.

It is characteristically orderly. For its matter is the phenomenal precipitate, which is an ordering of percepts according to extensions in space and time. So, if that human being should find apparent disorder in her world, she refers it to her mind for a remedy. But it is not the material mind alone that she refers it to.

The material is referred to because, insofar as the human mind is aware of its phenomenal precipitate—that is, insofar as it perceives and thinks in terms of the extensions of space and time—it employs its imaginative and logical faculties in an orderly manner. But the universal mind of spirit, on the contrary, is an eternal dynamic. It is not bound by the self-limiting character of secondary mind, which underpins the human mind. Consequently, it does not submit to such an order.

Since this universal dynamic is spirit, it is not material. For this reason, if its freedom is to be approximated by human understanding, this must be done by a non-discursive imaginative faculty of the human mind. That is to say, human awareness cannot determine the relations of percepts which are within the dynamic. But it can approximate their freedom in a less structured way than it does in the material mind. It may enter into a free association of percepts.

Thus the orderly pre-conceptual and conceptual arrangements of the phenomenal precipitate, which are material for the logical, discursively thinking mind, are in this way periodically critiqued, broken down, and restructured by the intervention of the free-forming imaginative faculty. Without this intervention of the imaginative faculty, human beings could not think creatively.

Nevertheless, this free-forming imaginative state of mind is not spirit. It is not the full spiritual dynamic but only mirrors the dynamic by permitting a certain amount of free association of percepts. All the same, it more nearly resembles the dynamic than does either the pre-conceptual mind or the logical mind. For though the pre-conceptual mind is imaginative, it is imaginative in an orderly manner suggesting the subsequent logical operations of the mind. So it is the free-forming imaginative process of mind which is responsible for creative thinking.

In common parlance, it might be assumed that a particular woman has a certain view of things. This view fits into a comfortable order in her mind. But, in the course of her contemplation of her view of the nature of her world, she may discover that there is an incongruence within her regularly accepted, orderly

The Immaterial Structure of Human Experience

arrangement of images and concepts of that world. Or, in the course of daily living, she may discover an incongruence between that imaginative or conceptual arrangement in her mind and her actual experience of the world.

She finds she cannot resolve this discrepancy in the usual orderly manner. Consequently, she has recourse to a more free association of percepts than she is generally accustomed to. In the midst of this free association, she encounters a hunch, a mental leap, an insight—some sort of unexpected connection that had not been previously thought of. This she plugs into her more orderly investigations and convictions. To her surprise, she discovers that it solves the problem by altering the relations of those constructs in some meaningful way.

But, to describe this process accurately, it must be observed that the new imaginative insight she has discovered has to be made to fit a logical structure. It must be put into logical form. This must be done prior to its being rendered useful to a mature mind. For she cannot remake the entire orderly structure of her world. So what is initially apprehended as an imaginative image or set of images made up of free associations of percepts in the mind is subsequently converted into a logical relationship consistent with the logical order of her world. In this way, it becomes a solution to the problem.

Thus a recourse to such free association must be translated into the order of the phenomenal precipitate. For the material mind never abandons its love of order for long. Its forays into the free-forming faculty of the imagination are all too brief, since it is order it is generally preoccupied with.

44. The material domain cannot be prior to spirit. Much of this philosophy hinges upon the fact that a recognition of the unity of consciousness is a foundation for the intuition of simple unity. The intuition of simple unity, in turn, makes material awareness possible. And that material awareness involves perception, imagination, conceptualization, and abstract thought.

So, if one were to attempt to explain the unity of human awareness from a material perspective, how might that be done? Can the materialist approach of modern science account for awareness, even if it were to be considered apart from the more enigmatic aspects of consciousness? That is, even if consciousness as such were simply assumed or ignored, can the manner in which one is aware of his world be explained?

Such a materialist perspective would be the reverse of the thesis of this work with its immaterialist point of view. For, though much of this work concentrates upon a representational analysis which might appear to be made amenable to a material approach to human awareness, that analysis is ultimately understood to be encompassed by the immaterialist philosophy.

Nevertheless, for the sake of clarification, let the issue be borne out from a material viewpoint. Thus, if a person were to attempt such an explanation, he might precede with the following conception. When the brain, or neural network, focuses awareness upon an object, that focus becomes a locus of heightened neural activity. In this way, the object of focus, as represented in a thought, becomes the content of consciousness. For it is this content upon which the attention of the mind is directed.

But what of this neural activity? What does it have to do with the *whole* of awareness as opposed to the mind's focus upon some content? The answer might look something like the following. Accompanying the heightened activity of the focus is a widespread neural activity, which has been involved in sensory processing and the generation of the thought.

The Immaterial Structure of Human Experience

So sensory impulses and other contributory thoughts and memories may still be underway, though perhaps fading in the physical mind. Thus they are in some degree registered, but are not at the focus of the mind's attention. Such would be the activity which is "surrounding" the heightened activity of focus.

In general, the mind's less intense awareness of other conscious or semiconscious neural activity can have two characteristics. On the one hand, it is either neurally linked to the object of focus. Or it is a result of unrelated but nevertheless in some degree active neural processes which are not associated with the object of focus. On the other hand, both the related and the unrelated activity are experienced in such a way as to produce a unity of awareness within which the focused object is felt to be present. That unity of awareness would be the "whole" of awareness.

The term "felt" means that a person is aware of this overall activity of his mind, though it is not brought to his immediate attention. It is not within his mind's focus. If some of the activity is far from the center of focus, or unrelated to it, he may or may not experience himself as being conscious of it. But he is in a broader sense aware of it. The term "aware" is used here to mean conscious of but not focused upon.

It is somewhat like a driver involved in a sudden road emergency. He is conscious of what is taking place on the road—say a car which slows sharply and unexpectedly in front of him. But he may not be conscious of what he is doing to adjust his own car to this circumstance. In other words, he may be aware of a need to apply his brakes and adjust his steering to meet the requirements of the situation. But this awareness may not include a consciousness centered upon the precise details of what he is doing.

In spite of this, some part of his mind is carefully applying the right pressure to the brakes and controlling the steering to keep him from losing control of his car or hitting the one in front of him. He may not appear to be aware of these actions. But in some sense he is. Nevertheless, the focus of his mind is on what is happening in front of him.

Describing the whole of such mental activity as a unity emphasizes its interrelated role as a unified sphere of awareness. For, though portions of the activity may be unrelated neurologically, the whole does collectively constitute a unified awareness. This is what is meant by awareness in the broadened context of meaning which is being presently employed.[44]

Overall, this might appear to be a reasonably good physical explanation of the character of human awareness, since it represents the whole of mental experience during any single and inclusive phase of such activity. But it does not work. For it omits a critical element which is involved in both thought and perception.

How can the human mind's ability to abstract—that is, to create the unity inherent in a concept—be understood by means of the materialist explanation introduced above? And how can the unity found in an object of sensory perception be accounted for? These two issues are related. For they both involve unity. That the individual percepts, red, round, and sweet, are perceived and conceptualized together as a ripe apple is due to an *a priori* condition of unity which precedes experience.

It ought to be asked in the case of perception in particular: how can one extract unity from disparate sensory input? It might

---

[44] It may be further noted that this awareness extends into the realm of what might be referred to as the active unconscious. That realm would constitute some portion of mind activity which is inhibited by complex neural means from entering the sphere of focus, or attention. It is nevertheless able to influence behavior. However, if viewed from an immaterialist perspective, this would constitute a theory in the same manner as Maxwell's electromagnetic theory.

be assumed that such unity already exists in the object of perception, which is the apple. But how does the mind perceive this unity by means of the senses? The senses do not register an apple. They register red, round, and sweet. As Kant noted in a manner similar to but different from what is put forth in this philosophy, the mind adds the element of unity.[45]

Even the shape alone of an apple, its roundness, needs an assist from an organizing intuition to be understood as a unified shape. Otherwise the mind would simply follow the contour along without arriving at a recognition of its unity as a curved surface. Unity can therefore not originate in terms of percepts. It must be brought to both thought and material experience from some other source, the intuition of unity. And the intuition of unity arises from the unity of consciousness, or spirit.

Thus the intuition of unity, being founded upon the unity of consciousness, is independent of any neural process. For, as the integrated work of individual neurons is disparate in origin, a recognition of unity cannot be an outcome of their collective activity. Rather, the ability to apprehend or discuss that activity as a unity results precisely from the fact that there is already a sense of unity.

For example, a sense of unity arising from disparate neurons communicating chemically and electrically with one another could no more be posited than that the scattered discharge pattern created by a shotgun could in any but the loosest sense suggest a unity. For the fact that it can suggest a unity comes from outside the pattern. The concept of unity is applied to it because all the shot came from the same source.

Consequently, consciousness might at best be said to parallel the neural process, to exist alongside it as an independent phe-

---

[45] Immanuel Kant, *The Critique of Pure Reason* and *Prolegomena*.

nomenon. For it cannot with any certainty be affirmed to originate from it. Such an assertion would amount to no more than any other unverifiable claim that brain chemistry is consciousness.

But, to proceed beyond the workings of the mind, let the full human organism be considered. Let any sentient organism be brought under scrutiny. It may in this way be discovered that the presupposition of a sense of unity is foundational to evolutionary theory. For it turns out that the acquisition of a particular variation, which would enable a sentient species to survive, requires that the individual creature must actively take advantage of its circumstances.

That is, the organism must avail itself of the new variation in order to prevail over its environmental circumstances and reproduce in a manner which will give it an edge over competitors. Otherwise, the margins of survival are often so slim and require such extreme exertions that any measure of indifference or loss of advantage would be fatal.

This must be all the more the case if the descendents of this creature are to continue to differentiate, radiate, and produce new species. To do this, each individual must express a will to exist. Such a will must precede the introduction of any advantageous physical or mental variation. For it is the guarantor of the full employment and survival of that variation.

Even a variation which gave a creature swifter flight or fleeter foot would not enhance its survival, if the creature did not "wish" to preserve itself. But why would it wish to preserve itself, if it did not have some sense of its individual uniqueness which required preservation? Would it not otherwise stand indifferently while it was devoured or destroyed in some manner? Thus, for such a will to exist, that will to exist cannot itself have

The Immaterial Structure of Human Experience

appeared as a variation. It must have been coexistent with the origin of life.

This is true even of a plant which, in a purely organic character, functions in such a manner as to parallel the effects of an intuition of unity. For a plant is an organic unity operating as an integrated whole in its own interest, even if it should not be conscious of that interest. However, the concern here is with sentient life. And vegetative integration is not enough to serve the interests of a creature which must act to survive. Sentient life is self-aware (though not necessarily self-conscious). Its organic unity is thus internalized in consciousness.

Every form of sentient life (if it is truly sentient) is in some degree articulate and self-aware, though, of course, not in an intellectual sense. The complexity of an insect's response to stimuli thus arises from its self-awareness. This complexity involves a feedback mechanism with its attendant processes of articulate sorting and choice on however primitive a level.

None of this insistence upon self-awareness constitutes a denial that much of an insect's behavior may be set for long periods in instinctive patterns. It merely asserts that not all of it can be so, if the sentient creature is to have the flexibility to survive, either as an individual or as a species. For insects are mobile. And mobility presents ever-renewed circumstances, which serve the interests of choice. In other words, the insect must at least be somewhat flexible in its detection of and response to danger and food sources.

Now, for the reasons just given, the success of life forms can only be accounted for by an inherent influence of some form of unity, either as an intuition in the "mental" life of a sentient creature or as an organic response in plant life. The organic response in plant life resembles the intuition of consciousness by means of its structural and chemical interrelations which approach its environment as an integrated unity responding to that environment in a self-referential, albeit unconscious, manner. In either case, this power orients the creature in such a way as to actively maintain and perpetuate its own organization.

What is this power? In sentient life, which is of chief concern here, it is the self-recognition of the creature concerning its own unique organization in opposition to its circumstances. In other words, it is its sense of unity as centered upon itself. It is a unity of consciousness, which then assimilates its physical character in identity with that unity of consciousness. This is what gives it the conscious organization and will to *be* the very unity that it is and to not lightly surrender such being.

This unity of self-awareness is referential in the following way. It involves a sense of unity which recognizes certain material aspects of itself as a central unity of importance. This is fundamental self-awareness. It need not be self-conscious in the intellectual human sense of that term. For this awareness, however rudimentary its powers of perception and information processing, is the organizational seat of a self-maintenance and self-perpetuation which can simply be referred to as "willed."

It is willed because self-referencing choices are made. Thus a sentient creature has a sense (or intuition) of its own individual unity because it is in some degree articulate and because it is a simple unity, both in its powers of awareness and in its physical organization. But the inherent unity of spirit and its effect upon the behavior of sentient organisms is prior to the will of that particular form of organism. Thus it has the same effect upon the natural selection of any sentient organism. It promotes it by giving it a context of self-unity.

The Immaterial Structure of Human Experience

For these various reasons—perception, thought, and evolution—the physical world, as it is encountered and responded to by human awareness, is subordinate to a spiritual principle of organization. In human beings, that principle fosters a sense of self-conscious self-unity. Specifically, it is the intuition of unity in human awareness as applied to the material manifestations of the person and his circumstances. Thus it cannot be demonstrated that perception and thought in human beings are no more than products of material processes.

45. Further thoughts on consciousness and its phenomenal world. It can only be cautiously suggested that primary mind should impose upon itself a limited perspective such as that which is labeled secondary mind. For no such theory of the working of spirit can be grounded directly in human experience.

It is only at best a framework which makes possible a closer integration of the material it enfolds by explaining it in terms of a purposeful source. This is necessary to supply meaning to experience. But the precise character of the derivation of material awareness from spirit must ultimately remain a mystery.

Nevertheless, a seed of doubt of this sort does not imply the nonexistence of spirit. For that is experiential. Human beings in deep meditation can and do produce within themselves what is sometimes described as an emptying of the mind. This emptiness of the mind is not a consciousness of nothing.

Rather, it is a state of mental clarity and emotional equanimity which is often described as a sense of fullness and well-being. It is this practice of the setting aside of the material without any diminishment of the faculty of awareness which is understood to be grounded in spirit. For the state of meditation is at least equal in intensity to any experience of sensory knowledge.

Furthermore, given the self-enclosing character of consciousness (there being nothing in awareness outside it), with its capacity for either encompassing or excluding material experience, there is sufficient reason for recognizing its dominance over material experience. For all that is known and experienced by human beings is known and experienced within the mind. Mind is thus prior to its content. Material experience may be temporarily set aside. But never awareness itself.

Awareness is itself. It is not understood in terms of anything but itself, but rather everything else in terms of it. It is consciousness. And in human experience it can be said to owe its existence to none other than itself. For it is prior to the experience of anything other than itself. It may even in a certain sense be said to be prior to the experience of itself. For that which is experienced must presuppose a ground for that experience.

To be conscious of something, one must be conscious. Thus, in comparison with such a role played by consciousness (or spirit) in human awareness, what human beings may otherwise be aware of—i.e., the realm of the physical, and even the inner realm of thought and imagination—is of lesser importance.

It is these considerations which merit a return to an assumption of the role played by secondary mind in its unarticulated presentation of percepts to human awareness. Here, in the earliest stages of infancy when the human mind first begins to respond to material impressions, there is observable evidence for the existence of a noumenal precipitate. For it characterizes a child's first experience.

However, the initial input of the noumenal precipitate is unstructured. It does not make possible any human interaction with the world of material experience. So, to create a ground for human knowledge and a distinguishing of a material self from that knowledge, secondary mind provides a means for the development of the phenomenal precipitate.

It is true that the noumenal precipitate, particularly in its earliest expression, is initially exhibited as an undifferentiated flow of percepts in an undifferentiated stream of time. Since these embryonic manifestations are obscured by later developments in the human mind, they cannot be directly apprehended by that mind in its mature state.

So the later developments constitute a clarification of the noumenal precipitate by means of the intuitions, which bring about the articulation of individual percepts and their associations. Most importantly, the employment of the intuitions proceeds further to foment a structural translation of the stream of percepts, as originating in the noumenal precipitate, into the extensions of the phenomenal precipitate.

The phenomenal precipitate is a construct of human awareness, much of the development of which can be directly observed. For it is an ongoing articulation of human awareness, an articulation which begins in infancy. Thus it is derived from something within consciousness. The noumenal precipitate is this writer's attempt to account for that something.

It is through the development of the phenomenal precipitate that the material world, as human beings experience it, unfolds. In order that human beings may interact with their experience and know themselves apart from it, the world they encounter bifurcates. It appears to become divided between consciousness, feeling, emotion, and thought on one side and perception of a physical world on the other. Thus it is principally within the context of a physical world that human understanding grows in its knowledge of the material self and of objective things in general.

It is also in the construction of such a world that the non-incremental time of secondary mind may be said to assist in erecting the scaffolding of space. It is this primitive sense of time which makes the construction of the extensions of space possible. For, under the influence of the intuitions, the flow of non-incremental time articulates the percepts and their associations, which in turn become the extensions of space. The construction of space then makes possible the identification—that is, the articulation—of incremental time.

But consciousness considered strictly in terms of itself is indeterminate. No knowledge of a finite world can be derived from this unlimited and indivisible field of awareness alone. However, it is within this indeterminate and unextended field of awareness—the unity of consciousness—that percepts are registered.

When sense impressions are generally spoken of by adult human beings, what is indicated is not percepts within the non-incremental stream of time, but rather percepts understood as sense impressions within the construct of incremental time and space. In this context of time and space, the mind's attention is drawn first to one then to another element of sensory input as a result of the consecutive impressions made by each of them upon the mind, or upon what are understood to be the senses.

However, the mind's attention moves quickly across closely associated percepts. These percepts are thus recognized as individual qualities which meld into properties, the properties being bound together in extensions which are equivalent in overall percepts to the associated percepts of the noumenal precipitate.

Nevertheless, it remains true that, at a more fundamental level, this upward gradation of awareness toward extensions in space is in fact the consecutive focus of mental attention on individual percepts. At this primal stage of awareness, there is no regard

The Immaterial Structure of Human Experience

whatsoever for a distinction between objectivity and subjectivity. For there is no incremental time and space. Rather, what is referred to is expressed in a different context than spatial awareness. What is referred to are the percepts of the noumenal precipitate.

The mature human mind is generally unaware of this process. But it is not always so. For such an accounting of isolated percepts may take place in physical experience, or in the objective mental contemplation of an object of thought, when the mind pauses to consider individual qualities. It is in just such a case as this that an inadvertent reference is being made by the mature human mind to the noumenal precipitate.

So it is apparent that both processes occur simultaneously: the focus on simple percepts in the noumenal realm and the awareness of the more complex structures of the phenomenal precipitate. For they are one and the same. The more fundamental process, which is a focus upon individual percepts within the noumenal precipitate, is the underlying character of the experience of a space and time delineated world.

This can be illustrated by a rudder which steers a ship. The rudder is identified with a pilot, as the pilot is the brains of the ship controlling the rudder. But the ship, which includes the rudder, also determines where the pilot goes, since the pilot must go where the ship goes. So it can be seen that deciding which perspective to emphasize is a matter of personal choice.

The choice is determined by whether or not one wishes to consider how a ship is made to move in a certain direction (emphasizing the brains of the pilot) or to consider how it is that all involved in the ship (including the pilot) move in a certain direction. One can choose to look at the bridge. Or one can focus on the boat.

Accordingly, one can be concerned with the underpinnings of the phenomenal precipitate, by looking at the noumenal precipitate. Or one can be concerned with how the phenomenal precipitate is made negotiable to human awareness, by looking at its temporal and spatial construct. The same mind deals with the same percepts in either case.

At this point in the present essay, it is useful to note that a clear distinction between the operations of secondary mind and those of the human mind has not always been consistently maintained. Human awareness has been spoken of as absorbing the operations of secondary mind into itself. And vice versa: secondary mind has been referred to as reflecting back on itself in the capacity of human awareness.

So it is that secondary mind appears to have been involved in both establishing and articulating the field of its activity. Thus the two operations—secondary mind and the human mind—are understood to be one in simultaneous functioning. That is why they can be referred to collectively as singly responsible both for the establishment of the noumenal precipitate and the mapping of the phenomenal precipitate. For human awareness, being itself the work of secondary mind, can be said to be developing the phenomenal precipitate as a simultaneous reiteration of the noumenal precipitate.

Nevertheless, when its focus upon the phenomenal precipitate is being emphasized, human awareness is generally referred to as mapping an existing noumenal substrate into a developing superstructure of incremental time and space. Thus a distinction is made. This is important because it is in mapping the noumenal precipitate that quantitative awareness may be said to be established.

The Immaterial Structure of Human Experience

So, for a closer analysis, let secondary mind be examined in its more restricted capacity of forming the noumenal precipitate. For, with the increasing diminishment of any adult human awareness of its activity, secondary mind can be thought of as being independently responsible for the initial establishment of proportion in the structuring of the noumenal precipitate.

This is accomplished by the operation of focus, which is the same fundamental faculty as that which is involved in the articulation of the phenomenal precipitate. As stated in previous entries, mental focus is the ground upon which the three intuitions—simple unity, plurality, and totality—are based. For these intuitions are modes of focus.

Under the influence of focus, the noumenal presentation of the content of consciousness sets each percept off against others in a manner which establishes the preliminary conditions for proportion. But this is not proportion as it is generally understood. For proportion is experienced by the human mind as characterizing the phenomenal precipitate.

Proportion, as it is present within the phenomenal precipitate, is a characteristic of extensions. It is encountered in a relation of extension to extension. It also arises in human understanding when the relation of one quality to another is considered apart from the extensions in which the qualities are found.

But, as is made clear in the proportional consideration of qualities, in either case it is the initial presentation of the content of consciousness in the noumenal precipitate which renders possible the human mind's effort at quantification as a means of articulating the phenomenal precipitate in terms of its extensions.

Focus establishes discreteness. And discreteness is necessary for proportionality [46] and the quantification which may ensue. For one thing cannot be determined as proportional to another unless the discrete character of each is determined. And that which is proportional is potentially subject to quantification. If the proportion is not numerically ascertained, then quantification does not occur. But it is only under such potential circumstances that a proportional comparison can be made.

In attempting to understand how discreteness provides an initial foundation for proportion, imagine a bag of thirty marbles. They are poured out upon a table. One observes that there are individual marbles. This is their discrete character. They are also round and share an identical physical extension. This indicates their proportional character.

Being of the same physical extension, qualities of color and transparency not being of any importance in this case, they are identical. So any one of them is the common measure of them all. Which indicates that they are in a one-to-one relation to each other. Thus any portion of them can be distinguished in terms of a common measure against any other portion of them, say one against the remaining twenty-nine. Or one against two. Or two against three.

These are all proportional relations, which can be discussed as such because the relationship is between extensions, which are physical bodies. Physical bodies can be commensurate or not commensurate with one another. They are commensurate if the establishment of a common measure is possible. That common measure is a matter of identical extension. So, in the example just given, a proportion of one to twenty-nine is one extension meas-

---

[46] As will be explained five paragraphs below, the term "proportion" is being used here in the sense of "ratio."

The Immaterial Structure of Human Experience

ured against twenty-nine which are identical to each other and to the one extension.

Thus the extension of any one of these marbles acts as a standard unit which applies to them all. Were it a case of proportions in the abstract, or ideal, character of mathematics, the standard unit would be the arithmetical unit one. Such a standard measure in either case, the physical or the ideal, makes commensurate relations possible. For these are necessary to the quantitative expression of proportions.

Mathematicians prefer to label the above relations—1/29, 1/2, 2/3—as "ratios." They reserve the term "proportion" for an equality of ratios, as in 1/2 = 2/4. But the common use of the term proportion, as employed here, is simply a commensurate relationship between two things. If one thing can be evenly measured by another, or by a part of another, then the two things are in proportion.

Statements, such as "His behavior is out of proportion to the situation," may also be made, in which no specific measure is indicated, but only implied. Nevertheless, the implication is important to the understanding of the comparison. Though a person's behavior and a situation of perhaps moral expectation cannot be physically or mathematically rendered in concrete terms, the statement implies that it might be, were it strictly necessary. And this gives the statement its meaning.

So, in brief, proportions are the inevitable outcome of some form of discreteness, whether physical, ideal, or implied. In two of the examples just discussed, since they are physical and numerical (or ideal in the latter case), and thus exhibit measurable commensurate relations, they may be understood in terms of quantification.

In other words, these two examples involve a discreteness of extension. And, as proportions between extensions must be commensurate, they require a common unit of measure. But such commensurability may also be implied without any sort of physical or ideal demonstration, as in the third example given above. However, where it is clearly understood that a common measure between extensions cannot be established, an incommensurate relationship prevails. Here a proportion cannot be be said to appertain.

But incommensurate relationships are vague. They cannot be given any sort of concrete expression by the mind. So the very fact that the term *in*commensurate is a negation of the term commensurate indicates the mind's inclination towards proportion. For the dominant concept is that which is negated.

Thus, in arithmetic, proportional relations (termed ratios) are developed on the basis of the arithmetical unit one. Where such a unit is not a fundamental component of a number—i.e., where it cannot form a multiple which is that number [47]—the number is irrational. Such a number cannot enter into a commensurate, or proportional, relationship with a number in which the arithmetical unit is such a fundamental component. Consequently, it cannot enter with a rational number into the expression of a fraction, or form a pattern-repeating decimal.

Rather, it must be expressed by an indeterminate succession of digits to the right of a decimal. The succession of digits to the right of the decimal is indeterminate because the digits are themselves rational numbers which (each in its appropriate decimal position) can be divided equally into arithmetical units.

---

[47] It is important to keep in mind that a number like 3/4 also forms a relationship of three arithmetical units to four, even though the fraction 3/4 is also less than one such arithmetical unit.

The Immaterial Structure of Human Experience

Thus they cannot fit evenly into the expression of an irrational number, which cannot be divided equally into arithmetical units. So they are repeated in ever smaller increments (decimal places further to the right of the decimal) in order to ever more closely approximate a rational number which they cannot express.

Now the two general operations of the mind—the pre-articulate, imaginative presentation of the content of consciousness in the early formation of the phenomenal precipitate, and the further intellectual articulation of that content—are what have been referred to collectively under the general heading of human awareness. For human awareness is usually equated with the phenomenal precipitate.

Secondary mind is clearly the source of the first operation because the transition from the noumenal flow of percepts to their imaginative reorganization in extensions is immediate and undetected by human awareness (except in the earliest stages of infancy). But the subsequent intellectual development—an overlay on the imaginative phenomenal precipitate—is clearly differentiated in human experience. It is a product of reason. And, as such, it is an ongoing process which human beings are daily aware of.

So it would seem as though secondary mind, the source of the first operation, were in fact the organ of general awareness, which in truth it is. Though it may be considered separately from the human mind, when an emphasis is being placed upon an exclusive definition of the latter, particularly as it appears in its maturity. For then the noumenal is fully obscured behind the operations of the phenomenal.

It is for this reason that the reader should continue to bear in mind that both processes together distinguish a single integrated mind. Secondary mind and the human mind are one and the same, except when brought under analysis. Together, they are human awareness. Nevertheless, it is the advantage of analysis to make it clear that quantification is not only dependent upon proportion among extensions in the phenomenal precipitate, but upon the initial recognition of discrete forms in the noumenal precipitate—i.e., the percepts and their associations.

However, let this analysis be set aside. For the moment, the noumenal may be allowed to slip into its place of obscurity behind the operations of the phenomenal. So, in the contemplation of the phenomena of maturing human experience, it can be observed that the growing human mind finds itself increasingly compelled to conceptually comprehend a world which appears to exhibit a potential for being expressed in proportions: proportions of physical extensions, to be exact.

This is to say that the intellectual mind begins to classify and reason about its experience. In such reasoning, a consideration of proportions occurs not only among extensions, but within them as well. Thus proportions are not always a matter of mathematics. Knowing that two pitches in music are equal in the hearing is a judgment confined to like qualities. These qualities are held in comparison in the mind as though they were commensurate, though this is not known. For commensurateness is only subsequently to be determined by means of dominant frequencies in acoustics, when the musical pitch is being physically described as sound.

In addition, there are the comparative relations of conceptual classifications. To state that "all dogs are mammals" is to include something smaller within something larger. But these are objects of thought, not physical extensions. Nevertheless, thoughts which are concepts are grounded in images. And images are representations of the physical in thought.

The Immaterial Structure of Human Experience

That is why such a relationship can be expressed with Euler's circles. It is not that the circles coincide proportionately with the images which support the concepts. They stand in for them. The circles themselves become objects of thought which attribute physical extension to the thought comparison. Thus it can be seen from this comparative use of the circles that a development of proportional awareness includes a classificatory recognition of inclusive, partially inclusive, and mutually exclusive elements of thought extension.

For example, among such circles (and like physical extensions) there are to be found relations of largeness, smallness, equality, more inclusiveness, less inclusiveness, congruence, etc. Consequently, relations suggesting proportion are created. They closely resemble commensurate relations, though they are not exact and are therefore not physical.

The circles can be any size relative to one another, so long as they are larger or smaller, inclusive or less inclusive of one another, as required. Equality and congruence are the standards of measure. Largeness and smallness take their comparative departure from equality, just as more inclusiveness and less inclusiveness take theirs from congruence.

In this way, the circles *appear* to suggest a numerical commensurability, which centers about equality and congruence in the same manner that arithmetic centers about the arithmetical unit. So, when such judgments are made, proportional thinking occurs, even when numbers or physical measures are not involved.

Thus relationships among qualities and thought extensions are suggestive of relationships among physical extensions. For it is the physical alone which is a foundation for the sense of proportion. This is conferred by analogy on the nonphysical. Such an analogy is most evident, and most redolent of the physical, in mathematics, which simulates the physical while not being physical.

In the numerical examples given above, there is a *class* of one, a class of twenty-nine, a class of two, and a class of three. In order to form proportional relations, these numerical classifications—which are, after all, conceptual—are related to one another by means of the arithmetical units which compose each of them.

Equal arithmetical units (the number 1) compose the numbers 1, 29, 2, and 3, providing for their commensurability. Thus there is a proportion of one unit to twenty-nine units, one unit to two units, and two units to three units. In other words, within the twenty-nine units, there are twenty-nine units of one, all of which are the same. So the twenty-nine units collectively may be "measured off" twenty-nine times by the one unit. Though this is not a physical measure.

Likewise, thinking in terms of Euler's circles, a classification of one unit is entirely enclosed in a classification of twenty-nine units. Or a classification of two units is entirely enclosed within a classification of three units. The two units cannot measure off the three units directly. But the individual units they are composed of can.

At the level of qualities, human image formation, and thus human perception, may not be concerned with proportions. For it should be noted that percepts do not combine in an object of thought or an object of perception (which is a thought image) on a one-to-one basis. So percepts at the phenomenal level do not function as individual units of measure.

As qualities, they may be compared to one another as though by proportion (say in degrees) when they are considered apart

The Immaterial Structure of Human Experience

from any extension to which they may belong. But, as components of an extension, they are blended into properties in such a manner that they cannot be individually quantified, not even by suggestion.

To better conceive of this, imagine a green stick. How many percepts of green are in the stick? If the stick can be divided in half, there are at least two green percepts. How many times can the pieces of stick be divided? This is not an abstract issue which results in questions of continuity. It is a matter of how far a mental image can be reduced.

Such a reduction depends upon two things: the relation of one extension to another in terms of the parts of a figure, and the relationship between separate extensions as exhibited in a spatial context. But it is no less complicated than the problem of continuity. So it is best to leave alone the matter of percept count in an object and its mental representation.

In contrast to the qualities of an image, thinking in terms of complete images or concepts is inherently proportional, or suggestive of proportion, in character. For these are extensions, be they thought or physical extensions. Referencing the objects of thought to physical extensions, even when the object of thought is not found among the physical, like a unicorn or a perfect circle, one sees that quantitative comparisons can be made or at least suggested.

As an example once again of the mind's conceptual predilection towards proportion, take an irrational number. The irrational number can only be represented with an indeterminate progression of integers to the right of a decimal. Are not these integers whole numbers? And are not whole numbers commensurate on the basis of the unit one? (Zero is, of course, a special case indicating the absence of a quantity or acting as a place marker for some integer deferred by a power of ten.)

So why is it the case that an irrational number can only be expressed in rational terms—i.e., involving an unending series of rational integers? It is because its indeterminacy cannot be grasped by the human intellect. The concept-producing mind must work with precise characteristics of finitude. Or it must at least imply that it is doing so.

Rational numbers are determinate concepts. A 3 is distinguished from a 2 and a 4 precisely because it is not a 2 or a 4. It is limited by the 2 and the 4. Or it is limited by other rational expressions, like 2 3/4 and 3 3/4, the latter three quarters building up toward the next whole number, 4. Thus these numbers, all being rational, are incremental.

In such cases, one rational number is bounded by another rational number acting as an increment of addition or subtraction. Both numbers are finite. That is what makes them rational. They can be apprehended conceptually because they are finite. So it can be seen that finitude is bounded by finitude. Moreover, finitude suggests proportion, which arises from its incremental character. Thus finitude and proportion are fundamental functions of the human mind. Without them, there is indeterminacy and disorder.

Now, in returning to a general analysis of mental properties, let it be observed once again that the noumenal precipitate presents human awareness with percepts. Initial focus upon each percept, and upon each association of percepts, makes a separate, consecutive impression upon the mind, inaugurating the flow of percepts as presented within non-incremental time. In turn, the sense of separateness produced by the successive appearance of each percept and of each association of percepts in non-

The Immaterial Structure of Human Experience

incremental time enhances a recognition of their individual character.

What is being spoken of here is secondary mind in its early, premature stage, insofar as human development is concerned. It is this which creates the noumenal precipitate. It represents a nexus, a point of transition from the infinite mind of spirit to the finite mind of humankind. But it is only a foundational stage in human awareness. For, as increased recognition of the character of each percept takes place, and as a greater appreciation of the grouping of those percepts into associations follows, this primitive stage of awareness is succeeded by a construction of the phenomenal precipitate by the human mind.

This results in the phenomenal precipitate becoming the principal, and eventually only, material structure for human experience. An important portion of this precipitate is understood as belonging to an objective, physical realm. The remainder is subjective. The imaginative, conceptual, and physical portions of the phenomenal precipitate undergo a continuing development, which is brought about initially by pre-conceptual and later by conceptual means. Thus the process begins pre-conceptually in infancy and continues into the conceptual articulations of adult life.

It progresses toward an increasingly sophisticated sense of space and incremental time. As this becomes predominantly conceptual with the development of the person, quantification is inaugurated. Of course, learning from others is involved in this process. For the discovery and use of proportions in thought and the invention of numbers are cultural phenomena.

Now, when, in the early development of the phenomenal precipitate, an associated bundle of percepts is recognized as an object or as part of an object, then each such associated bundle of percepts exists for the human mind as an extension in space or as an extension, or object, of thought.

But an extension in thought differs from an extension in space. It is not understood to be physical. Because it is not so understood, it is not recognized as physically spatial. Thus it is not fixed in a particular condition and position in relation to other such extensions, which condition or position cannot be altered by a human will without specific regard to the condition or position. In other words, it must be physically changed or moved according to specific laws governing the relations of physical phenomena.

For this reason, a thought differs from a physical phenomenon in that it is not governed by such laws. It does not appear to be independent of human will. But it does preclude other thoughts at the moment it is brought before the mind. And it focuses upon an image which is represented as extended. That is, the image exhibits the properties of a physical extension, though these properties are rendered independent of anything but the thought to which they appertain. It is in this sense that the thought is extended.

An example of either a mental object of thought or a physical extension in space would require that it be first of all an extension which involves an association of multiple percepts, as opposed to its being one percept alone. It would also involve figure (i.e., shape), such as the roundness of a snowball. But, if it is a physical extension as opposed to a thought extension, then in addition to these conditions is the following circumstance.

One would be tempted to point out that a physical snowball occupies a space which cannot be occupied by something else at the same time. But this statement must be rephrased. For to say that a snowball "occupies" a space is a matter of speaking meta-

The Immaterial Structure of Human Experience

phorically. In truth, extensions do not occupy space. Rather, an awareness of one object's exclusion of another, while they are both understood to be in a state of simultaneous existence, is what creates a sense of physical space.

Contiguity is physical space. In other words, an awareness of contiguous extension is prior to an awareness of physical space. Thus a snowball can be understood to be in a particular spatial relationship with other physical extensions which are contiguous with it. While it fulfills this condition, no other physical extension can do so.

But any single percept of an extended physical object can be understood differently from the combined percepts which are associated together in that extension. Individually, it is recognized as a percept of perception and has an independent identity. Such a percept in a physical object is a quality, which is in some ways akin to a feeling.

However, when a percept is understood in this manner, it is not experienced as interior to a perceiving person, as a feeling is. It is thought to be contained in the physical object. Nevertheless, in spite of the fact that it is not experienced as interior to the person, it exhibits the character of a single percept. Thus, when considered for itself, it is experienced as a direct single impression upon the mind. And it is in this respect alone that it resembles a feeling.

So a percept which expresses a quality is to be distinguished from its associated percepts among the multiple percepts which constitute the properties of an extension in space. Of course, all the associated percepts express qualities within one property or another. Otherwise, they would not be known to the mind. They would not be impressions upon the mind.

But as components of a property, they are blended together in such a way that, unless singled out as qualities, they may not express individual distinction. For example, an object exhibiting the property of turquoise coloration may not readily yield up its individual qualities of green and blue. These must be singled out with some effort. The sweet and sour flavor of an apple is a similar case.

Yet each type of percept may—sometimes with effort—be singled out. Nonetheless, as a whole, the total association of multiple percepts belongs either to a physical extension or an extension of thought. For both are objects in the sense that the former is experienced as a physical extension and the latter is experienced as a representation of one.

If a single percept is recognized as an unextended characteristic of an extension in space—that is, if it functions as an unextended characteristic of a property within a physical object—then it expresses itself as a quality. Any one specific quality is always a single type of percept among an association of other types of percepts.

So, in addition to possessing the characteristic of not being extended, the percept forms an association with other percepts within an extension. In fact, this association of percepts *is* the extension. And the percepts within it are organized into the properties of an object: either a physical object or an object of thought.

Characteristics peculiar to those extensions which are considered to be physical objects are some degree of impenetrability and a resistance to displacement. Recalling that physical extensions are themselves images presented within the phenomenal mind, it can be seen that these two characteristics do not have anything to do with the percepts which make up the object's composition. For in such cases, though parts of the object may be

The Immaterial Structure of Human Experience

redistributed in relation to one another or the whole of it may be moved to another location, its qualities are not affected insofar as their collective expression in the whole is concerned.[48]

Rather, the characteristics of impenetrability and resistance to displacement are directly imposed within the noumenal mind. Where these conditions appertain, they are brought about by a persistence in the mental representation of a particular association of percepts. It is this persistence in mental representation which insures a uniformity of character (impenetrability) and resistance to displacement concerning a particular extension.

If an extension is unchanged in terms of parts to the whole or in terms of its contiguity with other extensions, there is a persistence in its character and location. In other words, in the noumenal flow of percept input a particular association of percepts is repeated without any alteration in its close association with other repeated associations of percepts. This creates an enduring impression of physical uniformity and location. Consequently, there is a sense both of impenetrability and of a resistance to displacement.

Thus a brick in a free-standing wall supplies a sensation of resistance to a person's hand pushing against it. The sense of that brick's resistance to an alteration in its character and to its displacement may even increase if a more intimate encounter with it is assumed: say the hand is pushed harder against it.

In such a case, there are the sensations (i.e., percepts of feeling) of increased muscle tension and contact of the hand with the brick. This is accompanied by a persistence of the mental representation of that brick as maintaining its physical composition

---

[48] The present discussion is centered upon the characteristics of solids. Liquids and gasses present a more flexible situation, due to their elastic nature. But the same principles apply nonetheless.

amidst its contiguous accompaniment of neighboring extensions. As a result, the brick retains its character and its position with respect to the other bricks in the wall.

A yet greater pressure by some other means might succeed in penetrating or dislodging the brick. In the case of a penetration, parts of the brick will have been altered in their relationship to one another. For the parts, with their changed orientation to one another, are now recognizable as individual extensions which had previously formed the greater uniformity of extension of the whole brick.

In other words, they now appear in the noumenal stream as independent but mutually recognizable and closely associated associations of percepts. They are mutually recognizable because together they present the same family of qualities which had belonged to the whole brick. In other words, these more fragmented associations retain the qualities of the whole, which was the single original association of percepts.

A new circumstance has also been added. It is that each new fragmented extension in the phenomenal precipitate will exhibit its own peculiar figure which is yet capable of being integrated with the others in the original whole. That is, the parts, though individually unique in figure, suggest the possibility of being fitted back together to reconstitute the original extension. Thus not only the qualities and properties of the whole remain the same. But the fragments present figures which can be mutually integrated.

However, the fragments are independent extensions, spatially separated from one another. For this reason, some of the qualities may be distributed among them in such a manner as to deprive one or the other of a quality. These are the qualities which were already localized in the figure of the original exten-

The Immaterial Structure of Human Experience

sion. Say the brick was red in one place and reddish white in another. Now there is a red fragment and another fragment exhibiting both red and white.

In the case of the brick being dislodged, neither the parts nor the whole would remain in the wall. The brick, whole or in parts, falls to the ground. If the brick has been completely dislodged, the association of percepts which is that particular brick would henceforth appear elsewhere in the noumenal stream, either whole or in parts. For it is now contiguous with, and therefore accompanied by, those associations which form the various extensions of the ground. These locational associations were, of course, otherwise and varied as the brick or its parts fell to the ground.

To return to the general topic of qualities: since a quality in its individual character does not bring about the extension of a body, it can be differentiated from the body insofar as it is considered as a quality. Whereas, insofar as its role is to form an extension, it is not differentiated from the compound of percepts it enters into when it is experienced as contributing to the extension. For the extension is an expression of all the percepts together without a focused regard for the individual character of any one of them.

Thus any one quality is associated with multiple other qualities in producing the extension, much in the manner that an apple has red and green sections on the outside and white pulp and brown seeds on the inside. Such a division among qualities partitions the apple, so that multiple extensions can be recognized as parts within its one overall extension. It is this differentiation which makes figure possible.

Remember that, when regarding the immaterialist origin of material entities, even what is thought of as light and shadow on an object is a matter of qualities inherent in the object. As an artist knows, it is these types of variation which render possible a visual discrimination between what is one distinct turn of a figure and what is another.

But the apple is also both sweet and sour. And these qualities are often evenly distributed throughout a large part of it, though not all of it. So it can be seen that its qualities are, to a greater or less extent, unevenly distributed, like the red, green, white, and brown coloration, the different textures of skin, pulp, and seed, and the extensive, but not universal, distribution of flavor. Whereas it would appear that there is another characteristic which is uniformly expressive of the apple. This would be the spatial location of its colors, tastes, and textures within its figure.

The recognition of the apple's figure is not due to a consideration of the individual character of its various qualities. It results from an acknowledgement of a family resemblance between them, which arises from a repetition of these qualities appearing in close association with one another in the noumenal precipitate. So the unevenly distributed qualities of the apple identify its parts. And its figure unites them. Altogether the associated qualities and the figure they suggest constitute the extension, apple.

Insofar as they are performing the task of constituting an extension, the individual percepts exhibit no individual quantitative identity. For individually they have none. They are not individually extended. Though they may be separately located within the figure, like the color qualities of the apple.

Thus the simple fact that an object is quantitative, or extended, results from the associative influence of its constituent percepts. But its magnitude of extension (i.e., its relative size) arises from both the distribution of its qualities, which are separately

The Immaterial Structure of Human Experience

located within the parts of its figure, and from its spatial relationship to other contiguous extensions.

In the case of the apple, all of its qualities together constitute its extension. Whereas the magnitude of its extension—the visual magnitude, for example—is determined by the distribution of its different qualities, as in the colors—red, green, white, and brown—and the different shades of light upon it. Its tactile and other qualities behave in a similar manner.

It is important to note that, like the colors, shading is understood to exhibit qualities which are inherent in the apple, however much the shading may shift in appearance and intensity over relatively short intervals of time. These variations are considered to be changes in the apple. For they represent a modification of its qualities.

Of course, there are other qualities in the apple than those of vision, touch, and taste. Its qualities extend over the full range of what are generally considered to be the five human senses. But the few listed here are made to show how qualities work in different ways to determine both the fact of extension and its magnitude.

As previously mentioned, an extension's spatial relationship to other contiguous extensions also contributes to its magnitude. This is, however, determined as much by an experience of its ongoing identity amidst changes in location as it is by its immediate contiguous relationship to other extensions.

For example, why is it understood that an apple is the same apple whether it is seen from a distance or close up, regardless of whether it is in the same or changed surroundings? On the one hand, its magnitude would appear to be less at a distance and greater close up. But, on the other, a knowledge of its identity (i.e., the fact that it appears to be the same apple) and its physical context (illustrated by the observation, "that bowl and table cannot be so small!") would reveal it to be the same apple. In other words, due to the influence of experience, it is the latter observation which prevails.

Setting the problems of extension aside, the fact remains that each percept can be discerned as an individual quality within an extension. Thus one quality within an object may be distinguished from another. It is these qualities which combine to form the properties of an object. And relocation alone of the extension does not change them.

Granted that, in the case of shading, relocation in relation to a supposed light source does appear to produce an effect upon this quality. But it may rather be observed that the two phenomena—shading and position—are closely coordinated in occurrence. Their apparent causal connection, however familiar and consistent, is theoretical.

But what has been particularly set forth in this discussion is an explanation of why characteristics involving impenetrability and immovability must not be considered as qualities. Penetration and movement both involve motion. Penetration necessitates a displacement of parts, which requires a motion of the parts. And movement simply is motion. Motion cannot be a quality. For it involves a change of location. Change of location alone does not affect the appearance or disappearance of properties.[49]

---

[49] This statement must be qualified by the observation that chemical change would appear to involve the replacement of certain qualities or properties by others, as when water is decomposed into gases. But this involves a movement, not unlike a physical change, as when water turns to a gaseous state and its constituent elements move apart. Again, in the process of physical change, when water is converted to ice, there is understood to be a movement involving a crystalline structural alignment. This does alter the properties of the substance—i.e., from liquid to solid. However, in this immaterialist philosophy,

The Immaterial Structure of Human Experience

The whiteness, coldness, and heaviness of a snowball are individual qualities. Note that heaviness, like shading, is listed as a quality, regardless of the fact that it can be altered by a division into parts or a relocation of the object. The division into parts illustrates the fact that the quality is distributed amongst parts of the extension. And relocation simply involves the same situation as that of shading. Properties change coincidentally, but in a proportionately regular manner, in conjunction with context.

Without its qualities, the snowball would not be known. For qualities are percepts. And, without an image made up of percepts—those sensations by which something is perceived—an object could not be represented to the mind. So a quality must be a characteristic of an extension, but not of a motion of that extension.

It is the full complement of the snowball's qualities experienced together which is the snowball. Without them, there is no snowball. Yet it is also the case that, understood individually, a quality is not an extended entity. For no single percept constitutes an extension in physical or mental space. Rather, it is akin to a sensation or a feeling.

In consideration of this unique character, one cannot take a specific quality, say a particular sensation of whiteness, and add it to another instance of the same whiteness to obtain a spatial

---

what must be exclusively considered is what appears in the perceptual image presented to the mind. Here there is a change from one substance to another: liquid to gas or liquid to solid. In terms of the mental image, these phenomena essentially entail a process of replacement: water by gases and water by ice. Movement occurs, since water is seen to shrink in volume or to expand. But this apparent motion is a result of replacement, the new substance having different properties. Thus, though change can be said to entail motion, it is the alteration in substances which creates the appearance of motion. Whereas motion independently understood does not change the substance, but rather its context of reference to other substances.

extension. Two identical white colors appearing simultaneously must belong to separate spatial extensions. For there is only one whiteness of a particular hue and intensity either within a specific extension or within a part of that extension, however minute the parts must be understood to be.

A different whiteness demarcates a different part or extension. One particular whiteness is a single percept, which represents a single quality. If there is more than one such percept associated with an extension or its part, it serves only to increase intensity (i.e., saturation). In other words, it appears consecutively before the mind—in a staccato repetition, as it were—however rapid the sequence of that repetition.

Different variations of whiteness within an extension involve different color percepts in association with a white percept, much as an artist would combine yellow and white in an effort to create a cream. But two identical percepts of white are not combined together in the mind, except to increase saturation. Thus a close succession of one type of white percept appearing before the mind will only serve to intensify the whiteness. And the same whiteness in two separate parts of an extension results from the fact that the parts are individual extensions within the greater extension.

Since parts may be ever so minute in their appearance before the mind, subdivision seeming to be almost unlimited, what is referred to as a single extension, but which is made up of innumerable parts, may enclose ever so many identical percepts. But these identical percepts of whiteness must each appear in individual association with other qualities to constitute even the smallest part of an extension. Some of those associated qualities must be different. The identical percepts of whiteness cannot otherwise stand alone. Thus there will always be slight differences in

The Immaterial Structure of Human Experience

the associations of percepts, insofar as they constitute separate parts.

Again, an extension is necessarily formed from more than one type of percept. It is formed from an associated bundle of different percepts. The percepts are combined to create the properties of the extension. The combination of properties makes the extension. In addition, a bundle of associated percepts forming an extension can be added to another of a similar but not identical character to form a separate part of a greater extension.

Now it is a contiguity of physical extensions which contributes to the structure of physical space. This contiguity also contributes to the development of figure. For figure is derived from a differentiation between the qualities of one extension and those of another, each turn of the figure acting as an extension in contiguity with the next.

In this way, the articulation of an extension can apply both internally and externally to it. For it may involve a relation of parts or a relation of independent extensions. The qualities of each of these parts or of each of the independent extensions differ from one another in a lesser or greater degree. But they do differ.

The direct representations of sensations are what are of concern in immaterialist philosophy. Anything beyond these is conjecture. Indirect evidence cannot apply. Rather, indirect evidence forms the structure of material theories. Human beings find these material theories necessary to facilitate causal integration. Causal integration, in turn, renders the wonderful deeds of science possible for humankind. But it does not explain the ultimate origin of material relations. It merely takes advantage of certain regularities in material events.

One might be tempted to say that the mind's most subtle configurations of experience must be in terms of proportions. For proportion is the backbone of mathematics. And mathematics is the most subtle creation of the intellect. However, prior to intellect it is the pre-conceptual mind which sets up the foundations of the phenomenal precipitate in terms of images.

So, would it not be reasonable to assume that, in its attempt to investigate those foundations, the intellect should mirror the work of the pre-conceptual mind? But this cannot be so. For the intellect works with proportions. And it turns out that, insofar as proportions are assumed to be the origin of those foundations, difficulties emerge.

It is true that, up to a point, the relations found in physical experience can be mathematically understood. In other words, they can be mathematically expressed. Insofar as this is the case, the mathematical relations can be expanded by study, conjecture, and experiment. They can be theorized. But this theorization points up the fact that it is important to recognize that mathematics is a late human invention. It is a product of intellect, or reason. Whereas the underlying groundwork of the phenomenal precipitate is pre-conceptual, imaginative, and more subtle than reason.

The numerical relations which mathematics offers are ultimately confounded by an artificially restricted definition of number. For example, the whole number 2 is bounded in distinction from the whole numbers 1 and 3. Yet 1.999... is understood to be capable of standing in for 2. This implies that, in their practical relations, numbers are not always rigorously bounded.

Once this is accepted, it introduces the possibility of an employment of indeterminate numbers like the repeating decimal in 1.999.... An irrational number is also indeterminate. So a recognition of irrational numbers is soon to follow. Once irrational numbers have been recognized, they are granted a permissible

The Immaterial Structure of Human Experience

passage into mathematical reasoning. For they appear to reflect the subtleties of experience: those relations which proportions cannot be applied to.

But these irrationals then undermine mathematical relations in varying degrees. For they are not only indeterminate in expression, in the manner that a repeating decimal is also indeterminate in expression. Their precise character cannot be imagined, whereas the unending extension of the repeating decimal can at least be imagined, if not precisely realized.

The concept mathematicians employ for this latter, more complete indeterminacy is "infinite." Irrational numbers are supposed to be not finite in terms of their articulation. They can neither be written out in full nor imagined. So they cannot be understood in the way round numbers can be understood.

Their inability to be expressed in round numbers not only makes them inexact for the human intellect. It makes them incommensurable with rational numbers. They are, in fact, themselves found to be expressions of incommensurability. For they cannot be measured. The relationship between the sides and diagonal of a square is incommensurable. It reduces to $\sqrt{2}$, an algebraic irrational which renders a proportional relationship between the sides and diagonal infeasible.

Such is the case also with π, a transcendentally irrational number which forbids the formation of an exact proportion between the diameter and circumference of a perfect circle. So, in consequence of the resulting inexactness in numerical relations which this incommensurability produces, the precise character of the relations remains uncertain.[50]

---

[50] The irrational, or indeterminate, character of pi is due to the fact that an indeterminate number of radii would be required to establish the uniform curvature of the circumference of a perfect circle. For any distance whatsoever

George Lowell Tollefson

It is also understood that there are more irrational numbers than rational. For, since their formation is unbounded by definition, there is a very great possibility of them. Thus, even in the matter of numbers alone—an artificial system conceived by the human intellect—reality seems to creep in and force the numbers to lie outside the province of an exact expression.

That is to say, the mind's subtlety overreaches its inventiveness. In fact, the mind could not continue to be inventive, if this were not the case. And the fact that the mind is inventive is the clearest indication of the fact that it is the case. For yet undiscovered subtleties are where the few persistent minds are able to mine new inventions.

The mind continues to discover new, unthought-of relations. Therefore, in deference to this expansion of possibility beyond present intellectual means, a more flexible and forgiving statistical procedure must be resorted to in an attempt to represent the most minute structures of physical reality which might be en-

---

between any two radii would leave the uniformity of the curvature in doubt. In the case of $\sqrt{2}$, a problem arises because the irrational number is an algebraic root, which makes the cause of its irrational character less immediately evident, other than to concede that the number 2 will not break down into rational roots. However, as a square can be circumscribed by a circle, as the diagonal of the square is equal to the diameter of the circle, and as the sides of the square act in the role of chords which form segments dividing the circumference of the circle into four equal arcs, there is a geometrical correspondence between the circle's circumference and the perimeter of the square. For this reason, there is an implied numerical relationship between the transcendental number π and the algebraic root $\sqrt{2}$. Thus in some mathematical operations rational numbers resolve to algebraic irrational roots and these roots can bear a geometrical relationship to a transcendental number. By this means, among others, it can be seen that the rational system of numbers in general tends toward the irrational. In fact, *all things* lead to the irrational. For the rational is humankind's limited work. And the much great domain of the irrational is what humankind works on, classifying and defining, but never quite reaching the goal of completeness and consistency.

The Immaterial Structure of Human Experience

countered. Hence the seemingly counterintuitive developments of quantum science. New relations are found. But they do not fit the old.

To reiterate: Up to the point that this transition to a statistical treatment of experience was rendered necessary, an understanding of the structures of physical reality had been following a closely articulated quantitative path. A little fudging of the numbers here and there was covered over by the near approaches of infinitesimals and by an imposition of limits. And, in accordance with this quantitative approach, causal relations had been made to conform to more or less precise mathematical expression.

But now they begin to break down precisely because the numbers do not satisfactorily represent experience.[51] They do not provide a crisp and clearly discernible expression of what is observed by means of the original quantitative and mechanical approach. As a result, anomalies seem to appear in the physical evidence. For the anomalies themselves are mathematical creations and reflect the pitfalls thereof. Thus it is that certainty in both observation and reasoning is undermined. But certainty in terms of experimental result is retained.

In modern science, the mystery of the subdivision of experience is followed down to the atom and beyond. But the atom and its constituent particles is a product of theory formed from indirect observation. Even a plant cell, if it cannot be directly observed with the naked eye, is a product of theory, though it is clearly seen through a microscope. For there is the intervention of the microscope between the object and its image.

---

[51] This is not to say that modern statistical methods at the quantum level are not more precise in result. They are simply less clear in terms of a causal justification.

The production of the image depends upon theories of light. So the object and the image are united by a theory. Even if a cellular structure should be observable through no more than a magnifying glass, but yet not be observable without it, the object and the image would not be closely enough connected in experience to overthrow the present thesis.

In other words, the images are linked to their objects by an intellectual fabrication, no matter how consistent, widely applicable, and effective in prediction the theory may be. This is the case, though both the object and its image are clearly experienced: the one directly, the other indirectly. What is actually perceived as a linkage between them is the consecutive appearance of images in the mind. Independent sensations, or feelings, also accompany them.

Say there is a placing of plant material on a slide under a microscope on a table. The mind experiences this procedure as a series of images and impressions (i.e., percepts of feeling, as in the sensations of touch in handling the slide). Then there is an approaching and adjusting of the microscope until an image of a cell appears beneath it. The approaching and adjusting of the microscope and the image of the cell are also sensations and images brought before the mind.

These sensations and images are certain in experience. For they are what the mind knows directly. But the fact that the various sensations and images reflecting the process and the material are considered to be causally related because they appear in a consistently consecutive manner in the mind, must nonetheless be attributed to theory.

Finally, in returning to a broader consideration of the problem of figure, it should be noted that a liquid takes its figure from the figures to which it is contiguous. These are generally solids.

The Immaterial Structure of Human Experience

But it also takes its figure, or its peculiar flexibility of figure, from its own properties. However, these are properties which are not directly observed (i.e., not observed without instrumentation) and are therefore theoretical. What is directly known is that a liquid behaves in a certain way, retaining a flexible semblance of figure through an internal cohesiveness.

For example, molecular theory is employed to account for water surface tension. It also accounts for water's unique behavior when converting to a solid. But, as water is observed to expand and become a solid, the percepts presented to the mind change. Thus the ice is a different object which has appeared in experience in place of the original. This is so, even when the water is observed to freeze gradually. There is then a gradual replacement.

A gas, such as the air encountered in a wind, is unseen, unless accompanied by solids or liquids, as in smoke or steam. But it is certainly felt. And the fall leaves it purportedly whirls about are seen. It is experienced as a composite of sensations of relative dampness, coolness or warmness, pressure on and abrasion of the skin, even drying of the skin. These, when experienced together, identify it as a physical object, an extension. But it is an extension of conjecture. For determining what kind of extension it is is left to theory.

The human mind seeks correlations: The gas most commonly encountered is air. Is it made up of numerous solids in continual displacement? Or is it an unseen flowing liquid? Modern science has elected atoms and molecules as a means of relating gases to solids and liquids. For science attributes atoms and molecules as building blocks to all three. Thus air is in theory a residue. It is made up of particles of physically or chemically decomposed liquids and solids. And it carries within it a suspension of evaporated water, which is sometimes seen as steam, clouds, and fog. And sometimes it is unseen.

To proceed beyond either direct or indirect representation by an image in the mind, let an empty space be considered. Given the observations concerning solids, liquids, and even gases, all of which are conceived in some manner as extensions—though gas does not have a figure, and liquid does not entirely—it follows that a completely empty space is a figure which takes its shape exclusively from extensions contiguous to it. For it has no internal properties or parts.

An empty space is, in fact, an adjustment in the structure of the phenomenal precipitate made by the human mind. But what the human mind can do regarding it is of course limited by what is presented in the noumenal precipitate. For any contiguous physical extensions are determined in this way.

Nonetheless, given this limitation, the presence of an empty space in the overall structure of the phenomenal precipitate is an adjustment made to account for the not altogether smooth fitting together of the figures of the various extensions, particularly solids, which are composed of percepts and form images in the mind. Remember that figure is determined to a great extent by properties inherent in the object in question. Hence the irregular fit.

In other words, the figures of extensions are determined to some extent simply by the nature of their contiguity with one another in the overall phenomenal precipitate. But, even more precisely, the figures of various extensions are determined by their internal properties. Whereas there are no percepts to convey extension or figure to the character of empty space. Empty space does not exist for perception. It exists only as a construct of the mind, as does space itself. This construct results from a coordina-

The Immaterial Structure of Human Experience

tion of images and independent sensations which is predetermined in the noumenal precipitate.

Figures often do not fit together. Consequently, there is a gap between them. And nothing is perceived in the gap. Thus an absence of a sensation of touch confirms the lack of any visual imagery which would indicate the presence of something within a particular contiguous arrangement. In this way, though devoid of percepts itself, an empty space is bounded by extensions which do have percepts. So the empty space has dimensions derived from its surroundings.

As a consequence of its being bounded on all sides, it has a figure and resembles a physical extension. This must be held to be true of all empty space, in contradiction of the fact that outer space is generally assumed to be unlimited. For it too must be understood by the phenomenal mind as being bounded at some point by contiguous extensions, though they are not observed.

The phenomenal precipitate forming mind cannot imagine it to be otherwise. Though, of course, it can conjecture theoretically that it is otherwise. For anything is possible within the confined logic of a self-contained theory. But what the human mind actually knows is only that there is sensation (or the recognition of percepts and their combination in imagery, to be more exact).

Associated sensations must submit to some form of unity. They must become an extension, a physical or mental object. No extension, not even a bounded empty space, can be accounted for by a complete omission of percepts. However, a bounded empty space is not accounted for by percepts within itself. It is accounted for by the surrounding percepts of physical extensions.

All of what is being asserted here defies the common sense of modern materialism. This is because materialism is founded upon explanations of a deep structure which underlies physical experience. Much of this hypothetical structure remains unobserved until instrumental means, such as a microscope, high frequency rays, or a particle accelerator, are employed.

The workings of these instrumental means are explained by theories. For example, as previously mentioned, there is a theory for the behavior of electromagnetic radiation, which explains x-rays and the microscope. But this theory is itself indirectly confirmed by means of other types of instrumentation, thus leaving the evidence for an interpretation of immediate experience in an increasingly remote darkness.

Why is this important? It is important because consciousness is not considered. It is left out of the theoretical structures. Yet consciousness is by far the most impressive constituent of immediate experience. So it must be accounted for. That is why, in contrast to the indirect intellectual methodology described above—a methodology which avoids any serious consideration of consciousness—an immaterialism founded directly on consciousness is employed in this work.

It cannot be denied that the indirect intellectual methodology founded upon the senses is impressive in its immediate and useful results. But a philosophy of immaterialism possesses the advantage that it relies entirely upon, and is fully inclusive of, direct experience. Accordingly, it limits itself to consciousness, which cannot be overlooked, and to those percepts which are only encountered within consciousness.

The driving reason, the justification, for taking this approach is that, to be fully inclusive of experience is to be more honest. And perhaps in time disparities in present knowledge will be resolved by this more fully inclusive approach. Therefore, one must begin with consciousness, as all things are experienced within it.

The Immaterial Structure of Human Experience

Then and only then does it makes sense to proceed to the experience of the senses.

However, let it be unequivocally affirmed, as stated elsewhere, that none of this argument for immaterialism arises from an attempt to undermine science. Questions in science may often be pursued without regard to a comprehensive philosophy. For science is founded upon the given order of circumstances provided by spirit. Its conclusions rely upon a regularity in these circumstances.

But what the immaterialist philosophy attempts to do is to demonstrate the plausibility of an idea that the universe is ultimately an expression of spirit. For this accords better with the problem of the ever-present experience of consciousness and with the fact that it is the unity of this consciousness in human awareness which makes possible a human apprehension and organization of experience.

There is an additional observation which has not been considered in sufficient detail. It should be done. The observation is about qualities. An example of the problem is expressed in the question, how might a combined color be understood? Kelly green can be described as a yellowish green. So is it one color or two colors?

It is two colors recognized as one. Two color percepts, green and yellow, combine as one color. Yet they are each individual and can be recognized as separate qualities. So they do not lose their individual character. Nevertheless, they are also united in the object and recognized as one quality. In other words, they are two percepts functioning as one.

Significantly, this combination of two different percepts would not alone produce an extension. For it can exist within an extension without any necessary distinction of separate qualities.

Thus it would not produce an extension by itself, since it acts as a single quality. It can only produce an extension with other kinds of percepts, generally those which express qualities which are clearly differentiated from it.

This differentiation is what forms the extension. For an extension is a plurality of qualities. And a plurality cannot be recognized unless the individuals constituting the plurality are apprehended in some degree as individuals. Thus it is multiple qualities brought together in a plurality which is the extension. So the principal reason that the two percepts just mentioned do not form an extension is that they function as one percept of sensation.

As the mind apprehends an extended object exhibiting kelly green, its focus moves back and forth between the two percepts of color, registering green or yellow singly and not simultaneously. Thus the mind understands the one object alternately in two ways, as being either green or yellow, yet not as having two simultaneous colors.

For another example, consider a turquoise stone. Is it blue or green? A person looks hard at the stone in his attempt to answer this question. He generally decides on blue, as this quality seems to exist in it most, both in combination with green and without it. But it is a hard decision. For strong hints of green permeate the stone. And the precise location of their combination with blue is imperceptible.

Science would, of course, refer to these percepts as pigments. But pigments are not directly perceived as such. They are a product of a material interpretation of sensory data. What is directly known is what is in the mind. And what is in the mind are the percepts acting as qualities among associations of percepts which constitute mental and physical extensions, or objects.

The Immaterial Structure of Human Experience

Now it cannot be overlooked that the entire discussion concerning qualities has been partial to what the human mind comes to recognize as its visual sense. Visual representations in the mind are of principal importance to most human beings. So it is generally the case that human beings can be described as visually imaginative creatures. For they do not as a rule think with images of touch or sound. They think with visual images. Thus visual images are the principal ingredients of imaginative representation.

Musicians may beg to differ. Nevertheless, even dedicated musicians use a visual symbolism to record their aural sensations. Thus, if, in their musically creative activities, they are inclined to elevate sounds to a privileged status, imagining them in relation to one another without visual assistance, they nevertheless continue to reveal their underlying visual bias.

Accordingly, it is this unique role of visual images in imaginative representation which justifies the attribution of a special status for them. Such a privileged role elevates visual percepts above the other percepts made available to human sensibility, when in fact all percepts appear in equality in the noumenal precipitate.

So, to restate how a quality generally works: If a piece of wood, undifferentiated along its length, were to be painted two shades of green, the two shades of green would divide the wood into parts, even if its figure did not do so by other means. The piece of wood would be one extension composed of two differently colored extensions: one object in two parts, the two being differentiated by their peculiar shades of green. It is in this way that different qualities of a color, as in the two shades of green, or two or more other distinct qualities, can delineate specific extensions or parts of an extension.

It is for this reason that an artist can create three-dimensional illusions. Were it the case that color itself constituted an extension, rather than demarking an extension by functioning as one of its qualities, this would not be possible. A painter could not use color differentiation to create an illusion of three-dimensional extensions on a two-dimensional canvas. But, in fact, he does.

He does it by juxtaposing different colors or shades of color in ways which imply, or suggest, extended and overlapping figures. For the viewer accepts the quality as belonging to an extension or part of an extension and differentiating it from others. This occurs in spite of the fact that the pictorial illusion cannot be confirmed by any of the viewer's other senses, such as touch. He thus anticipates depth where it does not exist, but where a differentiated color lies.

That is, the differentiated, overlapping colors imply three-dimensional extensions which lie beyond the two-dimensionality of the canvas. When this technique is employed in a consistent manner, it is referred to as a form of perspective, though it may not involve a linear approach to perspective. Rather, it alludes to an imaginary set of displacements in three-dimensional space. Paul Cézanne's use of this technique for developing perspective is particularly notable.

Thus it can be seen that the implied extensions are not physically present where they are made to appear so. This illusion is possible because a particular quality of color is assumed by the viewer not only to belong to an extension or part of an extension, but to be uniform throughout that part. Consequently, where another quality of color appears, another extension is delineated.

There are, of course, different shades of one color. A painter may use white or black with a particular color to create them. Thus, from a painter's point of view, shades are mixtures of two colors. They are, in this sense, like the prior examples of green and yellow or green and blue. But they are considered to be shades of one color, as opposed to a combination of two colors. Of course, when comparing shades of the same color, one could see a relative presence of white or black in them, if one tried. But this is not the accustomed attitude. And attitudes have a lot to do with how colors are perceived.

As a color, it is not assumed that a particular shade of green is a whiter green and another is a blacker green. It is assumed that one shade is a lighter green and another shade is a darker green, which more strongly implies that these shades belong to one color. This is assumed, in spite of the fact that lighter and darker are no more than euphemisms for whiter and blacker.

Similarly again, there are the combinations of colors other than with black and white, such as is found in the green and yellow of kelly green. How then can a distinction be made between shades using black and white, on the one hand, and color combinations using yellow and green or green and blue, on the other hand? It cannot, except by convention. For they are all color combinations.

In regard to shades of one color, there are different combinations of green and white. Or there are combinations of green and black. Moreover, whether the mixture is said to include white or black often depends upon a reference to adjacent hues. For there is something of black or white in most, if not all, hues, rendering them available for such a reference.

In fact, so much are these blends the case, that a percept which is just white, black, green, yellow, red, or blue without an admixture of something else is hard to imagine. A "pure" color, considered strictly for its purity, and not for its saturation, does not exist for discrimination. Rather, a particular array of colors, like the scientific spectrum with its rainbow hues, has simply been chosen as a standard for color purity. And it is so chosen because it has been obtained in a certain way: by experiment accompanied with theory.

Thus, if a particular color is said to exhibit a specific frequency, that is a juxtaposition of the occurrence of a particular perception of color with experimental evidence for a frequency which is encountered in regular association with it. For example, blue refracts in a particular medium, such as glass or water, in a different manner than red or yellow. The way it consistently does so identifies it as having a specific frequency. But were this regularity of appearance between color and frequency removed, the association would become meaningless.

Combinations, such as kelly green, turquoise, or a particular shade of green, are brought together for human awareness in the phenomenal precipitate. However, the combinations are a result of the association of different color percepts in the noumenal precipitate. In other words, if they appear at first unassociated and then subsequently associated in the noumenal precipitate, or at first associated and then unassociated, this will be experienced in the phenomenal precipitate as a mixture of two independent colors. For the same colors are identified both together and apart.

So a painter may blend a particular shade of yellow with a particular shade of green to get kelly green. Or he may mix a particular white with a particular green to get a lighter green tint. Are the original yellows, greens, and whites he employs pure, unmixed percepts? Or are they also combinations?

Since the noumenal precipitate is the final standard of reference, and since it cannot be examined by human intelligence, it would be hard to say. Thus any standard of reference employed

The Immaterial Structure of Human Experience

can only be of an arbitrary character. And this is precisely because the noumenal precipitate cannot be examined.

This unavailability of the transcendent ground of human experience is a universal problem. That is to say, human knowledge is without exception provisional, due to the dependence of any one fragment of knowledge on other human knowledge, which other human knowledge is provisional in the same interdependent way. This unbroken interdependence gives human knowledge a circular character, everything being dependent on everything else.

But knowledge is a product of intellect. Whereas individual percepts are distinct and not interdependent. They only seem indistinct to the human mind when they appear in their relative relationship to one another. For they are most frequently processed in the mind in varying associations.

These associations are further processed in accordance with the conventions of intellect. But, in themselves, percepts are what they are, originating in their fundamental character in the noumenal precipitate. There is always this gulf between the exactness of experience and the vagueness of knowledge.

So color percepts exist in the mind both as individually distinct percepts and as combinations of those same percepts. However, in human experience, particularly in matters of determining hue to an unqualified exactness, it is not possible to ascertain with certainty what the proper character of an individual shade or variety of a color might be. For it is relative to other shades and varieties. And these are combinations of percepts.

46. The human mind. A thought is an extension of mental space. And mental space belongs to that portion of the phenomenal precipitate which the practical mind experiences as subjective. But there is a further qualification concerning a thought. Not only does mental space refer specifically to thinking. It does not refer to feelings or emotions. For feelings and emotions are not extended, as thoughts are, and therefore do not exhibit mental space.

It is the fact that thoughts are associations of percepts which renders them extended. So it is extension which gives them the characteristic of being (or "occupying") mental space. Each thought inhabits its own mental space until another thought replaces it. Thus the entirety of mental space at any moment is one thought. The thought can be an image or a concept.

Now one further observation should be noted. And this is again in regard to qualities. It will be observed, as mentioned in a previous essay, that a sense of the color blue may occupy the entire mind. But here it is a sense of the color which is spoken of, not a thought about it. That is, the color blue may occupy the mind as a pure visual sensation. As such, it is a feeling, apparently bearing no reference to any physical extension. Thus it is not an image and cannot be a mental extension. For it is a direct, unextended impression upon the mind.

Nonetheless, the color blue may, and generally does, act as a quality of an object of thought. In this capacity, it is expressed in an image, a representation of a physical object, imaginary or otherwise, brought under the attention of the mind. Thus there is this kind of flexibility of impressions on the mind. An impression may be a stand-alone percept, which is a feeling. Or it may be included in a composite of qualities in an image.

But the pure visual sensation of blue is not an extension like an imaginative image involving the quality of blue. Both express sensations. The sensations appear before the mind as percepts. But the former is a single percept, which stands alone before the

The Immaterial Structure of Human Experience

mind. Thus it is not a thought. The latter is a percept in association with other percepts. It is therefore composite within an image. It is a thought.

Now, if a person were to closely observe the workings of her own mind, she would see that the pure visual sensation of blue was first called to her mind as part of a more complex representation, perhaps the image of a blue sky. It was then subsequently abstracted from this reference.

In other words, mental focus removed all other content, translating a multi-sensational representation into a single sensation. In this way, a thought, which is a complex association of percepts, is reduced to one percept. It is accomplished by the mind's placing its focus upon that one percept. [52]

But circumstances are not so in the physical realm. In the physical realm, all directly observable phenomena are, as images in the mind, gathered into composites of percepts, or extensions. And all such extensions are understood to be physical. Thus there are no single percepts which are acknowledged by the practical mind as subsisting in the physical realm.

That is why it is said by some material thinkers that objects in the physical world are initially perceived as objects. Their qualities are not perceived independently and then combined into objects. Rather, as they understand it, the qualities are first discovered and identified in previously apprehended physical objects.

---

[52] As is stated periodically throughout this work, the discussion largely devotes itself to a representational theory of mind. But it should always be understood that an immaterialist perspective shifts the emphasis from the individual human mind to the realm of spirit, whence all phenomena originate. Thus the human mind's focus is, in fact, a determination of spirit. And this determination is expressed in the noumenal precipitate, where the character of mental focus is laid out, as it were, in advance of phenomenal awareness.

However, this argument belies the fragmentary character of sensory input, which sensory faculty they must nevertheless insist upon. For, even if a physical object were held to exist completely intact in its independence of the perceiving mind, that mind would still have to put sensory pieces together to get a whole image of it.

Those pieces would be the percepts. To perceive an object, the mind would have to re-associate the percepts (the supposed sensory impressions) within itself as an image. In other words, the mind would have to recreate physical reality in order to perceive it. This is a redundancy which cannot be demonstrably supported. Hence one of the many reasons for the immaterialist argument.

Nevertheless, though it is true that any composite perception must be rendered composite in the mind, physical objects do appear to be more rigorously arrayed relative to one another in the physical realm. Physical objects are extensions. And the rigorous relationship of these extensions is that of a contiguous, mutually limiting character.

This results in a fidelity of parts to the whole which resists the intervention of an individual human will. That is why the physical realm is experienced as being independent of the mind. And it is also why a three-dimensional space is posited to encompass all that is physical. Space itself is extension. It is a composite of extensions. Thus contiguity and mutual limitation of extensions compose the greater structure of space.

There are no independent percepts in the physical realm. So an experience of the color blue is confined to an extension. An extension is a composite of percepts. Thus the mental representation of blue will exhibit it as a quality of an object. Nevertheless,

The Immaterial Structure of Human Experience

it remains the case that a physical object can only be known to the mind as an image.

The confinement of the color blue to an object, either in physical or mental space, results from the fact that the practical human mind cannot register a solitary percept of blue as something to be objectively experienced, either as a physical object or as an object of thought (which resembles a physical object). It is only when the percept is to be subjectively experienced for itself, and not in relation to an object, that the mind can do so.

Consequently, blueness in its individual character cannot exist independently in physical space. Nor can it exist independently of its object in the mind's representation of that object. For either circumstance would make a single percept a physical object or a mental representation of an object.

Since as a single percept blue is a feeling, it is unextended and cannot be a quality of a physical object or a thought. The need for it to be a quality of an extension is the reason that, in the less flexible physical realm, it is always a quality of some object. In the more flexible mental realm, on the other hand, it may be singled out for mental awareness. For a feeling alone, without reference to an extension of thought, can be a focus of mental awareness.

So, as it was in a previous essay, let it again be assumed that the color blue might be experienced as an all-pervasive presence. Just blue in the mind. This is the manner in which a blue sky may be imagined to be experienced by a parachutist shortly after his leaving an aircraft at high altitude, assuming he does not look down at the ground or up at the aircraft or at any clouds. But the blue he experiences is not truly all-pervasive. It is still a quality of the sky which, however expansive and all-encompassing to the parachutist, is a finite physical entity. The sky is an object.

In other words, the sky is a physical extension: an object bounded by other objects—ground, horizon, clouds, and whatever might be assumed to lie above it in this case. If the parachutist were to look down at the distant ground, he would experience this limitation. He would acknowledge that the sky had a boundary.

Thus he would assume other boundaries, completing its finitude as an extension. And, because he could see that the seemingly all-pervasive blue he experiences is, in fact, a quality of a bounded object, he would know that this blue is a quality of something which is subject to measure.

The reason the color blue is subject to measure is that the sky is subject to measure. The color extends only as far as the sky does. It characterizes the extension of which it is a quality. The blue is expressive of the sky extension and not of some other extension. It is in the sky and not in the ground. So its measure is the measure of the extension of which it is a quality.

That is the reason why the blue quality of a physical extension is less flexible than a pure mental experience of blue can be. The quality of the former cannot truly occupy the entire mind in the way the latter can. Not even if it seems that way. For, to do so, it must be entirely without reference to limitation.

Whereas the extent to which it seems that way is the extent to which it appears to have been converted from a quality to a pure sensation. But if the conversion is incomplete, if the mind knows better, if it knows the sensation is a quality of the sky, the sensation is definitively contained.

As in the case of the pure sensation of blue, a human being can imagine the all-pervasiveness of a quality of blue, if no evidence to the contrary is admitted by the mind. For then it in effect becomes a pure sensation of blue. But, inasmuch as it remains a

The Immaterial Structure of Human Experience

quality, it belongs to something physical. So it is not held in the mind as a pure sensation.

A blue sky can be experienced as unlimited only when the imaginative representation of it is reduced to a single sensation, or feeling, and it no longer references a sky. But then it is not an imaginative representation. It is a pure sensation, a feeling. And it is not expressive of limitation. It is "seen" because the visual sensation is a feeling of blue.

But, if physically or mentally it remains a quality, it is necessarily limited. It is seen as pertaining to an object. Anything that is an object is limited. And anything that is limited is quantifiable. That is why the blue of the sky is held to be quantitative, like everything else in the physical world.

But emotions are more complex than feelings. So, although they are composed of a sequential coalescence of feelings, they must be examined in a different light. As being composed of feelings, they are intimate and personal. In fact, they are so closely associated with the general experience of being human, they are often confused with a sense of self. "I am happy" can appear to mean "My entire self is suffused with happiness." For this reason, it is more difficult to ferret out the precise character of emotions than it is to define feelings.

Emotions present the most complicated form of an object of human awareness to be brought under any sort of definition. They are a coalescence of individual feelings which appear before the mind in sequence and not simultaneously. Yet the coalescence associates them as one in experience. Nonetheless, they are not compound, as thoughts and material objects are compound.

Accordingly, since emotions are not compound, they are not thoughts (concepts or images). They do not occur as a mental space. Nor are they physical objects expressing physical space. The color blue, which has already been mentioned, is a quality which can, from a strictly mental point of view, be labeled a feeling. But take the emotion which is joy. Joy is not a feeling in this sense. It is an emotion, which is a coalescence of feelings: elation, fulfillment, optimism, etc.

These feelings do not include those which might also function as qualities, like the color blue. For qualities can be objective. And the components of an emotion are strictly subjective. Nevertheless, like the color blue, an emotion does have the power of independently filling the whole mind. Or it can be experienced as accompanying, one might even say blending with, a thought or an act, without being a constituent element of either.

This latter characteristic is a result of the fact that emotions often accompany thoughts and acts somewhat in the manner that qualities accompany extensions. But emotions do not contribute to either the extension of a thought or to those physical extensions which make up the circumstances of an act. Nevertheless, they can be experienced almost as if they were an integral part of either of these two types of extensions. Though they blend differently with each of them.

So, in reference to the character of emotions, it must be said that they behave somewhat in the manner of qualities. But emphasis must be placed upon the term "somewhat." For there are caveats. Because both thoughts and emotions take place in the mind, a person can experience a joyful thought involving such a close association between the emotion and the thought, that it can be hard for her to distinguish their separate occurrence. The emotion can, in effect, act as an attribute of the thought, as though it were a quality included within the thought extension.

The Immaterial Structure of Human Experience

However, it is not quite the same when emotions accompany actions. For emotions accompany acts in a different way. They persist in remaining separate from those physical extensions which collectively define any act. This is due to the illusive veil which falls between subjectivity and objectivity.

In other words, emotions are experienced as occurring in the mind, while acts are experienced as occurring in the physical realm. Nevertheless, through this veil a vague sense of connection is made. It is not strong enough to resemble a quality. But the emotion does closely insinuate itself into the circumstances of the act.

In contradistinction to this is the matter of emotion to emotion. Here there is no resemblance to either of the aforementioned cases. Emotions do not associate as closely with one another as they do with thoughts and acts. One emotion can only appear in the most casual way to be experienced as accompanying another emotion, such as in the case of the emotion of joy appearing to be accompanied by the emotion of gratitude.

This appearance is due to a lack of attention being paid to the manner in which these emotions are experienced. It can be described as an oversight. For, insofar as any two emotions are concerned, there is a pointed relationship of independence between them. Each is isolated from the other in articulation.

Each is felt distinctly. So upon close scrutiny, it will be observed that, rather than arising simultaneously in the mind, the two distinct emotions are experienced alternately in a close sequence like intermittent links in a chain, much as the individual feelings which coalesce into a particular emotion are. But in the latter case, the sequence is so rapid and integrated as to coalesce into the one emotion. Whereas, in the former case, the separate emotions are not as rapid in sequence and therefore do not coalesce.

Separate emotions never appear simultaneously in the mind. That is to say, there is no means by which they can be considered to be contiguous to one another in a single mental expression, like two apples in a thought image. Nor can one emotion function as a property of another, since neither is a set of percepts which can be combined into the property of an extension. Only an extension, like a thought or a physical object, can have qualities. And only an extension can take on properties.

Rather than being extended, emotions are a sequential coalescence of feelings. Specific elements in such a sequence may reappear in that same sequence numerous times. But the feelings remain discrete within the emotion. So the emotion is not extended in mental space, as a thought is. Nor is it extended in physical space as an object is.

The same is true of multiple emotions. They appear before the mind in a sequence. Thus a close sequence of two emotions is proximate in time, while remaining sequential. And, only if each emotion is steadily repeated in the mind in an alternating fashion, can the two emotions appear, albeit falsely, to that human mind to be simultaneous in experience. For this is not even a coalescence of the two emotions.

However, there is one peculiar type of arrangement by which several emotions may be understandably mistaken for a compound emotion. An emotion can take part in an association of several emotions held together by a concept, such as occurs with the concept of duty when it embraces the emotions of loyalty, fear, and determination. But this seeming compound of emotions is not itself an emotion. In fact, it would be better referred to as

The Immaterial Structure of Human Experience

an attitude. For here the governing mental object is the concept of duty, which ties the several emotions together.

But this apparent compounding of several emotions by means of a concept is, to say the least, a unity of challenging complexity. For while the images supporting a concept can stand before the mind as pluralities of percepts, emotions cannot be expressed together as such a plurality. They are intimately linked to a concept by the power of that concept to evoke them individually, as that concept stands before the mind. But they are only linked to one another sequentially through time. Thus they cannot appear before the mind simultaneously with one another.

In other words, emotions are not extended. Thus they cannot be properties embedded in a concept. Nor can they join together as though they were a compound of images supporting the concept. They cannot present themselves to the mind as a compound of emotions. Though it remains true that they can individually present themselves in a linked appearance with the concept, which evokes them one at a time in alternating sequence.

For example, the concept of duty may, as has been indicated, call up emotions of loyalty, fear, and determination. So the attitude is the linking of these emotions with the concept. It is the emotions *and* the concept. Thus the attitude is not the concept alone. Nor are the emotions compounded together in the way the percepts of a physical object or thought are. For the individual emotions of loyalty, fear, and determination remain independent and sequential in articulation. Nevertheless, they are each individually linked to the concept of duty, thus collectively forming an associative unity with that concept.

So that is why it must be said that such an association of emotions by means of a concept uniting them to itself is only loosely referred to as an emotion. It is in truth a general attitude.

Nevertheless, like the feelings of an emotion, the emotions of this attitude may, by means of short-term memory, impress themselves upon the mind as an entirety. [53]

In other words, at some point the mind appears to be aware of the full implication of the attitude of duty. For there is sequential recall of the emotional elements of that duty. This sequence along with the concept is subsumed under an enlargement of mental focus. But, to be precise, the concept at the heart of the attitude is what is consistently before the mind, not the emotions.

The situation becomes yet more complex. For this attitude involving a concept and several emotions may appear to be accompanied by other emotions as well, such as joy or antipathy or an anticipation of either. Consequently, due to such a varied complexity of the attitude and its accompanying array of mental impressions, it can be hard to focus the mind's attention sufficiently to see that no one of the emotions or feelings involved appears simultaneously with any of the others before the mind.

Thus this law of the mind, as it were, a law of alternating sequence as regards feelings and emotions, can encompass an increasingly large array of emotions and feelings. In this way, an emotion of joy or antipathy can be associated with the attitude of duty along with the other emotions already mentioned. In fact, a number of such emotions or feelings may be appended.

Though the number cannot be so great as to dilute the effect of the principal emotions. For, though associated with the attitude, any additional emotions and feelings like these may be deemed not integral to an attitude's primary expression. Howev-

---

[53] It is important to recall that memory itself is a repetition of impressions upon the mind. Since feelings in an emotion are a repetition, emotions in an attitude are a repetition, and short-term memory is a repetition of these repetitions, this involves a complex redundancy of repetitions.

The Immaterial Structure of Human Experience

er, they do increase the complexity of the mind's experience of the attitude. And due to the felt unity of this experience as a whole, the mind mistakenly understands itself to be experiencing something like a blending of numerous mental impressions into one.

Reverting now to a discussion of individual emotions, it might be asked, how does emotional intensity occur? That is to say, how is the intensity of an emotion presented to the mind strictly in terms of percepts and disregarding any physiological explanation? The short response would be that varying degrees of emotional intensity are experienced as a result of an iterative process.

At greater length, it can be explained that the overall effect of the varying intensities of a lingering emotion is not the work of the differentiated feelings which compose that emotion, when their percepts are considered individually. For the individual percepts of a particular feeling are indistinguishable from one another as percepts. There is but one kind of such percept for each feeling.

So it is rather the case that the variations in intensity result from a cumulative effect among percepts of each kind. The word "cumulative," as opposed to "collective," is chosen to express this relationship because the effect of increasing or decreasing intensity is achieved over time and not in simultaneity.

How is the effect achieved? In several related ways. If a significant number of percepts of all the feelings associated with one emotion appear in alternating sequence without a break, or without much of a break, and with the breaks not occurring often, a greater intensity of the emotion will be experienced than would be the case if the breaks were of a longer duration or occurred more frequently.

A break would have been caused by the appearance before the mind of any percepts of a feeling which are unrelated to the emotion in question. Or the break might occur because the emotion is set aside by a focus upon a train of images of perception, imaginative images, or thoughts. Anything which distracts the mind from a recognition of the feelings associated with an emotion for a sufficient duration of time would constitute a break.

Conversely, a buildup in the experience of an emotion is particularly intense if the emotion is both persistent in avoiding long breaks and extensive in duration between any breaks which should occur. In other words, it is the case if the breaks are brief, far apart, or both. It is also true if the emotion continues for some time.

This is so because an uninterrupted, or little interrupted, frequency increases the effect of intensity—i.e., it increases a person's awareness of the feelings and emotion. And a long duration increases a person's sense of having continuously undergone the feelings and emotion. Thus the combination increases the overall intensity and impact of an emotion.

On the other hand, too many short breaks in the sequence of percepts of the various feelings associated with any one emotion will lessen the intensity, not only of the feelings, but of the emotion as a whole. This is generally caused by the frequent passing of the percepts of other feelings or emotions before the mind, when they occur between incidents of the original percepts in question.

Thus a lessening in the intensity of the entire original emotion, with its pattern of feelings, is caused by such interruptions. It occurs when all the feelings involved in that particular emotion undergo these interruptions. But, even if only one of those feelings were to undergo such interruptions, it would alter and could

The Immaterial Structure of Human Experience

destroy the overall emotion. For the emotion is the expression of its full complement of feelings.

In extreme cases, a prolonged duration of any interruption of all or some of the feelings belonging to an emotion will discontinue any sense of continuity of the emotion. On the other hand, breaks in the sequence of percepts of all the feelings characterizing an emotion, should they occur neither too often nor too rarely, and should they be neither too large nor too small, will create a continuous, moderately varying, middle range intensity of that emotion.

Much has been said here about the sequential character of feelings in their role of producing an emotion. So it should also be emphasized that, contrary to the manner in which they appear in the phenomenal precipitate, contiguous physical objects are not unlike feelings and emotions in the manner in which they are initially recognized by the mind. For they are not truly experienced in a simultaneous manner either.

Rather, human awareness constructs the contiguity of physical objects in space, creating an illusion of simultaneity. But the fact that physical objects are initially displayed before the mind sequentially is amply illustrated by the flow of percepts and associations of percepts in the noumenal precipitate. This sequential flow is due to the mind's limited powers of awareness, which reduce it to an exercise of focus.

Focus confines the mind to a temporal experience. In fact, temporality implies sequence. Thus the human mind does not perceive many things at once, but in sequence, moving from a small range of focus to another small range of focus. Consequently, this may seem like a contradiction regarding statements asserting that the mind grasps a unity of percepts as an extension and multiple such unities as physical space.

But it is not a contradiction. For, as stated from the beginning of this work, there is a mechanism of translation which renders both interpretations possible. Within the noumenal precipitate there is a process of repeating associations of percepts within a repeated context of other associations of percepts.

This is what establishes the contiguity and permanence of place among physical extensions in the phenomenal precipitate. For the phenomenal precipitate, by means of imagination and intellect, employs this feature to establish contiguity and a buildup of a sense of physical space in human experience.

That is why physical objects, when apprehended in daily experience, are not generally recognized in the minute terms of their individual percepts. Such a process, if it were to occur on a regular basis, would be arduous and time-consuming and not conducive to an effective human response to experience. So how physical objects are approached by the mature human mind may be roughly illustrated as follows.

If a person sees an automobile from one side, she observes only the features of that one side. The rest of the car remains out of her line of vision. And this results from the order in which percepts are presented in the noumenal precipitate. First, it may be the percepts for the headlights and front bumper which are presented. Then percepts for the fender and front tire appear, etc.

But even this side portion of the car is not seen in detail. For the observer, by virtue of the generality of her vision, cannot be aware of every dent and ding on that part of the car. So her immediate knowledge of what she sees is inevitably limited in any one sighting. Either the sighting covers much with less detail. Or it covers less with more detail.

But should she choose to observe exact detail, she must focus on a very small portion of the car. For details can only pass

The Immaterial Structure of Human Experience

through her mind one at a time. If she should choose to note a relationship between two things, the process will be the same. She will limit her observation detail by detail to what joins the two things. So, whatever she does, the focus of her mind limits what passes before it.

Though the focus may appear to be her own, responding to variations in her will at the material level of her awareness, it is, in fact, determined by what secondary mind presents to her awareness in response to the once and for all instantaneous act of her spiritual will. It is in this way that, certain associations of percepts (i.e., certain objects), having become familiar in her experience, are subsequently grasped in their entirety by only a few details. Those few details are sufficient for the whole to be recognized.

Thus it can be seen that the physical objects of the phenomenal precipitate are not fleshed out in a concrete grid work of space, as might be imagined. For the phenomenal precipitate presents a process to the mind, not a fully realized construct. It is never whole and complete. It is always undergoing construction and modification.

Yet such is the consistency of spirit in presenting experience to the mind through the percepts of the noumenal precipitate, that any attempt to deliberately examine this experience in detail, as it would appear in a fully realized phenomenal precipitate, would complete the grid work of the precipitate in proper order up to that moment.

If this were not so, no anticipation of future circumstances would be possible. For it must be based upon an assessment of past experience. It is this continuity and appropriateness of integration in the flow of percepts in the noumenal precipitate which makes interaction between a person and her world feasible. Thus experience is always made full. For the noumenal precipitate will, at every point, meet the demands of experience with the appropriate percepts and associations of percepts.

In other words, having seen what is on the right, a person turning left will see what is on the left because the noumenal precipitate will have immediately supplied the percepts both for the turning and for whatever is on the left. Turning back to the right, the percepts for the right will be resupplied.

So, again, a few impressions upon the mind may be sufficient to call to mind a whole range of them, as contained in an object. Under a material interpretation, this might, of course, be said to involve memory. The person encounters a few details and remembers the whole. But, when understood in terms of the noumenal precipitate, the memory is nothing more than that precipitate's responsiveness in meeting the demands of its own buildup of circumstance.

In other words, it is spirit which supplies experience to the human mind, should that experience involve the apparent making of a decision or should it involve a simple reliance on memory. The noumenal precipitate will rise to every such occasion, supplying the percepts and associations of percepts needed. For the human will is located neither in the noumenal nor the phenomenal precipitates. It is grounded in spirit itself. Thus it is from spirit that the order of experience is put forth.

However, human awareness, especially in maturing years, experiences itself as existing in the midst of the phenomenal precipitate. It is convinced that this is so. Thus the development of the phenomenal precipitate, with its spatial features and its features of incremental time, becomes the character of human experience.

The Immaterial Structure of Human Experience

These features influence awareness. For a sense of space creates the sense of a physical self and its placement in that physical space. Physical space, with its complement of change, renders time incremental. This time can be physically measured by means of a comparison of relative changes in physical extensions. So incremental time, in turn, creates an articulated before and after. As a result, the human mind consistently appears to recall the past into the present.

This apparent recall function is memory. So, since memory seems to be involved in any person's awareness of her experience, she is inclined to rely upon memory for a portion of that experience. Thus she finds herself in the midst of the phenomenal precipitate, the material realm, which is understood as the immediate ground of experience.

But, in fact, memory is simply one of many phenomena to be discovered in the way the phenomenal precipitate is constructed. It is associated with incremental time, subjectivity, and the self. And without this incremental time, this subjectivity, and this sense of self, it would not exist for the mind. So it must be said in truth that memory belongs to the precipitates, deriving its origin from an orderly noumenal presentation of percepts to the mind and discovering its function as memory in the reworking of that noumenal presentation in the phenomenal precipitate.

The initial construction of the phenomenal precipitate is accomplished by a child. For it is the child who may be said to create the structure of her own experience of the world in phenomenal terms, however much this may ultimately be dependent on the noumenal stream of percepts. Thus, however rudimentary and imaginative it may be, the origin of the phenomenal precipitate early in human awareness is what makes human experience a construction involving human participation.

It supplies the sense of a memory of the past, which allows for a unique present, and a future—in short, a personal history.

But this building of the phenomenal precipitate in early childhood might appear again to imply a preexisting function of memory. For how can a person construct something, if she does not remember where she placed the initial building blocks? So it would seem that memory is one of the ways in which a child constructs the phenomenal precipitate.

In this light, it would appear that the development of a memory both influences and follows from her experience. In fact, one does not precede the other. Memory comes into existence simultaneously with the articulation of experience. It is in this way that her experience seems increasingly to surround her.

So, however early its development within the phenomenal precipitate, memory is itself a part of the phenomenal precipitate. It is constructed with it. As percepts are presented to the child by the noumenal precipitate, those of memory included, and, as she works them into her vision of reality in the phenomenal precipitate, she experiences herself as existing in the midst of them.

Constructing some portions of the phenomenal precipitate, while being shaped by others already constructed by her, her mind becomes increasingly enclosed within the structure. Thus she comes to see the process as one of discovery on her part. She discovers her world and, in the midst of it, her memory.

She is involved in the construction of the phenomenal precipitate from the materials presented to her by the noumenal precipitate. But, more importantly, she herself, her decisions, her actions, and her participation in the formation of the phenomenal precipitate, are a part of the development of the phenomenal from a noumenal origin. For all, in the final analysis, is the work of spirit.

The Immaterial Structure of Human Experience

47. Because the concept of energy is a measure of material change, it can only be predicated of the material domain. Within the circumstances of material experience, it must be held that energy is no more than a concept for the measurement of change. Thus energy, as an experiential entity in its own right, does not exist. For it is merely a conceptual apparatus for measuring what does exist, namely change.

In contrast, the dynamic of universal spirit cannot be thought of in terms of energy. For it cannot be reduced to relations of change in any way resembling those of material experience. Rather, it may be imaginatively (but no more than imaginatively) conceived as a system in which a thing and its change exist together. Thus it cannot be understood in terms of material experience, in which change involves the replacement of one phenomenal circumstance by another.

The inner workings of spirit are concealed from human awareness. For spirit is the realm of the infinite, or not finite, as opposed to the finite. Accordingly, the infinite is not accessible to a finite mind, other than as represented by the inscrutable mystery of pure consciousness. For pure consciousness, considered only in itself, is without limit and indivisible. These are the characteristics of spirit. Nevertheless, when human consciousness is considered in terms of its content, nothing is revealed concerning the origin of that content. The content exhibits a limited character and nothing more.

On the other hand, because the content of human consciousness exhibits a limited character, it is clearly manifested in terms of finitude. But, since the origin of this content and its finitude is not clear, changes in the content must be understood in terms of something outside its domain. This is the dynamic of universal spirit. For the spiritual dynamic, involving change without replacement, supplies an unlimited potential to the ever-changing actual of the material realm. Without this unseen potential, the actual could not change.

Moreover, as the phrase "unlimited potential" suggests, the spiritual dynamic's domain of possibility is much greater than the material realm's domain of the actual. Thus the spiritual dynamic may be imagined to be so complex that, were it possible for it to be accessible to human analysis, no apparent change within it could be brought under the limited circumstances necessary for submitting it to any kind of measure.

This arises from the fact that change without replacement can be subdivided into ever so minute increments in a progression towards recognizable change. Consequently, a thing and its change become one. The change and its change become one. Etc. So such subdivision indicates an integrated unity which is seamless. And there is no means of determining the limits of where one thing ends and another begins. Yet these are the requirements of finitude and thus of material measure.

Hence no determinate concept, like that of energy, can be applied to spirit. For measurable change, the source of the concept of energy, is only conceivable within a finite relational system. That is, it is only conceivable within a system composed of finite entities. The fact that energy is a measure of material change arises from the fact that there is something finite to provide the basis of comparison which is required in the exercise of making a measurement.

48. Change is ultimately seamless within material experience. In human experience there are no discernible increments in change, just as there are no precise increments in the measure of

The Immaterial Structure of Human Experience

time, which is based on that change. One may choose one state of an event and compare it to another state of the same event, such as a comparison between the two states in a physical transformation of water into ice. And one may observe that they are marked by a difference: water is liquid, ice solid.

But the process of change from one state to the next, like the transition from one moment to another in time, is seamless to observation. So it should be asked, exactly when can it be understood that water becomes ice? In which moment might this occur? Or at what point has a sufficient portion of the water made the transition? At an observable point, no doubt. But at precisely what point does the change become observable?

The same can be said concerning an explosion of gunpowder, the consumption of a log in a fire, or the change of uranium into lead. Overall change can be measured at any point, but not the exact moment or location of its occurrence. For human observation and understanding, there is always an element of imprecision, so that an identification of change cannot be exact. Thus to consider a precise increment of change is no more than to offer up an arbitrary isolation of a phenomenon for the sake of convenience in observation and analysis.

49. Change and the spiritual dynamic. As stated in previous entries, in an immaterialist philosophy there can be no such thing as energy. For what are presented to the mind are percepts (perceptions, or impressions on the mind), extensions composed of percepts, and changes in the character or context of these extensions. So there is only the measurement of change. Thus the concept of work is no more than a practical way of describing change.

The concept of energy, or force, is a quantitative way of accounting for it. The concept of energy takes cognizance of proportion in change. That is its purpose as a concept. These statements have profound implications for understanding the difference between primary and secondary mind. For none of them has relevance to the relations of primary mind.

Primary mind is spirit. It is all-encompassing and universal. This is to say that all of material reality emanates from it. Spirit not only originates, but permeates the character of all things. Secondary mind is self-limiting primary mind. Thus it is also spirit, but under a transformation. Its immediate expression is in the terms of a non-incremental stream of time.

Focus, the principal limiting characteristic of secondary mind, is the cause of the sequencing of percepts in non-incremental time. Thus it brings about the human need to recognize and express limitation. For the sequencing of percepts in non-incremental time determines the human mind's segmented approach to experience. It is this which informs the buildup of the fundamental structure of the phenomenal precipitate in terms of finite entities.

As a result of this sequencing of percepts, non-incremental time becomes the source of alterations in the relations of objects in space. That is, by means of non-incremental time, one association of percepts is made to follow another in the noumenal precipitate. These associations of percepts become individual objects both in mental recognition and in physical experience. They constitute the phenomenal precipitate.

Appearing in sequence with variation, they become the changes and movements of mental and physical objects. For the variations in them and in their relationship to one another become events. And events are a product of change. That is to say,

The Immaterial Structure of Human Experience

changes are interpreted as events, be they considered as occurring within or without the mind.

An example of variation in an object would be chemical or physical change. An example of variation in the relationship of one object to another is motion. Of course, chemical and physical changes are motions, since there is a displacement of qualities or properties within them. This displacement is the meaning of the word motion.

At an early stage of human awareness, change is merely experienced. It is not understood. But, by means of incremental time, the recognition of which follows upon the experience of change, one state of things is understood to follow another. With increased experience, the human mind seeks to identify proportion in these occurrences. This is the recognition of measure in change. Hence the concepts of energy and work are born of measure. They are derived from an observance of quantitative relations between physical objects and between different states of those objects.

Proportion is an orderly expression of limitation. Without its development in human awareness, human existence could not have arrived at its present condition. But primary mind, or universal spirit, is not confined to such a limited and fragmented sense of reality. Rather, primary mind is a spiritual dynamic, which can only be understood by human beings when it is imagined to subsist independently of any precipitate.

This difference is due to the fact that the noumenal precipitate can only be said to describe the activity of secondary mind. It is an activity which is immediately prior to, and foundational to, the formation of the phenomenal precipitate. (This is to say that it is logically, not temporally, prior.) So, though it is yet within the domain of spirit and thus outside the domain of a mature material awareness, it does not refer to primary mind.

Rather, it pertains to a "process" lending itself toward a material awareness. It is delineated by percepts. And these are experienced as harbingers of finitude. Thus, being composed of finite entities undergoing change, the noumenal precipitate fosters a system of operations. These arise from the working of focus in non-incremental time and the logically subsequent working of focus in incremental time as well.

Primary mind, on the other hand, is universal spirit. Represented to the human mind as the experience of pure consciousness alone—the finitude of percepts and their combinations being set aside and not pertaining to it—it appears to human sensibility as devoid of any content whatsoever.

Thus, as a spiritual dynamic which is prior to both limitation and change, which are recognized in the noumenal and phenomenal precipitates alone, primary mind can only be imagined as self-sustaining and opaque to the human mind. For its manner of proceeding cannot be conceptualized.

All concepts merely point to it as that unity which bears a relationship to the unity of pure human consciousness. In fact, it *is* the unity of pure human consciousness. For there is but one spirit, simultaneously manifesting itself in one universal consciousness and in innumerable limited states of consciousness.

It is this unity which makes the formation of mental images and concepts possible. For, without a prior sense of unity, these mental operations could not occur. The perception and organization of experience would not be feasible. In addition to these distinctions, and taking note of the fact that all experience of the material world is mental, it can be seen that primary mind, in the form of self-limiting secondary mind, must encompass the whole

The Immaterial Structure of Human Experience

of material experience for any one human being and for all sentient beings collectively.

Now both image formation and conceptualization are rendered possible by the intuition of simple unity, which is derived from the unity of spirit. Because of the limitation of mental activity which is set by secondary mind, focus is the mode of activity which this intuition of simple unity takes. Or, to state the point conversely, the intuition of simple unity is a mode of activity which is focus. They are essentially one and the same.

It is by means of focus that concepts of the material world are formed. But, since focus is an expression of the limiting role of secondary mind, these concepts are confined to an articulation of finitude. For this reason, there can be no concepts which adequately describe the internal workings of spirit. Consequently, its relations, whatever they may be, cannot be definitively grasped by the limitations of the human intellect.

So, when the mind is looking upon spirit, or attempting to do so, the occluded nature of its lens results from the fact that human awareness is a product of the faculty of focus. Focus blocks awareness of the character of spirit, allowing only a pure consciousness to pass through. But this human awareness of pure consciousness does not grasp the comprehensiveness and complexity of the universal spirit which that consciousness reflects. For such an insight cannot be an expression of the limited human mind.

Thus it is the sense of limitation in unity, or the intuition of simple unity—i.e., focus—which acts as a screen. For this intuition, which is focus, is necessary to the development of human knowledge. Focus articulates material experience. But it does not reveal what the origin for the percepts of that experience might be. The percepts simply appear within consciousness.

50. Indeterminate change and free will. As self-limiting spirit, or secondary mind, spirit precipitates the phenomenal world, which is material. Accordingly, it can be said that the finite emanates from the infinite. On the one hand, when considered within itself, the spiritual dynamic is indeterminate change. For it is infinite. On the other hand, when the finite limitations of the precipitates are considered, there is determinate change.

The indeterminant cannot be known from the perspective of the determinant. So, from the perspective of the precipitates, the spiritual dynamic presents itself as an external source for change. This source is easily overlooked. And, when that is the case, such change as occurs within the precipitates appears to be determinate. For it is mistakenly understood to be arising from material relations alone.

Now, when the spiritual dynamic and its precipitates are considered not separately, but together as a whole, as though they were a single, integrated unity, that all-encompassing unity may be held to be neither exclusively determinate nor exclusively indeterminate. For both conditions are expressed within it.

Thus arises a world made known to thoughtful human sensibility. It is a realm exhibiting characteristics which are both causal and free. And it is the free characteristics which cannot be incontrovertibly explained, since every attempt to do so must employ a matter and manner of thinking which is drawn from the causal characteristics of the material.

Matters of spirit are otherwise than those concerning the realm of the finite. The finite appears causal and therefore determined in its integrated relations. But the indeterminate process of change in the spiritual dynamic characterizes a realm of limitless potential. That is what the spiritual dynamic is: a realm of limit-

The Immaterial Structure of Human Experience

less potential. In other words, where no possibility has been determined, all possibility exists.

That is why the spiritual dynamic is understood to be a limitless potential. No limits can be placed by the human mind upon its range of possibilities. Though such limits may appear to be deducible from the determined relations of the phenomenal precipitate, they cannot be guaranteed.

But there is a caveat which must be considered when speaking of the spiritual dynamic. It is that ordinary terms rendered appropriate within a material context are easily misemployed in a spiritual context. Thus, in regard to the spiritual realm, the apparent suggestion of motion in the word "change" can only be considered to be illustrative.

For change within the spiritual dynamic is not something which can be interpreted as a product of energy. That is to say, such change as takes place in spirit is not an expression of those mensurable proportions which underlie the concept of energy. In fact, the concept of energy has no function whatsoever in spiritual matters. For this reason, the spiritual dynamic is not to be understood as an expression of energy.

Energy implies material change, such as is found in physical motion. However, the word "material" encompasses more than the physical. It refers to the full realm of the phenomenal precipitate, which includes both the physical and thought. It also refers to impressions on the mind which are neither, such as those feelings which are not incorporated in extensions.

Thoughts are included in the phenomenal precipitate because human thoughts and their succession in the human mind are extended and limited, or finite. Thus their succession one after the other is as material as is a change from water to ice or the change of locations discovered in the motion of any physical object.

Thought, physical change, and motion are all material in the sense that they either exhibit or involve extension within the phenomenal precipitate. Extension implies a division into isolated entities, which are not fluid in relation to one another.

But the spiritual dynamic is not material. Since it is a single unity which is indivisible, unbounded, and infinite (i.e., not finite), it does not express extension in the material sense. For material extensions, though temporally and spatially coordinated, are not integrated in the fluid manner of spirit. They are understood as self-enclosed and independent of one another.

The integrated workings of spirit are permeable in reflection of one another and of the whole. They do remain individual. But, though it is true that these elements work together as though separate, they are one. So internal changes in spirit do not take place in the manner of a precipitate. Rather, the spiritual dynamic is extraneous and prior to the precipitates, which latter are derived from the spiritual dynamic's self-limiting character as secondary mind.[54]

Now let the human mind's place within the phenomenal precipitate be considered. This perspective is cut off from spirit. Here the concrete elements of human experience are all limited. They are the individual percepts and the compounded ones forming the extensions of the phenomenal precipitate. Accordingly, it can easily be observed that the human sense of its own limitation is a product of the precipitates. For the human mind observes itself within the relations of the phenomenal precipitate alone.

---

[54] As previously stated, to assert such things as this about spirit is purely speculative. But it does provide a convenient means of illustrating the contrast between spirit and matter. And the general tenor of this contrast is made clearly evident in a comparison between human consciousness and what it is conscious of.

The Immaterial Structure of Human Experience

It sees itself as delimited by the extensions of that precipitate. It finds itself here and not there amongst the extensions. It notes that other conscious minds are rendered opaque to it. They appear and perish within the phenomenal precipitate, like every other extension in that precipitate. Consequently, the human mind concludes that it must itself be so limited.

The phenomenal precipitate is, in truth, an expression of the spiritual dynamic. It is so by means of the self-limiting character of spirit. This self-limiting character of spirit is expressed through secondary mind and its noumenal precipitate. The noumenal precipitate is the presentation of percepts in non-incremental time. The phenomenal precipitate is the presentation of those same percepts in the form of extensions. These extensions come to be measured by incremental time, thus obscuring their origin in non-incremental time.

So it is by means of this circuitous route that the phenomenal precipitate becomes a distant reflection of the spiritual dynamic. For though the dynamic is its ground and origin, the phenomenal precipitate no longer reflects the indeterminate character of that dynamic. This is what the work of spirit's self-limitation has accomplished. It has drawn out the finite from the infinite.

So what is the connection between causation in the material realm and the origin of the material in spirit? The causal connection originates in spirit and not in the material. And, though causal relations are determined in the material by means of an orderly presentation of percepts in non-incremental time, they are expressed in a mature human awareness by means of extensions in the phenomenal precipitate. The physical extensions can potentially be understood in proportional terms, though this is not to say the physical realm is ever entirely proportional.

There is a consistency in the manner of this material presentation. For there are repetitions of individual percepts and associations of percepts in the noumenal precipitate. But there is only this suggestion of a pattern. Nothing else can be known, since human awareness cannot penetrate the workings of spirit.

Yet human understanding requires, as a result of its finitude, as a result of its being blocked from any definitive experience but the material, that there be order in that experience. Being confined to an unfolding of time, it must act in one finite moment upon an expectation of the outcome of present exigencies in the next. So not only must there be order. There must be an intellectually apprehended order which allows for prediction.

In particular, reasons must be given for events in the physical order: reasons which provide satisfaction and security in anticipation, since what is yet to occur is unknown. So there must be an explanation for the pattern of change in experience. It is in this way that, when it is brought under intellectual development by the mind, the patterned structure of the phenomenal precipitate begins to exhibit a causally interwoven fabric.

Nevertheless, it must be emphasized that such laws as are to be found within material experience are valid only in a practical sense. For there is a deeper order than this law. It is a spiritual order, an order rooted in the infinite. For example, the concept of energy may work well—even necessarily so—in practical and intellectual matters. Thus it should be employed in any human endeavor to understand the material order in useful, predictive terms. Yet such causal formulations as result from such reasoning are nothing more than useful explanations for patterns of change in the phenomenal precipitate.

As for change in the spiritual dynamic, the situation is different. This change is prior to any precipitate. For it is an inherent

The Immaterial Structure of Human Experience

condition of spirit. But spirit is unextended, unbounded, and indivisible. So there can be no definitive limitation, no complete separation and isolation of elements in spirit.

As the characteristics of spirit are an absence of extension, boundary, and definitive separation, so these must apply to changes within it. Thus change in the spiritual dynamic is unextended, unbounded, and indivisible. Yet to speak of change in this way is, of course, incomprehensible to human understanding. So its precise character must remain unknown.

Nevertheless, it can be asserted that the spiritual dynamic does produce the percepts which are the building blocks of material awareness, since they originate in primary mind. However, in any sense that human beings might attempt to conceive them in a spiritual state, they remain unarticulated and unlimited. They exhibit the characteristics of non-extension, unboundedness, and indivisibility. For, though individual even in spirit, they exist in a unified and fluid state.

But, when they are introduced to human awareness, circumstances are otherwise. In order for the percepts to be made present to human awareness, secondary mind is tasked with the purpose of rendering them available to that awareness as finite entities. Thus their origin is inaccessibly hidden in the veil of secondary mind, where there can be no human awareness of their source. So they appear, as it were, unannounced as vaguely articulated, but nonetheless limited, impressions on the mind.

This initial limitation results from their sequential apprehension by the mind. But they are subsequently given a greater definitiveness through mental focus, which acts in its capacity as the intuition of simple unity. Thus it is mental focus which provides them with the full attributes of finitude, just as it had initially brought them forth in a sequential manner. The full attributes of finitude are extension, boundary, and division (or definitive separation between percepts). Consequently, when expressed in the human mind, they are finite.

All this is initially accomplished within the sequential order of non-incremental time. There are single percepts of feeling, coalesced single percepts of emotion, and the associated percepts of physical objects and objects of thought. The associated percepts are modified further into the extensions of the phenomenal precipitate. Out of the complex spatial structure of the physical portion of the phenomenal precipitate and the presence of change within that structure arises incremental time.

As stated above, in the spiritual dynamic these percepts are unformed in any sense that human sensibility could apprehend. They have no determined relationship to one another and no finitude in themselves. For determined relationships are a characteristic of the finite and thus only occur in the precipitates.

Or at least it must be conceded that this is as much as human intelligence can confidently determine. For human imagination is limited to finite percepts, associations of these percepts, and the relations which result from them. Human understanding is likewise confined to concept formation, which depends upon a grounding in the images of the imagination.

Thus, in regard to change within the spiritual dynamic alone, there can be no environment of reference such as is found within the phenomenal precipitate. There is no structure by which to proclaim the origin, the character, or even the existence of any particular change. Accordingly, it can be seen that, inasmuch as human awareness is concerned, an assertion of change in the spiritual dynamic is no more than an intellectual provision for unlimited potential. Consequently, when change in the spiritual sense is spoken of, what is being referred to is potential.

The Immaterial Structure of Human Experience

Such change may be described in this way: change in the spiritual dynamic involves an innumerable supply of available alternatives for human experience. Some of these alternatives are made accessible for inclusion in the phenomenal precipitate. As alternatives arising in the spiritual dynamic, they are indeterminate. But the specific alternative selected for inclusion in the phenomenal precipitate enters into a determinate relationship with all that appears within the structured context of that precipitate.

The number of alternatives which is available within the dynamic is unspecified. But, once an alternative has been included in the precipitate, the one which appears is clearly specified. Most of the other alternatives in the dynamic may never be known to the human mind. In some cases, one or two of them, which were involved in a choice, may be recognized as potential, or as possibly called for by the orderly presentation of percepts in the mind. But most alternatives will not be recognized.

As previously stated, the spiritual dynamic is infinite. But infinite has only one meaning for human awareness. So, for human understanding, spirit is infinite in the important sense that it is pointedly *not* finite. Its potential cannot be enumerated. Therefore, metaphorically speaking, change in the dynamic is simply all possible change, all change within and beyond imaginative reference, including, but not limited to, that which occurs or might occur within the phenomenal precipitate. Thus it also includes those changes which never occur in the phenomenal precipitate.

It is the entire spectrum of potential alternatives taken together. They are, for human understanding, an indistinguishable mass, a white light in which every conceivable and inconceivable color is present. Thus no single alternative, nor any specific set of alternatives, can be specified in terms of spirit. For it cannot be identified amidst such a blended plenitude.

Nevertheless, in material terms—more specifically, in terms of the phenomenal precipitate—time and space are an unfolding material domain in which points of reference exist which do have meaning. Time and space provide a context within which, and in terms of which, change is observed and calibrated by human faculties.

Here, when one alternative or another occurs, it appears to the human mind to be physically caused. Sometimes it appears to be selected by human agency. Thus it appears either to be determined by physical circumstances or by human thoughts and actions. Either way, it occurs on the basis of what can be recognized and known. But what is known to human awareness is limited.

So, given this limitation, what are experienced are alternative developments, which arise as integral functions of the phenomenal precipitate. They are either understood to be determined as part of a causal structure (if they occur) or as part of a logical structure (if they do not occur). Or, where human agency is involved, they are seen to partake of both. For a person may appear to think, then cause action in the world. Conversely, an action may appear to influence a person's thoughts.

Thus one may say, "It rained today because of a buildup of clouds." Or, "It did not rain today, in spite of a buildup of clouds." The first is a causal phenomenon which occurred. The second is a logically expected causal phenomenon which did not occur. In the latter case, the causal relation is recognized in thought, rather than in an event. One may also say, "We seeded the clouds so it would rain today." In this case, human agency has been introduced.

The Immaterial Structure of Human Experience

But even when causes (mentally expected or physically occurring) cannot be discerned by human understanding—i.e., when causal antecedents cannot be distinguished—it is nevertheless assumed that such causes exist. For example, the fact that it both rained and did not rain upon a buildup of clouds suggests undetected causal influences which must accompany the buildup of clouds to make it rain.

So alternatives—something caused, something else caused, or something not caused—are not assumed to appear without a cause. For the absence of a cause is also a cause. It is the cause of something not happening. Everywhere there is a recognition or expectation of a cause. For something to happen without a cause would be classed as a miracle, which is a matter of faith, not involving the expected functioning of the world.

Miracles, where they are thought to occur, are ascribed to an intellectually unapproachable trans-material status. So, in general, normal events and their alternatives clearly occur in an environment of change which is defined by context, that context being either physical or logical or both.

Conversely, when change is considered from the point of view of the dynamic state of primary mind, or spirit, it is unlimited and unspecified. Accordingly, the spiritual dynamic and its potential alternatives can be seen in illustration as being like a molten subterranean pool, concealed from finite awareness. From this subterranean pool arises a volcanic rupture in the spiritual quietude, out of which the extensions of time and space, with all their specific relations and limitations, are brought forth.

For the spiritual dynamic is the indeterminate source of all percepts which are made present to human awareness in a determinate manner. Thus the existence of the phenomenal precipitate—a medium of time and space and relational change. To human awareness, it is always in the process of being formed. And it is always known by what has already been formed.

The precipitates are an emanation which may be said to be both encompassed by spirit and projected from spirit. When considered simply as an expression of universal spirit, they must be seen as encompassed by primary mind. For primary mind is their ultimate source. But when seen as a product of universal spirit focused toward human awareness—i.e., as a product of self-limiting spirit—they must be understood as projected by secondary mind.

In short, change in the spiritual dynamic may be conceived as unspecified, unlimited, existent possibility. Unspecified in the sense that it is indefinite, or cannot be defined. Unlimited in the sense that it is indeterminate. That is, it cannot be assigned determined limits by human understanding. Existent possibility in the sense that it exists in the spiritual dynamic and is potential for the precipitates.

As an illustration, dynamic change could be said to be reflected in a human being's time- and space-bound sense of the future. This future is a set of events which shall be, but which is as yet unspecified in being. The implied change is potential. It is not yet actual. For it has not been registered in human experience. It does not appear to human sensibility to be enclosed within the phenomenal precipitate.

On the other hand, change which has already occurred has occurred within the precipitates (as human sensibility perceives it) and is registered in the human sense of the past. It involves events which are specified in being. What has occurred in the past can be stated precisely. And what relationship one event in the past has to other events in the past, including those which have preceded it, can also be stated. This is change within the

The Immaterial Structure of Human Experience

phenomenal precipitate, as mature human beings experience it. Change within that precipitate belongs to the human past.

Yet, secondary mind sees the entire phenomenal precipitate laid out before it at once. For secondary mind is spirit, albeit self-limiting spirit. It is this full awareness which, by means of focus, it offers piecemeal to human consciousness. For secondary mind is the author of non-incremental time, the unfolding of percepts in the noumenal precipitate, and therefore of events within the phenomenal precipitate and their unfolding in incremental time. It is the foundation and origin of any sense of time.

But now, for the sake of a speculative interest, past and future may be considered together from a human perspective, thus not only from the perspective of secondary mind. They may be considered as one continuous, existent phenomenon. Nonetheless, for quotidian human awareness, past and future are an awkward wedding of unequal partners. For, when this speculative view is put forward, a human being cannot specify past and future together without denying the unspecified nature of the future, which latter she must nevertheless acknowledge as existing, or having previously existed, beyond her reach.

In other words, since her judgment is rooted in past occurrences, she is unable to assert the character of the unspecified future without rendering its unspecified nature in doubt. For, inasmuch as her awareness is limited to material experience, it is limited to the past. So the unspecified character of the future must be discovered in that experience. Thus it is inevitably located in her past, making it a specified past event. For this reason, to such a sensibility as hers, it is only the future, while yet independent of her experience, which is unspecified.

Conversely, in the case of considering the whole strictly from the perspective of the future, the actual of the past must be exhumed and placed by her mind in the larger domain of the potential, which is the unspecified future. For she knows the whole of her experience comes from the future. Thus the specificity of the past is brought into a condition of the non-specificity of the future. And this non-specificity renders it inaccessible to the finite mind.

Consequently, as a result of attempting either comprehensive view, she finds herself caught in a dilemma of specificity and non-specificity, of determinism and freedom. For events known to her appear determined within their material context. But events as yet unknown to her remain undetermined to her awareness.

So she must choose between them. Yet this she cannot do. She cannot have all of one without the other. And, as the future is continually converted into the past in what would appear to be a seamless manner, she is obliged to concede that *neither* past nor future is fully determinate or indeterminate.

Now, from a strictly material perspective, the past is clearly specified. All its parts are in a pattern. But the building of that past from unspecified elements is incomprehensible. So the future must in some sense be specified. Yet the future is unknown until it is in the past. In other words, if the past is determined, it would seem that the future must be determined also.

Likewise, when the whole, past and future, is considered from the perspective of the future, it is indeterminate. The past is simply the unspecified future now assumed to be expressed in a specified manner—i.e., now brought under the mind's eye in a certain pattern. It is a mystery why it should be made present to human notice in the way that it is.

In either case, a person is forced to make a concession to what she cannot know—i.e., the working of secondary mind, its representation of what *was* the future (and no longer is the future)

The Immaterial Structure of Human Experience

in the past, its concealment of what *is* the future in the present (for, as it comes to be recognized, it is no longer the future or the present), and its non-revelation of the future itself.

Accordingly, the past is not specified in the future, insofar as can be determined by human awareness. For human awareness cannot conceive in terms of the potential how it is that an actual event comes to be. Limited to the material, the mind conceives that the actual event can only be understood to have come about by means of previous material causes. Yet the effect of these causes is inevitably deduced after the event, not before it. So any seemingly predictive pattern in the organization of experience is merely coincidental. For the causes are dredged from an inert past. They are not deduced from the future.

More precisely, the problem is this: The fact that there is a regularity of occurrence in material events implies that future events may be predicted in terms of prior events. But it does not necessarily indicate cause. For a causal connection cannot be determined from a material relationship. The connection, however often repeated, is not certain.[55]

Neither among material events are predictable outcomes, in which there may be more than one alternative, bound in the future by any relations which human awareness can descry. A person would therefore not be so bold as to assert that the future is determined. This could not be justified simply because events can be found in a specific order in the past.

Thus it turns out that, for human sensibility, the past is not a mere illustration of the precipitates, some unillustrated portion of which is presumed to extend into the present and future. It *is* the precipitates, insofar as human awareness is concerned. For the

---

[55] David Hume, *A Treatise of Human Nature* and *An Enquiry Concerning Human Understanding*.

precipitates, as presented to the human mind, are always set in their relations. This is precisely the defining characteristic of the past.

But, on the contrary, the precipitates are wholly fixed, both past and future, in secondary mind. They are fixed prior to their presentation to human awareness. For spirit sees the past and future together. Consequently, determinacy is a characteristic which is true of the precipitates in secondary mind.

However, the sense of the word "determined" as applicable to secondary mind is quite different from what it is in terms of the material mind. But, since spiritual relations are not made clear to human intelligence, it is permissible to refer to them as determined, so long as the reference is understood to be tentative. For these relations, whatever they may be, are an expression of spirit. And it is inconceivable that human understanding could form an image or concept of them in any manner other than to assume that they are determined.

So a human being should consider her understanding of the precipitates to be incomplete when regarded from the point of view of secondary mind. For she acknowledges that the completed, or full, phenomenal precipitate is already determined in the mind of universal spirit. But she realizes that it, or a portion of it at least—i.e., the future—remains undetermined to her human sensibility.

Thus the future is spirit. For it is only found in spirit. As such, it is entirely independent of human experience, since it lies outside of human awareness. Human sensibility cannot detect any of its workings. To the human mind, spirit is indeterminate potential. It is not actual, and thus determinate, in the manner that human awareness of the precipitates is. So, insofar as human understanding is concerned, the indeterminacy of the potential is

The Immaterial Structure of Human Experience

the defining characteristic of both spirit and the future. For this reason, that which has just been referred to as determinate is, in fact, indeterminate for human awareness.

Spirit is thus both determinate and indeterminate. It is determinate to itself and indeterminate to human awareness. But to say that it is determinate to itself is not to assert that it is determinate relationally, as the phenomenal precipitate is. Spirit is a dynamic known only to itself. So what it means to say that it is known to itself cannot be understood within the limited, finite circumstances of human awareness.

In this way, it can be seen that the past, which for a mature human sensibility is the phenomenal precipitate, becomes a platform for making judgments. For reason is thus given specific relations among which to choose and a certain order in their presentation to encourage choice. By this means, the past leads into the future: regularity of some relations within the phenomenal precipitate augers an *apparent* predilection toward some future events as opposed to others. But it does not guarantee them.

As a consequence of this lack of a guarantee, the precipitates lie open to free will. In other words, they lie open to indeterminate change originating in spirit. For it is spirit which acts as a potential source for what subsequently appears to human awareness to be determinate change occurring from within the phenomenal precipitate.

Possibility is thus engaged. Possibility is potential, which is spirit. It is indeterminate change. Yet its products are seen by the human mind as operating amongst the relational circumstances of the phenomenal precipitate, within which change may be determined. There in the precipitate—particularly if the relationship is observed to occur frequently enough to be considered a causal relation—material change is often mistaken for a product of prior events in the precipitate.

It thereby becomes increasingly clear that the phenomenal precipitate is not only a necessary, but a limited, platform for human awareness. Because it is limited, it is a source of illusion. For human understanding finds itself to be constrained by those material circumstances which are the phenomenal precipitate.

However, there is a spiritual yearning in the midst of these material conditions. Though the yearning originates from outside the precipitate, it acts within it. For it is derived from the experience of simple unity in pure consciousness. Yet it has no field upon which to work except the content of that consciousness.

That yearning, if it is fortunate enough not to seek an easy refuge in material egoism, becomes a drive for knowledge, eventually rising toward wisdom. For it is this desire—to become engaged in events and develop an understanding of them—which, as a knowledge of the interconnectedness of things broadens, may eventually allow for an expression of the sense of a universal unity of experience. And this can lead to a discovery of the unified self as an expression of that experience. Such a unified self is a mirror of universal consciousness.

It works in the following manner. The more a finite mind can organize the materials of its awareness, the more it brings them under the umbrella of unity. The more it brings the materials of its awareness under the umbrella of unity, the more the mind rises in its efforts toward its own transcendent sense of self-unity. That is, the more the mind's content becomes unified, the more that content takes on the character of the unifying consciousness which unifies it.

In other words, the more the conscious human mind sees unity in everything which has been united by its organizing power,

The Immaterial Structure of Human Experience

the more it sees unity in the organizing power of its understanding. Everything becomes bound, as it were, in concentric circles to itself. This self is the unity of pure consciousness. Pure consciousness recognizes itself as unlimited and universal spirit. In this way, the human mind comes to rest within its unlimited and universal self.

This is the culmination of the expression of human yearning. It is a resurgence of spirit amidst the limitations of the material. Seen in practical terms, it is the human will acting within the phenomenal precipitate. Acting within the precipitate necessitates a knowledge of the past. For the phenomenal precipitate is experienced as the past. So it is upon the past that the human mind must found its understanding of the material.

To do so, it must build prognostications. By the building of prognostications, the mind establishes connections between past and future events, between the phenomenal precipitate as it is experienced and the phenomenal precipitate as it will be experienced. For those future events will become a part of the experience of that precipitate—i.e., a part of its past—and must therefore be considered. Thus it is prognostications such as these, insofar as they are successful, which make possible the human mind's sense of bringing all things into unity with itself.

However, it should be noted in passing that this is not a process which finds a termination in some future state of human culture. Rather it is a process which produces an increasing cultural maturity. It moves toward a state in which human beings find themselves in a more harmonious accord with themselves, one another, and their circumstances. But, as human intelligence is inherently limited to the finite, it cannot arrive at a final state.

An issue which has not been addressed in the foregoing discussion is that of the character of the present. It seems to stand between the past and the future and to partake of each and nothing else. So the difficulty lies in determining which it is. Or is it a peculiar amalgam of the two which turns out to be something altogether different?

Human beings sometimes call the most recent past the present. But of course, when the problem is examined in conceptual terms, there appears to be no present beyond the indistinguishable nexus of past and future. The present, or what *is*, is what has already been. To put it another way, the past, in the illusory form of its being taken for the present, is instantaneously slipping away the moment it appears under scrutiny. So there is no present. There is only a future unfolding directly into the past.

Thus, since the human mind cannot capture an instant, the present does not intellectually exist for it. Consequently, insofar as can be understood by the human mind, human beings must make practical judgments concerning the past in order to determine actions for a yet undetermined future.

In short, the judgments themselves are realized from the materials of the past, while proposing themselves to be wrought out of the vapors of the future. And the person, not truly finding herself to be living in any sort of present, is caught in an incomprehensible threat of insignificance. She either was or will be, but is not now.

But the character of spirit as a whole presents a different outlook. Simply because the past is a necessary platform for limited human awareness, it does not follow that it should be unequivocally asserted that the past is in any way a ground for understanding spiritual being. The past is no more than the phenomenal precipitate, insofar as human awareness is capable of recognizing it. It is that portion of the phenomenal precipitate which has been laid down in non-incremental time in the noumenal precipitate.

The Immaterial Structure of Human Experience

In other words, insofar as the conscious human mind appears to human awareness to be bound by matter, spirit cannot be apprehended. For an awareness of spirit cannot be derived from matter. But neither can human consciousness be derived from matter. So to find itself the human mind must ascend from matter to its own consciousness. For it is consciousness that is spirit. And it is consciousness which lies at the core of that person's awareness. Consciousness *is* the person.

Matter, on the other hand, is encompassed within spirit, just as the content of consciousness is encompassed within consciousness. This priority of spirit is rendered all the more obvious when it is considered that the spiritual dynamic must be held to precede the phenomenal precipitate in being. For out of it flow the impressions upon the mind which are the noumenal precipitate. Recognizing such a precedence in being is a manner of conceding that spirit is prior to matter.

Thus, when regarding matter and spirit together inclusively, matter is understood to be dependent upon spirit. For this reason, human decisions, and therefore human will, must be understood to belong ultimately to the spiritual dynamic, where there is no sequence in time and no order of events.

Tracing the human will to this source, it can be seen that human decisions are "eternal" in the timeless sense of that word. That is why the seat of the will may be said to be undetermined—that is, free. And it is also the means by which a person finds herself to be eternal and fully immersed in an eternal now, a present which is not bounded by past and future, but is that within which past and future have their limited origin.

The human will thus finds the ground of its being in an environment of indeterminate change, which is the spiritual dynamic. Yet, due to the limited material vision of the human mind, confined as it is within the phenomenal precipitate, the will appears to be expressed within an ordered environment of determined change, which is the phenomenal precipitate. Thus it appears mistakenly to be caused and not free, as the Baron d'Holbach would have it.[56]

In life, human existence is bound within the limits of human understanding. Those limits are encompassed by the percepts and their order of appearance in non-incremental time. The spiritual dynamic therefore does not exist for the human mind. Accordingly, neither does the future, except in earnest and hopeful expectation. This creates a dichotomy, which human understanding alone cannot surmount. But human awareness is greater than human understanding. For, beyond the materiality of its experience, it is found to be spirit.

Thus there are conflicting levels of human awareness, the one material, the other spiritual. So it is that the will, as well as the spiritual dynamic in which it is truly embedded, can neither be said to be determinate nor indeterminate. They are neither understood to be fully caused nor fully free. For will and spirit (the latter confined in human experience to pure consciousness) appear to immediate experience to be both. They remain unspecified to the human mind. Rather, they are experienced in a specified world.

This is why the spiritual dynamic (universal conscious awareness, the ground of human consciousness) appears to be contained within the limits of what in truth emanates from it: the phenomenal precipitate. For this precipitate is, after all, only a manner of perception and thought. It is an expression of limited awareness, a world introduced in non-incremental time.

---

[56] Paul-Henri Thiry, Baron d'Holbach, *The System of Nature*.

The Immaterial Structure of Human Experience

However, human awareness, when understood as pure consciousness without regard to its content, cannot be limited. Though its origin remains opaque to human understanding, it is clearly not an order of being which is determined by the material. That is, it is not an isolated articulation of spirit. It is the whole of spirit. It is consciousness. It is only the content of consciousness which is a specific and limited articulation.

The appearance of human consciousness as limited in a material world—that is, of its being limited by its own content—is simply a consequence of time- and space-bound perception and thought. Thus it is in the spiritual dynamic, in a milieu of unbounded creativity, not in a context of material limitation, that the human will may be seen to be exhibiting its fundamental role of freedom.

51. Speculative thought. A general rule of thumb may be applied to the work in this book. It has been suggested in previous entries. In full detail, it is as follows. If a thinking person is, or thinks he is, drawing his concepts and theories about human experience exclusively from that experience—that is, from the phenomenal precipitate alone—then he is looking at life from the perspective of practical human awareness, as presented by secondary mind. That is the narrow view of empiricism, the one which governs the investigations of science. And it is the general method of science. As such, it ignores consciousness as a part of human experience.

But, conversely, a person may choose to think in a deliberately speculative manner. For this reason, he may look at human experience from the point of view of human consciousness. And, because consciousness is found to envelop any perceptual input, he is likely to feel compelled to recognize consciousness as something wholly independent of and greater than the perceptual input it encloses.

For this reason, he decides to extend his view of individual consciousness to embrace a greater universal consciousness. Having done so, he discovers that, not only does consciousness play a role in experience, it becomes the focal point for his understanding of the totality of that experience.

Consequently, he finds himself engaged in an attempt to project reality from the perspective of primary mind, which is universal consciousness, or spirit. In doing this, he will, of course, draw upon material experience. He must because his thoughts are an expression of the percepts of material experience. They are limited by these percepts. For both imaginative images and concepts are associations of percepts, the former directly, the latter by reference to the former.

So, for the purpose of a deeper explication of experience, he will permit himself to go beyond the standard empirical view. But, because he is limited to percepts in his thinking, he will use those percepts to construct an enlarged reality—i.e., a reality which extends beyond the phenomenal precipitate. His purpose is to explain the experience of the phenomenal precipitate without omitting the role that consciousness plays in that experience.

Nevertheless, it cannot be denied that there is nothing about primary mind which can be demonstrated. But viewing material experience from the perspective of primary mind does provide a means for understanding matter in terms of spirit, instead of ignoring consciousness altogether. It suggests an exploration of sensory data in terms of consciousness. In this way, consciousness is included in the thought project.

Now sensory data, in the broadened sense in which the concept is presently being used, are not to be understood as confined

The Immaterial Structure of Human Experience

to the content of an individual consciousness. They are not being considered as occurring as an integral part of one person's, or even a collective, phenomenal precipitate. For they precede the precipitates in their origin. Sensory data are prior to any materially conceived person who would perceive them.

Thus sensory data cannot in this regard be defined in terms familiar to the physical senses. Rather, the individual percepts of sensory data are understood as originating in an unarticulated form which is prior to the possibility of any conceptual analysis of them. These are the percepts which are projected to human sensibility by secondary mind through the stream of non-incremental time.

It is only upon entry into the stream of non-incremental time that they become individually articulated. As a result, some are arranged in close association with others. But this introduction of percepts into non-incremental time is prior to their recognition as qualities of extended objects, either physical or of thought.

To be more precise in this explication, let the perspective be shifted a little. Set primary mind aside and consider only secondary mind. The concept of sensory data, taken in this narrowed sense, is thus drawn from the perspective of secondary mind alone. In this state, the data has undergone some, but not total, limitation and delineation.

In practical terms, secondary mind is the noumenal precipitate. So it is logically prior to any development of the phenomenal precipitate in human awareness. Of course, in this prior state, secondary mind is only vaguely distinguishable from primary mind. For it has yet to put its self-limiting powers into full effect. What finite means of articulation have occurred are rudimentary.

Nevertheless, what can be seen is that sensory data can be understood to originate in universal spirit, albeit that it is universal spirit under the self-imposed condition of self-limitation. That is, the data are to be recognized in a spiritually embedded role as a characteristic of spirit. However, though this perspective may be convenient for speculative purposes, it is far from a practical view of experience. For it seems to be strictly theoretical.

In fact, when weighed in terms of the limits of the human mind as to what it is directly aware of, the notion of a noumenal precipitate comes up light in the scales. But it does register some weight. For in the early and nearly forgotten experience of a very young or newborn child, it is briefly experienced. However, for the most part, it cannot be demonstrated to the adult mind without a carefully considered inspection of early childhood experience. So it must be conceded that to most people the working of the noumenal precipitate seems imagined rather than perceived.

But imagination is not an illegitimate tool. Reason itself is nothing more than disciplined imagination. For example, upon evidence obtained from very precise but indirect experimental procedures (which are valued in terms of the effort expended and success achieved in obtaining that precision), human beings have imagined quarks and electrons and have accomplished a good deal with them. What has been accomplished with these ideas has been taken as further evidence of their validity. Thus they have been inserted into chains of reason, long entertained, which would now be barren without them.

Any confirmation of the reality of these concepts, though they have been experimentally verified and arranged (even discovered) according to mathematical proportions, is nevertheless highly speculative in character. For all forms of experimental verification of these particles have involved a complex array of concepts which must have been assumed prior to the experiments which verified the existence of the particles. And though many of

The Immaterial Structure of Human Experience

the concepts preceding the concepts involved in the experiment were themselves confirmed empirically, such verification was also preceded by prior assumptions.

Thus the very process of thinking, or conceptualization, becomes an unavoidable participant in perception. For there is something of this procedure in even the most mundane sorts of encounters. For example, it was once assumed that electricity was two fluids, which hypothesis was made to account for its polarity.

Accordingly, or perhaps in the absence of a recognition of this presence of the role of imaginative supposition in thought, a hidden assumption is often erroneously maintained. For, if it fits in with experimental verification and other evidence, it may long remain in the scientific lexicon of thought, where it does no immediate harm. But in a future progress of the science it will influence other findings, until finally the evidence clearly contradicts experimental observation. By this time the weight of a buildup of past structures of thought is either too much, or almost too much, to overcome.

This problem ultimately concerns philosophical assumptions restricting pertinent data to that which is drawn from physical experience. In this frame of mind, the physical is understood to be categorically distinct from the mental. For, from the perspective of common human awareness, the mind seems to be opposed to the physical realm and to operate independently of it, contemplating its relations without subjective bias. Thus the subjective attendants of thought (emotions, values, etc.) would appear not to be of concern in the investigation of the physical.

A further potentially injurious assumption is that the human mind has an initially clear and unvarying grasp of what it perceives. What it perceives is both the physical realm and its own mental operations. But these appear to be distinct and independent of one another. Thus, for the sake of empirical consistency, another assumption is made. It is that the operations of the mind are an indirect derivative of the physical realm and are therefore subject to the same relations, or laws.

Of course, this can only be suggested by parallels between brain and mind states. It cannot be definitively verified. For the leap between brain and mind is unbridgeable. So, as a result, a serious investigation of the mind's relationship to the physical is set aside. Thus the physical is left to stand alone as the field of principal concern in empirical science.

Now, if the human mind is assumed to be clear and unvarying in its grasp of what it perceives—that is, if it is assumed that what the mind perceives is all that there is—then the physical is held to be simply what it is. It must only be properly thought about and investigated to determine its nature. Such a view as to scientific procedure can be found in René Descartes' *Discourse on the Method of Rightly Conducting the Reason.*

But, in the intervening period of nearly four centuries, modern science, in its increasingly mechanistic inclination, has superceded Descartes' method. Even mathematics, a highly abstract science, has come to be looked upon in a mechanistic manner in its application to physical phenomena. Though it is employed in a more subtle way than the cruder physical models used in forming hypotheses.

Going beyond Descartes to an assumed derivation of mind from the physical, which he certainly did not advocate, one arrives at a reductionist position. All is ultimately physical. So, on this basis, it is understood that there is a common experience of a purely objective world, which is unshakable in the clarity of its facts. For, if proper investigative procedures are followed, there

The Immaterial Structure of Human Experience

can, it would seem, be no variation in individual apprehensions of physical experience.

Thus it is the explicit purpose of science to clarify matters concerning the physical. The untrained mind may be confused. But the senses and reason are not. Science is therefore a species of organized thinking in which the common experience of the physical is brought before the tribunal of disciplined observation and thought.

But, in spite of these assurances, the methodology of science cannot be airtight. It leaves a good deal of room for doubt concerning some of its most fundamental insights. The reason for this is that those insights rely in varying degree upon common experience. But what is "common experience"?

Certain questions must be asked: Can physical data be accurately apprehended? And can the validity of that data be demonstrated by means of a systematic use of "common" experience? Can this be the case, even when that experience is considerably refined by an objective reliance upon experimental investigation?

Is there no room left for doubt when the thinking is logical and the experimentation is carefully inductive? Is the assumption to be maintained, that there is something which is irreducibly common in human experience which supports both the logic and the inductive inference?

Certainly, it must be agreed that, if such an assumption is to be held, science must search out to the last degree where a line of verification for it should be drawn. This is what Descartes attempted to do. But his method is incomplete. For beyond such a line, wherever it is drawn, doubt continues to linger.

The task of such a shoring up of objectivity has not been performed with anything approaching the degree of affirmation often assumed by the defenders of the scientific method. In fact, it cannot be done by science at all. For it is ultimately an epistemological problem. And what is epistemological is metaphysical, unless any appearance of metaphysical speculation is to be meticulously avoided for form's sake. That is, unless any appearance of metaphysical speculation is to be suppressed because it does not appear to resemble the scientific method.

So questions concerning the validity of the scientific method of investigation are raised. But what then? What ground can science comfortably stand upon? Is there such a thing as common experience? If so, what is it? These questions, particularly the latter one, shift the issue to a matter of definition. What must be defined is the character of common experience.

So it must be asked, what is common experience? Is it an indisputable fact that everyone gets the same input from experience and understands at least its rudiments in precisely the same way? Or does that experience include the influence of common sense almost from its inception as experience? In other words, is there a sort of general consensus (not always strictly adhered to) as to how the world should be experienced? If this is so, can it be honestly maintained that common sense is no more than an integrated component of common experience, adding nothing to it?

Or is something more than physical experience implied by the term "common experience," that something being a common viewpoint which augments common experience in various ways? It not only augments, it suffuses common experience in such a manner as to obscure its own presence in the mind of the beholder.

For common experience, were it conceived strictly in terms of sensory experience, would be no more than what human beings commonly perceive without assistance from one another's opinion in the matter. But it is clearly the case that common sense

The Immaterial Structure of Human Experience

is something more, and that it influences experience. It is a cultural item inevitably and ubiquitously present in human experience.

For it is what human beings commonly receive to be true of their experience. That is, it is what they have come to accept as true. So there is a considerable divergence between the two concepts—common experience and common sense—though the latter is generally overlooked as a component of the former.

This divergence between the two results in an ambiguity which is inherent in the phrase "common experience," since common sense is generally included in the meaning of that phrase. For the phrase "common experience" can and should express bare sensory experience. But whether it ever does is a doubtful matter. Or, which is more to the point suggested here, it can mean that same experience, but as commonly received according to general opinion.

It is a fact easily observed that human beings almost inevitably attach themselves to the latter case. They adopt a habit of confounding opinion with experience. This predilection results from two things. First, the phenomenal precipitate (or a closely coordinated plurality of phenomenal precipitates, to be more exact) is the common milieu through which all human beings experience life. This is the perceptual portion of the formula, insofar as it has to do with what is generally thought of as sensory experience. Second, human beings are social animals with a ready faculty of speech and a sharing of opinions. This is the common sense portion of the formula.

An example of this would be a modern physicist who believes that every object remains in a state of uniform motion or a state of rest until an outside force acts upon it. However powerful and universally confirmed in its practical results this view is, it is, at best, indirectly verified. The practical results are the proof.

For there is no incontrovertible demonstration of inertia as a principle in itself. Perhaps there is no incontrovertible proof of any physical occurrence in this way. In any event, prior to its adoption in the seventeenth century, there was the long held opinion, derived from Aristotle, that an object moves only insofar as a force is acting upon it. [57]

It is undoubtedly true that the law of inertia has yielded better practical results than the earlier Aristotelian view. And much in the way of theory and practice has been built upon it, all yielding greater practical results, until it seems almost impregnable as a principle of fact. But, matters of empirical expediency aside, such a view as this is held for reasons other than truth. It is held because science cannot proceed without a systematic development. It needs a reliable basis of agreed upon concepts and terms.

So convention decrees that a view such as this can only be overthrown by experimental evidence, or by a new interpretation of existing evidence which is convincingly to the contrary. Science is, after all, a milieu of intensive social interchange. And sociability is an engine of uniformity in language and manners. Its product is culture: literature, art, philosophy, science, and mathematics. Physical science and mathematics are especially careful about their terms, even rigorously so.

So the systematic development of any science means the scientific investigator must employ a conventionalization of terminology. That is, he must socialize its concepts. Once an acceptable amount of experimental verification for any term has been established, he promptly does this. For to repeatedly re-verify every previous concept back to the dawn of human experi-

---

[57] Aristotle, *Physics*.

The Immaterial Structure of Human Experience

ence would, of course, mire the process of scientific investigation in needless repetition. That is why, once the validity of a term, or set of relations indicated by a term like inertia, has been accepted, it is no longer seriously contested. And in time it sinks deep into the thought patterns of the investigator.

But unfortunately some of the concepts buried within accepted terms remain unverified. For example, the concept of energy which is involved in any idea of motion, be it uniform motion or otherwise, could be called into question. What exactly is energy? Given its reliance in this case upon a more general concept of energy, which includes potential energy, and upon its more abstruse, but still proportional, character in such an instance as gravitational force, it would appear to be a term which does no more than describe proportional relations of change which are consistent in their quantitative measures. These relations may be in occurrence or potentially so.

A uniformity of change is observed and can be subjected to experimental verification by altering the uniformity with another force. But the concept of force (a word closely akin to energy) is a form of conjecture. Furthermore, what is the ground for a reliance upon an observed consistency in a train of events? In other words, other than a consistency under observation, which has so far proven to be regular, what is the justification for the idea of cause and effect?

Nevertheless, in spite of such a vague, but not unimportant, insinuation of doubt, the accepted terms have become second nature to the investigator. And the partially unconfirmed character of their origin is soon conventionally overlooked. Thus they are carried into future investigations and experimental confirmations. These, in turn, are followed by further investigations and experimental confirmations based on the previous ones. The situation eventually becomes one in which they are treated as though they were the substance of perception itself.

Another such example is that of the concept of the infinitesimal, so critical to the development of the modern calculus which is derived from the mathematical investigations of Isaac Newton and Gottfried Leibniz. The philosopher, George Berkeley, raised questions concerning the vagueness of the concept of the infinitesimal. [58] In response to this, the idea of limits was eventually "settled" through the efforts of Karl Weierstrass and his theory of irrational numbers, which were defined by means of a convergent sequence of rational numbers. [59]

But has this justification of mathematical limits really resolved the issue? Or does the fact remain that the infinitesimal has simply been tucked out of reckoning into the number of the limit? For a whole (in fact, any rational) number does itself prove to be inexact under close investigation. There is clearly room between it and any adjacent number for an infinitesimal variation, without altering it as a number, as in the case of 1.999... and 2.

Moreover, do people even know what they mean when they speak of the infinite, let alone the infinitely small? Can a string of natural numbers, where each number is a finite multiple of finite mathematical units, and where, if the counting stops, the result is a finite number—can this result in an infinity? Is this not an indeterminacy instead?

What on earth could be a ground for assuming that something strung out indefinitely in imagination is definitively not finite in character—that it is infinite? Let alone attempting to justify such a number by means of a convergent sequence of rational numbers, which are themselves inexact? Nevertheless, this

---

[58] George Berkeley, *The Analyst.*
[59] E. T. Bell, *Men of Mathematics,* p. 431.

The Immaterial Structure of Human Experience

having been said, the calculus does yield wonderful results. It fits in smoothly and logically with other calculations. So why disrupt the furious pace of progress?

Some inherited concepts, such as the idea that infinity has to do with an indeterminate largeness or smallness, reach back in time as far as Aristotle. Others, like Galileo's assumed principle of inertia and Newton's law of the same, are more recent, this one being only slightly less than four hundred years old. It is relatively young.

But it has become a cornerstone of modern physical science. So understandably it remains in use. Who wants to pull out the stone that will make the entire structure collapse? Yet eventually it may be necessary to do so in order to clear a path for a more comprehensive understanding of experience—a less isolated and mechanistic one.

But why this absurd idea of infinity? Is it so physical scientists can have it both ways—a universe which is material and finite, yet infinite, thus implying some sort of awe-inspiring universal extension to what remains mechanistically analyzable? Or do mathematicians simply wish to place all quantitative matters into neat little boxes? An indeterminacy is messy and undefined. Transfinite numbers are not.

This is not an attempt to undermine the brilliant work of Georg Cantor.[60] It would simply be more convenient (and honest) to define transfinite numbers as indeterminate and not infinite. For infinite means *not* finite. Under such a conceptual rehabilitation, Cantor's wonderful insights would largely remain intact.

---

[60] Bertrand Russell, "Mathematics and the Metaphysicians" and Hans Hahn, "Infinity" in *the World of Mathematics*, pp. 1583–1587 and 1593–1605.

However, in regard to physical science, the theoretical explanation of experimental results is not quite as simple as this. For objects may not lie. But interpretations of their relations can and often do, particularly when systems of thought become so complex as to seem impenetrable. Here it becomes increasingly evident that accustomed practice treats familiar interpretations as though they were fact.

Whatever the reason, it is in these various ways that social interpolations of meaning from the past are fit into what is perceived now. They are felt to be indispensible. They are subtly legitimized by the complex medium into which they are repeatedly invested and by the practical results obtained. Every part of the grand formulation supports its partners. So none can be dispensed with.

However, there is an issue more disturbing than the intrusions of common sense and conventional habit into science and mathematics. There is a direct epistemological issue. For it is clearly evident that the phenomenal precipitate alone cannot be expected to suggest a way of tying together such disparate phenomena as consciousness and the content of that consciousness.[61] So there remains the problem of what to do with consciousness.

This is particularly troublesome because consciousness hides itself in unexpected places, such as in the human faculty of conceptualization. Here consciousness provides the experiential basis for the intuition of simple unity. That intuition is necessary for bringing disparate phenomena into the unity of a classification. And classification is conceptualization.

---

[61] The issue is the same even if one does not speak of the phenomenal precipitate as the content of consciousness. If one assumes a material realm utterly distinct from human consciousness, but somehow responsible for it, it is no easy matter to explain consciousness in terms of the material realm.

The Immaterial Structure of Human Experience

Thus, given its material limitations, the phenomenal precipitate alone cannot supply an explanation for the uniting of the elements of a concept. For there is more to a concept than the direct perceptual elements found in what is generally understood to be sensory experience. The perceptual elements are only percepts. They do not of their own power unite themselves in a concept.

Even in something as simple as perception, with its image presentation before the mind, how is it that human beings are able to determine that such and such percepts belong to this object and not to that object? Granted there is a coordination of experience which might assist in this process. For example, there is the case of touch corroborating sight, the percepts for these two faculties appearing in the noumenal stream in a prescribed order conducive to their mutual reference in experience.

But repeatedly encountering the properties of a physical object in a certain perceptual order cannot overcome the problem of determining their unity in an object. Why should anything be in unity with anything else? So, in spite of an assist in the order of perceptual experience, a person might never form a single image of an object if something within him did not unify its properties in that image.

The sense of unity is also the means by which concepts employ powers of abstraction. For example, the concept "mankind" is an abstraction from the concept "man." Concepts are classifications. Classifications are unities—unities of properties, which in turn are unities of percepts, or qualities.

Now the mental faculty which makes such unities possible is spiritual in origin. And it is this same faculty which provides the power of abstraction. That is to say, the intuition of unity, which makes the transformation of sensory experience into images and classifications possible, also facilitates the movement of classificatory thought up the scale of abstraction—as in a thought rising from the specific classification "a man" to the more inclusive "mankind."

Another example of a mental transition toward greater abstraction is as follows. The concept, or classification, "dog" is an association of properties characteristic of dogs. The classification "mammal" is an association of some of the properties characteristic of dogs with some other related properties pertaining to cats, horses, etc.

In other words, the concept "mammal" selects only those properties which these species have in common. It does not select barking, meowing, and whinnying. For these are what are referred to as accidental properties, insofar as the classification "mammal" is concerned. They pertain to certain mammals, but not to all.

This mode of association of properties into classifications, and then further association of classifications according to properties of similitude as opposed to those of difference, is the means by which the human mind negotiates its way through the flood of perceptual experience. For a differentiation, identification, and hierarchy of classifications makes possible an intellectual organization of experience.

Some concepts originate directly in experience, such as from a person's encounter with particular dogs, cats, or horses. Other concepts are added to these according to the method of abstraction. Thus the concept "mammal" originates in specific animals sharing traits of warm-bloodedness, lactation, etc.

The total association of properties in any one thought is either imaginative or conceptual. Imagination produces images. And concepts are derived from imaginative imagery through the application of a definition. Thus a visual image of a chair may

The Immaterial Structure of Human Experience

appear in the mind, accompanied by other sensations associated with that object.

Some of these other sensations involve the activities of some person making a chair and another sitting upon the chair. The various sensations involved in the image of the chair combine to make up its properties. A chair is something made. A chair is something sat upon. It is made of a solid material. Etc. This composite of properties in an image is the initial perceptual form of a mental representation. It pertains to that particular chair.

In time, however, several other similar images may arise in experience and appear in the mind, each differing in some critical details from the others. Perhaps, for example, some chairs are made from materials which differ from others, say leather and wood or Naugahyde and metal. But they all have in common the characteristics that they are made of a solid material and made by a person for a person to sit upon.

So these images are collectively transformed into a single concept when the definition, *an object made of solid material by a person for a person to sit upon,* is emphasized as representing the series of images. For the definition signifies what they all have in common. More importantly, it asserts what they all *must* have in common to fulfill the meaning of the concept.

So it can be seen that even a simple image of an object, like that of a chair or a dog, must undergo some degree of abstraction to become a concept. Thus all concepts are abstractions from imagery. Further advances to higher levels of abstraction involve increasingly selective associations of properties. Accordingly, dogs, cats, and horses are mammals because they share the properties of warm-bloodedness and lactation. But they do not share barking, meowing, and whinnying.

In the same way, chairs, beds, tables, and dressers constitute furniture because they are made by people for people to rest themselves or useful objects upon or within. Here the original property "sitting" has itself been generalized to a higher classification as a form of rest involving people inclined in different attitudes, such as sitting or lying down. It also includes human owned objects as things needing a place to rest. These are properties relating to the furniture. So a conceptual abstraction may involve an abstraction of properties as well.

These concepts, their similarity, their difference, and their often hierarchical arrangement serve an important purpose. For they constitute the intellectual structure of the phenomenal precipitate. In other words, they organize experience. Organized experience facilitates recognition and underpins a knowledge of what to do in the midst of that experience.

So it is consciousness itself, brought under secondary mind's limiting faculty of focus, which is responsible for the subtleties, not only of perception, but of sophisticated mental life. Focus is what narrows consciousness towards a finitude of its content. It is also what provides a means for the articulation of material experience. It does these things by means of the intuition of simple unity.

Thus the intuition of simple unity (as well as the accompanying and closely related intuitions of plurality and totality) originates as a faculty of secondary mind, which is responsible for non-incremental time and its initial presentation of percepts. But these three intuitions are also recognizably present in the phenomenal operations of human awareness. For the mental acts of association, differentiation, and abstraction concerning objects, or extensions, are their work.

The Immaterial Structure of Human Experience

Though classifications have been mentioned as concepts, they do, in a broader sense, include images. For there are both open and closed classifications. Open classifications are flexible and readily subject to change, a few properties at a time. Closed classifications are not. This is the difference between an imaginative image and a concept.

Since a concept is closed, there is an assurance that it will not vary. As it is stabilized in this way, it can be logically manipulated. Whereas, because imaginative images may vary freely in the mind and blend imperceptibly into one another, they cannot directly serve the purposes of rational thought. They must first be converted into closed concepts by means of a definition.

So, when it is said that the early processing of human experience is pre-conceptual, what is meant is that the construction of the phenomenal precipitate is quite fluid and imaginative, allowing for subtle adjustments which would be more difficult to obtain conceptually. But, even so, the formation of imaginative associations also requires a sense of unity. For an image is a loose association of properties. And a recognized association is a unity.

On the one hand, it is this fluid, less structured type of thinking which builds up a child's reality in images, both perceptual and imaginative. But, on the other, it still involves the faculty of focus. For the intuition of unity determines the fundamental character of both imaginative imagery and concept formation. It forms either a fluid unity of association or a fixed unity of association limited by a definition. Definition is what settles the unity into one invariable meaning and makes it a concept.

A child begins by thinking fluidly in images, only later translating those images into concepts. Nevertheless, the contribution to the child's mind of these images is the structuring of a reality which, at a later time, concepts, propositional statements, and systems of thought will be predicated upon. For not only concepts, but propositional statements and systems of thought are closed classifications.

A proposition combines subject and predicate in a single closed classification, [62] which is a concept. "Horse" is a concept. "Mammal" is a concept. But so is "a horse is a mammal" a concept. Likewise, multiple propositions are systematically united in such a manner as to bring themselves collectively under a single classification, which embraces a system of thought. Thus the concept "relativity" evokes a series of propositions. It was also in such a way that the various observations of Charles Darwin were drawn together under the principle of natural selection, which can be expressed simply as a concept.

So childhood experience and adult conceptualization are both necessary to human development. For the latter rests upon the former. By means of this process, images lay the groundwork of the phenomenal precipitate. Subsequently, as the human mind is matured with experience, concepts are overlaid onto this pre-conceptual precipitate. Then, as a result of repeated practice and acceptance, they are sewn into the fabric of the individual's perception of reality. But neither the image foundation nor the conceptual overlay can be said to be always reliably accurate.

For example, a person may assume an apple should be green because that is all he has ever seen. He may therefore conclude that greenness is an essential characteristic of apples. He would, of course, be wrong. And it is the general experience of others which might possibly correct him. Yet this general opinion may itself be wrong. For it may hold that apples are always red, at

---

[62] Aristotle's syllogistic logic is most often used in this work because of its simplicity of structure and verbal clarity of relations.

The Immaterial Structure of Human Experience

least when ripe, while further experience would reveal that they can be green, gold, and red when ripe.

So imaginative representations in young children and intellectual concepts in adults are likely to be in varying degree unreliable components of cumulative experience. That experience is built up by two factors. The first is oneself. The second is one's community. Either is subject to error. Thus both must be brought under a careful scrutiny. Every element of each must be carefully examined.

But, for the most part, it is consciousness, as the most thoroughly unified part of human experience, which is of central concern. Consciousness under focus plays a dominant role in the earliest childhood acts of perception and image formation. For it supplies the unity necessary to encompass the percepts of an image, as focus limits them.

The process determines which percepts should be included in mental representations of objects or events, and which should not. Where it does so wrongly in terms of the overall expanse of experience which is to be built up, it beclouds philosophy and undermines science in ways which are generally unseen. Yet this early role becomes the least apparent form of influence which consciousness exerts upon human awareness.

Why is it that the input of the noumenal precipitate, with its associations of percepts, should not completely govern the recognition of objects in the phenomenal precipitate? It would seem that it should. But in the translation from noumenal to phenomenal there is the exercise of the individual human mind.

This exercise sometimes alters the understanding in what appear to be insignificant ways. The example of the green, gold, and red apples above is sufficient to illustrate this. From such a small beginning greater errors can proceed, as the mind enters into its conceptual development. Then error upon error compounds the matter.

So, in addition to the roles of consciousness and focus in thought formation, it should be observed that the phenomenal precipitate is a complex and layered structure. Most notable in regard to this complexity is the fact that it is subdivided by the human mind into subjective and objective realms. As a result of this subdivision, there is in human experience an apparent isolation of mental life from the physical environment.

Since human experience is encompassed within an ongoing environment of change, the bifurcated reality results in a need for interaction between the internal and external realms. To accomplish this, a person must be both intermingled with and stand apart from the external realm. He must simultaneously be a part of it and not a part of it.

Thus the phenomenal precipitate may be conceived as a single entity which is divided in character. It is an interactive milieu, subdivided into subjective and objective realms, concerning which line of division there can be no certain discernment. Consequently, the question arises: how much am I of the body and how much not? This uncertain divisiveness in experience is not, of course, the point of view of spirit, which views thought and physical matter as an indistinguishable whole. But it is certainly promoted by the limited awareness which secondary mind imposes on human understanding.

Now, from the perspective of a contemporary empiricist in practicing his science, or especially in positivist philosophy, consciousness either does not exist or is of little concern. For it is viewed as background noise. In other words, consciousness is at best that which receives but does not participate in experience. It

The Immaterial Structure of Human Experience

is an indifferent whiteboard upon which sensation is momentarily inscribed.

Nevertheless, as has been shown, consciousness is anything but inert. It gives shape and purpose to focus. For focus is simply the unity of consciousness functioning under the constraints of finitude. To focus upon something, there must be something to focus. It is consciousness which is being focused. Working together, these are the intuition of unity. So consciousness is far from inactive.

Rather, it is intimately involved in perception and in the thought process. Consequently, since the role of consciousness is generally ignored in its image representation of perception and in its development of imaginative images and concepts, something about empirical evidence is left unexplained. That something is consciousness and focus and their active role in image and concept formation.

So, although ignored, consciousness is nonetheless invariably concealed within theoretical and speculative assumptions. It bespeaks a realm of experience which is not purely mechanical. For this reason, if the truth is to be fully weighed in empirical and philosophical matters, consciousness in its active role must be brought into the light and considered as a part of any such study. If it is not so considered, it will nevertheless exert a hidden influence.[63]

---

[63] As has been previously mentioned in other contexts, the present argument takes a representational form. However, if viewed from an overall immaterialist perspective, the above described acts of focus can be understood, not as products of an individual human will acting in time, but as instantaneously predetermined by a deeper will, still individual and still human, but embedded in spirit and not in the flow of material experience. Material experience is thus decided as a whole and not as parts in a temporal progression.

52. Experience, individual and common. To facilitate interaction between a person and his environment, a subdivision is made in human experience between thought, emotion, and feeling, on the one hand, and physical objects and events, on the other. But, in addition to this necessary distinction between subjective and objective realms, experience is also presented according to each person's individual perspective. Nevertheless, though this is so, it remains the case that, in its general character, the greater part of physical experience is common to everyone in the same environment.

In other words, the particular sequence of personal encounter among physical phenomena is experienced from an individual point of view. For example, in approaching a bowl of fruit, one person may first take note of the pears, another of the apples. But the objective relationships remain the same: all the pears are located among the apples. None of them are next to the oranges.

Only the apples appear next to the oranges. This is true for anyone who comes upon them. Thus the general order of physical phenomena is transpersonal. The pears, apples, and oranges lie together in a fixed orientation to one another and to other objects, such as the bowl, the table, the room, and each of the persons viewing them.

This is to say that physical objects may fall into their sequence in a slightly different experiential manner according to person. But the overall structure of the physical realm is fixed and common to all. So are those physical events which are not dependent on the person, such as the gradual ripening and overripening of the fruit. This means a great deal is left unaffected by individual caprice. It is in this way that people can exist individually in one and the same physical world.

The Immaterial Structure of Human Experience

To assert that the physical realm is transpersonal is to say it is common to humankind. For, as presented in the non-incremental time of the noumenal precipitate, it is grounded upon associations of percepts which represent physical objects. Roughly the same associations of percepts are given to anyone who encounters a theater of experience in common with another person.

So it is these which are shared by humankind, not in their particular sequence of encounter—for individual approaches may vary—but in the types of properties the objects encountered may possess and in their spatial contiguity to one another. How they are observed to be modified, with or without human intervention, is also shared in common experience.

According to individual experience, one physical object might precede or follow another in its sequence of presentation in the noumenal precipitate. Thus it appears in that person's experience in a personally unique order. But for all people in that environment physical objects are the same in their character and in their spatial relationship to other physical objects.

Likewise, thoughts will vary from individual to individual. But the physical objects and events which directly or indirectly provide occasions for those thoughts will not vary significantly in character to any human awareness. It is this independence of character from any particular person which relegates physical objects and events to the objective realm in the first place.

Thus, though the objects and events of the physical realm are common in general character to everyone who encounters them, and the objects of thought are directly or indirectly reflective of objective experience, individual thoughts are personal. One person will not necessarily perceive and mentally represent the same objects in precisely the same manner as another person.

Nevertheless, these personal deviations in experience are minor. For the greater uniformity of physical experience serves to unite humankind. In other words, human beings recognize the same general patterns of experience. Thus the systematic intellectual constructions made possible by these patterns—i.e., plans for hunting, gathering, and farming, as well as for weather prediction, science, and philosophy—are mutually accessible to everyone who has been educated according to a common system of thought.

With adequate cooperation, patience, and study, physical experience may be communally shared. For this reason, complex interpretations of ever broader relationships can be transmitted from person to person with an expectation of their mutual comprehensibility. For these intellectual constructs do follow the course of human experience as logically understood.

53. Natural insight. Natural insight is not readily accessible to most human beings. For it is a matter of making connections between images or between concepts without the benefit of an immediately recognizable association or a logical explanation or logical foreshadowing. This is to say that natural insight is not a result of imaginative associations which are based on clearly recognized relations. For such clearly recognized relations are the foundational building blocks of the phenomenal precipitate. A clearly recognized relation is what a natural insight is not.

The clearly recognized relations of properties originating in experience are what occur as physical perceptions, external events, and thought. Thus they are registered in the phenomenal precipitate. For this is where these phenomena take their final form in relation to one another. The fact that such phenomena are registered in the human mind as experience—as something which

The Immaterial Structure of Human Experience

has occurred and therefore lies in the past—is what constitutes the phenomenal precipitate.

Accordingly, though physical perceptions, external events, and thoughts originate in the noumenal precipitate, having done so, they immediately appear in the phenomenal precipitate as experience. For the phenomenal precipitate takes the form for human awareness of a reflection of experience. It is what has been experienced by that awareness and is therefore what exists for that awareness.

For what exists is either what a person has actually experienced or what she believes belongs to the character of experience as she has encountered it and come to know it. Thus her beliefs partake of the character of experience. For they enter into its structure. Or perhaps it should be said that they enter into its superstructure, amending immediate experience as, for example, scientific belief amends experience.

What this means is that within the phenomenal precipitate readily accessible experience is made available for the mind's perusal. In other words, there is never a present but only a past in human awareness. For an experience to be registered in the mind, however minute its content and immediate its duration, it must take the form of having occurred—i.e., of belonging to the past.

Nevertheless, the ground of the initial appearance of any experience is the noumenal precipitate, or non-incremental time. That is to say, individual percepts are subjective feelings and emotions. Associations of percepts are thoughts and physical objects. These are the elements of material experience.

But in their origin they are an expression of the noumenal precipitate. Furthermore, it is only the associations of percepts which are formed into the extensions of the phenomenal precipitate. Hence, it is these which constitute the extended and, as it were, visible portion of experience. By "visible" is meant that portion of experience which can be directly represented in a mental image. The image is generally visual. But it is supported by tactile, aural, and other mental impressions. All of these together constitute the extension.

It is in the phenomenal precipitate that extensions are encountered, both those of thought and those of physical objects. And it is in the phenomenal precipitate that changes are observed to take place in incremental time. For these changes, founded upon extensions and increments of modification among them, are encountered as the phenomena of experience in the phenomenal precipitate alone.

Consequently, it is here that their relations are recognized and determined in human understanding. So it is also here that those relations are reviewed and studied by the human mind. They are relations which are common to all who seek to understand the character of phenomena in human experience.

Conversely, natural insight exhibits no universal basis for its appearance. Rather, it is a gift, given to few and often rarely possessed even by them. For the man or woman of consistent natural insight is to be counted among the rarest of the rare. Such a faculty would constitute genius.

This distinction is due to a simple fact. Though natural insight is drawn from experience, it is inaccessible to the awareness of the majority of people. For it does not appear to them in a readily identified manner. On the contrary, it appears in unlikely links between properties which are generally dispersed among different physical objects or objects of thought. These most people would be inclined to miss.

The insufficiency of any readily recognizable link between these properties is such as to make the possibility of such insights

The Immaterial Structure of Human Experience

unknown to most people. That is, not only is each revelation of natural insight rare in itself. But the possibility of that revelation remains undisclosed, until it is brought forth by one who is in possession of the gift of insight.

An example may be taken from Charles Darwin's publication of *The Origin of Species*. This book had the effect over time of completely reorganizing biological science. Such a revolution was not the result of introducing the concept of natural selection alone. It was a result of the manner of defense of the concept which was developed in the book.

The concept was, as it were, put to the test in numerous insightful ways. Disparate facts were brought together in surprising combinations to support the argument. These insights were the product of an exceptional mind. And the sheer weight of the material Darwin presented was a tour de force of natural insight.

In fact, the argument was so admirably put forth in such multiple and variant detail, its effect was to remove all reasonable objection to the general thesis. Regardless of minor disagreements over particular points which remain to this day, the general theory holds because of the richness of insight in Darwin's presentation.

But not only is it the case that natural insight is rare. It is valid to say that neither is it derived from experience in an ordinary way. This has already been suggested by the observation that natural insight appears in a recognition of unlikely links between disparate properties, which links most people would be inclined to miss.

It is due to the fact that for common sensibility the grounds for experience are found in the accustomed relations of objects and events. Whereas the grounds for natural insight are not. Thus they cannot be readily accessed. But, for those possessed of an unusual perspicacity, they do exist.

Here they are found in a manner generally overlooked by all but the keenest of minds. This is so because objects must be seen in terms of their various component properties. The properties must be singled out. For it is these, their relationship recognized in spite of their position among different and unrelated objects, which can be brought together in the mind to form unexpected links.

Since they are not easily recognized, such links are not contributed to the structure of-the phenomenal precipitate by the ordinary working of the human mind. In other words, they are not registered as ordinary experience. Because of this, it is reasonable to say that natural insight does not, at least initially, follow the logical course of human experience and expectation.

By "human experience" is meant both thought and physical experience. But they are not unalike. For physical experience is apprehended in thought. To the human mind, physical perceptions and events are images in the mind. That is how such things are perceived. Any concepts which may be derived from these are more highly articulated levels of thought concerning the same. Lodged in memory (as it would seem to human awareness), these thoughts registering physical experiences become a basis of future expectation. In other words, they are the foundation for the common processes of induction and deduction.

Thoughts are mental extensions directly or indirectly referencing physical extensions, depending on whether the thought is representational or purely imaginative. It can also be said that those directly involved in perception simply *are* the physical extensions they represent. For all forms of perception are apprehended in the mind. Here what is spoken of is what is commonly

The Immaterial Structure of Human Experience

referred to as taking place in the present, though of course it is immediately registered as past upon its expression in the mind.

Thus, even when present experience is unfolding in the mind, that experience can only be said to be made up of past thoughts registering past physical experiences. Emotions and feelings also fall under this rule, though they are excepted from consideration as belonging to the phenomenal precipitate. For, though they are experienced, they are not extended. Thus they cannot be represented in a mental image. So it is the relations of extensions which are of concern in matters of common apprehension and understanding.

Common understanding is accomplished by association in imagination and by logical entailment in reason. The latter is dependent upon the former. For concepts are based upon images. Frequently, they are several images of properties which have been brought together and collectively restricted as to their individual character as properties and their manner of association with one another. This formalization is wrought by a definition.

These concepts, their similarities, their distinctions, their combinations within a proposition (propositions are also concepts), and the derivation of propositions from other propositions, are not a source of natural insight. This is due to the fact that, in the initial appearance of a natural insight, conceptualizations do not provide a ready support for that insight.

Nor can it be said that natural insight results from new imaginative associations of properties derived from prior associations of properties which are already incorporated as images in what is generally thought of as memory. That is to say, natural insight is not a product of common imaginative free play between images.

Nor, as indicated concerning concepts, does it occur in logical inference. That is to say, it does not do either of these things initially. Though such operations may occur subsequent to a natural insight. For then the insight is simply being developed, which is to say it is being integrated into imaginative and intellectual experience.

It does not arise by association or inference because it cannot be derived from a commonly recognizable relationship between phenomena, be the relationship imaginatively or intellectually apprehended. In other words, it is not a consequent of ordinary imagination. Nor is it a consequent of logical thinking.

It is neither of these. For an ordinary imaginative process implies that prior imaginative associations were clearly registered in the mind as past images of thought. And concepts are based on these. So, were these processes the source of natural insight, natural insights would flow smoothly from them, which they do not.

As to the process of logical thinking, it must be remembered that concept formation follows upon imaginative thinking. It is simply a more rigorous, or controlled, form of it. Thus, if logical thinking led to natural insight, natural insight would be founded upon the relationship of a new thought process to the clear expression of a previous thought process. And this would mean it was based upon a foundation which is common in human experience. Therefore, it would not be a natural insight.

In short, a natural insight is not a derived image or concept. That is, it is not an image or concept which is carefully developed from the properties of other images or concepts. For such derived insights cannot be characterized as unexpected gifts of the mind. They are the result of study. Thus they do not have the aura of spontaneity characteristic of natural insight, but are the work of careful observation and thought.

Nevertheless, in spite of these objections, natural insights, like the more common imaginative associations and intellectual

The Immaterial Structure of Human Experience

inferences, are, in fact, destined to become an integral part of experience—i.e., a free image or an image which is an integral part of a concept. That is, they will be used to form images in the mind from which concepts may be derived.

Of course, as has already been pointed out, the fact that they form images which can become concepts is also true of the common forms just mentioned. Both natural insights and common associations and inferences take their final form as new free images or new images within concepts. Yet natural insight differs from common insight in its manner of initial recognition.

So let the character of the common form of insight be reiterated. A new image can be formed in recognizable relationship to other images. It is an imaginative reassignment of properties drawn from two or more existing objects of thought. In other words, the new image is constructed from images already embedded in what is generally understood to be memory. Since the original images appear in the mind as familiar objects of thought, it is the obvious relationship of the new representation to the old ones which makes them mutually common derivatives of experience available to most minds.

But this form of intellectual creation is unlike a natural insight precisely because it is common to the experience of most people. It is readily accessible within ordinary mental activity. That is to say, it is ultimately based upon and blends easily into recognized experience. This is so regardless of how far it may appear in its final form to differ from the images which had suggested it.

The image of a unicorn suffices to demonstrate this. The fact that unicorns do not exist in nature does not mean that the newly formed image of one is entirely original or spontaneous. For narwhals and horses do exist in nature. And it is something like the mental images of these which might have supplied the new imaginative image with its character, when the properties within a narwhal and a horse were rearranged associatively in imagination. Thus the new image is not so far removed from its natural sources, be they the narwhal and the horse or something similar. So the new image does not express a great leap of the imagination, since precedents for it are readily encountered.

In accordance with these remarks, it may be said that new images or concepts of the common type can be logically explained as soon as they are laid down within the mind. That is, they can if they fulfill one condition. It is that they are images or concepts which resemble already existing images or concepts closely enough for the new ones to have been readily suggested by the old ones. In other words, the new images, and any subsequent concepts derived from them, can be explained as soon as they become experience. For they can be immediately understood in terms of prior experience.

Likewise, the same thing can be said about entire fields of complex human knowledge, such as are found in the arts and sciences. It can be asserted that their images and concepts have a derivation similar to the above. For new imaginative images and concepts, as well as any associations and implications which occur between them, commonly result from a careful study of preceding experience. Thus they can be logically explained as soon as they are laid down in final form within the mind. That is, as soon as these new images or concepts themselves become thought experience, they can be explained in terms of previous thought experience.

Accordingly, a work of art, a school of art, or a science, insofar as it proceeds from common investigation and practice, and not from an unexpected insight, is a form of readily accessible

The Immaterial Structure of Human Experience

development of thought. In particular, this is the character of science: it can be referenced to common experience, or at least to the experience common to scientific investigators.

Of course, natural insight does play a role in science. If it did not, progress would be insignificant. But when this occurs, it is strikingly evident. However, since art remains directly imaginative, and thus is more freely associative, the distinction between common association and original insight is more difficult to ferret out.

However, it is precisely in respect of this relation to experience that natural insight differs from the common forms of association. It is true that a natural insight will come to reflect the proportional relations of physical and mental experience. For it is natural. But due to its spontaneity and initial novelty, a full recognition of its role in the natural order of things is delayed.

Any connection between the insight and common experience is generally unseen. Rather, it is recognized in a flash of illumination. So, initially, a natural insight defies definition and explanation. It is as though it came from outside human experience altogether. Nevertheless, this is not the case.

The rarity and spontaneity in the appearance of a natural insight is due to its relatively obscure origin. It must be grasped by human awareness when first encountered, before it slips out of notice. And this is generally not what happens. So a natural insight is not by nature a part of general human awareness. For most people it remains submerged in experience.

Some possible associations between properties of separate objects are too vague to command notice. In other words, they are too far apart in experience, as they are generally involved in other more prominent types of association. But a subsequent repetition in the mind of the normal relations in the elements of experience, when these are generated in the reflective moment of an acutely attentive sensibility, may spontaneously exhume a vague connection by bringing disparate properties into a more noticeable proximity to one another. A connection between them may then be apprehended. Thus these connections can occasionally be seen and recognized by a sensitive mind, though they are generally passed over in most situations.

However, when such connections are made, as does occasionally occur, they are ultimately logically explainable. For, as the newly associated properties are integral to existing objects, the unforeseen relationship which has been discovered between existing objects will, of course, lie within the proportional structure of the extensions of the phenomenal precipitate.

This is why such insights are useful. Though not fully defined at first in terms of their relationship to experience, they will be so defined. For the extensions where the properties originate will retain their common relationships. Added to this will be the connection discovered between previously unassociated properties.

So natural insights do make sense in terms of ordinary human experience. This is why a natural insight (generally apprehended as some form of urgent and convincing conjecture) seems plausible once its full character has been recognized. It fits into the structure of experience and may be logically explained in terms of it.

For, however obscure they may initially appear to be, the newly associated properties of a natural insight are ultimately derived from experience. So the insight is well grounded in experience. Accordingly, since what is already known in experience is thus enhanced by a new relationship fortuitously apprehended, the insight's growing importance will eventually be understood.

The Immaterial Structure of Human Experience

More and more relations will follow from the spontaneously apprehended insight, which arose in recognition of only one or a few disparate connections. These relations will multiply until the new insight is thoroughly woven into experience. But the fact remains: the defining characteristic of a natural insight is that it is not obvious to most minds.

54. Spiritual insight. Spiritual insight is another matter altogether. It is not natural. Its source is a spiritual experience which bears no relationship to the natural working of either the noumenal precipitate or the phenomenal precipitate. It is derived directly from consciousness. However, the experience is temporally finite. It happens. It is gone.

So, though it is directly derived from consciousness and is therefore a spiritual experience, it is a spiritual experience which is something other than the experience of pure consciousness. Yet it cannot be said that it is a state of mind. Rather, it is a condition of consciousness which is experienced within consciousness.

For its direct affinity with consciousness is essential to its character as an experience. That is to say, it is as if consciousness were a river that ran unexpectedly through a stony channel and became turbulent. Nevertheless, it is the same river. It holds the same fish, just as consciousness and its condition hold the same percepts of the noumenal and phenomenal precipitates.

Thus the spiritual experience which is the source of spiritual insight is as ineffable an experience as consciousness is. For it is a condition of consciousness. No language derived from the material realm of the phenomenal precipitate can ever truly represent either one. It can describe neither consciousness nor its condition. For example, to say that pure consciousness is infinite is to assert of it nothing but what it is not: it is not finite. Consequently, spirit remains ineffable, though it is the ground of what is experienced and known.

So what other language is there to describe consciousness or its condition? There is none. Only their effects are known. The origin of those effects remains shrouded in mystery, though that origin is clearly experienced as individual consciousness or its condition. It cannot be mistaken for anything else. So it can truly be said that, since the source of spiritual insight is spirit and not the phenomenal realm, it is another matter altogether than natural insight.

Should a spiritual insight be held to be valid for human understanding, the validity of the spiritual experience which induced it could not be logically or empirically demonstrated. The very fact that the spiritual experience ever occurred could not be affirmed. For the ground of a spiritual insight is not derived from the realm of percepts.

Thus, since the ground of a spiritual insight proceeds from spiritual as opposed to material experience, the importance for human life of the resulting spiritual insight is strictly a matter of faith. For this reason, such an insight has much in common with the character of a miracle. The verification of its source is true only for the one to whom it occurs. For she alone can verify such a source of conviction within herself.

To distinguish this spiritual experience which leads to spiritual insight from the experience of pure consciousness, it should be called a *felt* spiritual experience. It is felt in the sense that it awakens an awareness toward some particular orientation of the person who experiences it. She must say something, do something, etc.

Thus for purposes of assimilation into human understanding, a connection between the felt spiritual experience and phenome-

The Immaterial Structure of Human Experience

nal experience is made by the mind of the one who has the felt spiritual experience. This connection is the spiritual insight. Nevertheless, the relationship between that felt spiritual experience and the phenomenal experience it is translated into—i.e., the spiritual insight—is in no way evident insofar as it is possible to demonstrate that a felt spiritual experience could be the origin of a resulting spiritual insight.

This process of translation of the felt spiritual experience into phenomenal experience is called a spiritual insight. The phenomenal expression is the insight. It occurs because spiritual experiences must be interpreted in some way. It may be said that there is an urgency of interpretation in the felt spiritual experience. Such a felt spiritual experience is an inscrutable disturbance of the mind. It is motivational without an apparent cause.

It is the phenomenal realm which supplies the materials for explanation. That is, the phenomenal realm provides the expression of the insight. The insight spells out a practical course of action. Nevertheless, though such a course of action may be motivationally expedient, it is intellectually unsatisfactory. For, from the moment of inception of a felt spiritual experience, it is understood that it cannot truly be interpreted in terms of phenomenal experience.

As previously stated, a felt spiritual experience does not originate from either the noumenal or the phenomenal precipitate. Yet the resulting spiritual insight implies such a connection. It implies that something has occurred in the phenomenal precipitate which necessitates or suggests a course of action. The course of action takes the form of an expression of the spiritual insight. But nothing has occurred in the phenomenal precipitate which necessitates or suggests such a course of action. No such material circumstance exists. Rather, in its place is a felt spiritual experience.

So when the felt spiritual experience is considered from the point of view of the precipitates—i.e., from the point of view of material experience—its relationship to such must be said to possess the character of not exhibiting any sort of precedent. To assume such a relationship between it and a course of action (the expression of a spiritual insight) is to posit a connection between an apparent nothing and that course of action. Thus the course of action which the spiritual insight suggests is without precedent.

So to say that a person is "impelled" to a course of action by a felt spiritual experience is not to characterize what that action should be. The individual person having the felt spiritual experience makes an interpretation without external reference. In other words, she decides what direction she is being impelled in. And she does this without phenomenal authority. She does it by fiat.

But having made the decision, she cannot justify it to herself by any experience common to both herself and other human beings. Nor can she justify it to others. For in the eyes of others, it is as though she had not had the felt spiritual experience. They are forced to take her word for what they do not see. Neither does she see it. For she, it would seem, only remembers that she had an inexplicable spiritual experience.

Thus a relationship between a felt spiritual experience and either the noumenal or phenomenal precipitates is not recognizable. For a felt spiritual experience does not arise from human phenomenal experience, but rather enters into it. In sum, the union between a felt spiritual experience and its derivative insight is unnatural. It is extra-empirical (in the narrow, precipitate-bound sense of the word empirical) and extra-rational. It is extra-rational because it cannot be explained.

The Immaterial Structure of Human Experience

As regards the noumenal precipitate, a felt spiritual experience does not arise from non-incremental time, not even vaguely. It is not a matter of its being missed or overlooked. It is not an issue of some percept or even a number of percepts passing unnoticed into experience. It is simply not there. For it is not composed of percepts. At least, it is not so represented until thought about and represented after the fact, somewhat in the manner that pure consciousness can be represented to the human mind (albeit in negative terms).

So a felt spiritual experience is not in any way built into the phenomenal precipitate, since all percepts of that precipitate arise from the flow of percepts in non-incremental time. This includes percepts presumably introduced as new combinations constructed out of old ones by the human mind. The new combinations are, in fact, registered independently in their own right in the flow of percepts in non-incremental time.

Thus a felt spiritual experience does not originate in the noumenal precipitate. Nor is it constructed from elements within the phenomenal precipitate by being overlaid upon it, then eventually worked into it, in the manner of a scientific hypothesis. For this would also require its appearance in the flow of non-incremental time.

Nevertheless, a strong inclination does arise in the person who has such a spiritual experience. The experience must come from somewhere. But she knows not where. It is a powerful sense of something experienced. And it results in an involuntary turn of her own mind (what is generally referred to as a regeneration of heart).

Initially, this felt spiritual experience is not figured forth in any manner but is only experienced as the vaguest sort of an occasion for an inner clarification. It is more like an emptying of consciousness, a removal of its content. It marks a turning of the mind, in which it does not include within itself, but is almost immediately followed by, an emotional response. Yet the spiritual experience occupies no time span, except by reference to preceding and subsequent thoughts and events. For time is a function of the presentation of percepts in non-incremental time.

The mind at this point contains no percepts, and can only be said to be in a state of rest without any sort of reference to duration. But it is a state of rest which occasions restlessness. For it lacks material content. The lack of material content is an unsustainable vacuum. So it is into this material vacuum that emotions flow, initiating a new sense of purpose. The new sense of purpose constitutes an altered stream of percepts, which is a re-materialization of the mind. It is a correction of past convictions. That correction is the turn of mind, the "change of heart."

Thus it is this breach that is the experience which leads to a spiritual insight. For the spiritual insight is the re-materialization of the breach. It is the attempted connection made by the human mind between what came before the felt spiritual experience and what follows it in the realm of human motivations and acts. For even in a quiescent human state, there must be motivation and action, as in the mental conviction: I have determined not to act.

For this reason, it can be said that the spiritual insight is itself the working out of the correction, a filling of the breach. In other words, the felt spiritual experience occurs without precedent. Thus it is thought to inaugurate a new purpose, to mean something regenerative. It appears to indicate that a person should do something to implement a turnabout of the mind, or heart.

As has already been pointed out, connections are thus made by the human mind. The felt spiritual experience occurs. And a new motivation is found. New paths of action are laid out. Even

The Immaterial Structure of Human Experience

when such connections are construed as no more than redefinitions or explanations, they turn the human will in some direction. For they become motivational guides. To bestow meaning upon something is to determine a course of action.

In other words, to define something is to decide how one should act in relation to it. If a person thinks in a certain way, that person has made a volitional determination based on something known and defined, the character of which she has either previously or presently determined. She may think: "This is a chair. A chair is for sitting. Therefore, I can ignore it for now because, knowing what it is, I do not wish to sit." Thus an act of will is consequent to an act of discernment.

So what gives urgency to the felt spiritual experience is the fact that it is a breach. The breach demands a definition of the circumstances of the breach and consequent determination of the human will in relation to it. It is a reconnection and continuation of purpose, even though the purpose may be a reversal of some previous position. For the breach is experienced as a gap in a material context. And the material context must be restored.

The breach must be fitted in some way into material experience—i.e., into the phenomenal precipitate—however improbable a connection that may occasion. For when a breach in the flow of material experience has occurred, that breach must be filled. Otherwise, such an experience would have no meaning. It would be as though the person were suspended in nothingness. Such a state of awareness would result at best in confusion, and at worst in disorientation and indecision.

There is an exception: only if the breach is deliberately pursued, as in a state of meditation, can the circumstances be otherwise. For the state of meditation arises out of purpose. It results from a predetermined act of the human will. And the material emptiness of the state of meditation is held deliberatively in the midst of a material context. It is, as it were, surrounded by purpose. It is not an unexpected and inexplicable breach in material awareness.

So, in all other cases, it is from an attempt at definition (and therefore clarification) in terms of phenomenal experience that a motivational obligation proceeds. In other words, from this attempt to understand the spiritual experience in terms of the everyday material world, meaningful importance is assigned to the spiritual experience. There is a growing conviction of what must be done, of how one must orient one's future attitude and behavior to what came before the spiritual experience.

Thus a connection has been made, albeit not a logical connection. A course of action is decided upon. And it must be carried out with the force of the original spiritual disruption. In this way, the practical connection becomes a spiritual insight. It is applied to one's life. It is a spiritual insight which gives the spiritual experience direction and meaning. As a result, the spiritual experience becomes attached to the motivational life of the spiritual percipient.

This means that the insight, however improbable a connection it represents, must be expressed in material terms. It must be related to prior events and motivations and accordingly be made comprehensible to the person involved and to others where an explanation may be warranted. That is, it must be explained in terms of the phenomenal precipitate.

Often these practical connections are made instantaneously in the mind of the percipient. There is no recognized delay, or gap, between the spiritual experience and the resulting insight. For it takes the immediate form of a representation of some sort. In other words, the percipient experiences a vision, which is the

The Immaterial Structure of Human Experience

instantaneous and combined work of spirit and her own mind. That is to say, it is the instantaneous and combined work of a condition of her consciousness and the content of that same consciousness.

Yet the fact remains that the vision, or the rationally comprehensible connections it represents—i.e., the spiritual insight—is not logical in terms of past experience. The vision is not a seamless continuation of reality. It is but a figuring forth of something incomprehensible in terms of what came before it. In other words, it does not fit logically into the structure of the phenomenal precipitate and cannot truly be satisfactorily defined in terms of it.

For example, a person may have a vision of being given a new spiritual law or of being introduced to an entirely new spiritual order. She feels compelled to convey this revelation to her fellow beings. Yet she cannot explain the source of her authority. She must simply speak in terms of it as though the authority were already understood.

The law which she has conceived, or the spiritual order with which she has become acquainted, or indeed the very language of expression which she has "heard" and must employ in presenting the revelation to others, is drawn from the materials of the phenomenal precipitate. They are her own. Thus they are thoroughly human in expression and execution.

But the specific character of their unfolding, the compelling sense of their truth, and the knowledge of the direction in which the force of that truth must be employed, cannot be explained. They must be assumed. Unauthorized by any logical or material precedent, they must be figured forth in image and manner, which is the matter of the vision and the consequent execution of its purpose.

But they cannot be affirmed, except by means of the radiant heart and bearing of the message giver. Thus a seemingly improbable connection between a felt spiritual experience and the phenomenal order is made by means of a spiritual insight. It is explained as best it may be within that insight. It is expressed in terms of a connection between the spiritual experience and the mundane. Most importantly, it is expressed *as though* that connection were between the mundane and the mundane.

But this connection is not demonstrable. For it appears, as it were, out of nothing. Its necessity cannot be proven from the materials of prior human experience, though its efficacy in terms of subsequent human hope and comfort can be observed. For these practical consequences are realized by the followers of the revelation. They experience them.

Thus the relationship formed between a spiritual experience and its practical consequences constitutes an insight, which is not a relationship which is demonstrable in terms of any prior human experience. For there was no foreknowledge which led to the insight, no logic of phenomenal experience which might have suggested it. It is for this reason that the elements which constitute the vision are not logical in terms of the structure of the phenomenal precipitate. In other words, the insight is not rationally definable. Rather, it is proven after the fact by its effect.

For an example of the confirmation provided by the effect of a spiritual experience, imagine the following. While confronted with an emergency situation, an individual hears what she imagines to be the voice of God. She cannot explain it. For the voice she has experienced is not embodied. So she wonders: am I momentarily schizophrenic, or hearing voices, due to emotional distress? She can never be certain. But years later, she remains certain of what she heard. It was not a normal human experience.

The Immaterial Structure of Human Experience

Though it was not a normal human experience and has never become logically demonstrable to her mind—i.e., though it could not and still cannot be used to explain ordinary occurrences with which she either was or is familiar—she has accepted it as spiritual. For her, its spiritual character was subsequently confirmed in experience by faith and practice. She heeded its warning, which may have saved her life and those of others who were with her at the time. Since then, being of a skeptical, but not an unbelieving, cast of mind, she has long pondered its implications.

As demonstrated in the example, the heard voice is of course intellectually indefensible. The voice is not a voice the recipient can give a plausible accounting of. For a felt spiritual experience is entirely random and individual. So is its representation, as in this case the voice. It cannot be impressed upon another as evidential material. That other person has no experience of it. It makes no sense to him.

But let another glance be given to the voice and its cause, the felt spiritual experience. Insofar as the possibility of a felt spiritual experience is admitted, something more than a material definition must be realized, if that spiritual experience is to be granted validity. That something more takes the form of an enlarged sense of reality, a reality which includes the possibility of such an experience.

For the enlarged sense of reality is the insight which expresses itself in a vision and its consequences. It is extra-material in what occasions it. Thus the enlarged sense of reality is more comprehensive than that which the phenomenal precipitate alone can support. For the enlarged sense of reality includes a felt spiritual experience.[64]

What is meant by the "consequences" of the vision? In the example just given, this would be that the person's actions paid off. Her acceptance of the voice appeared to have saved her life and those of others. At any rate, it led to her doing what had that effect, which is precisely the same thing. Though there was no prior experience to account for the voice, her subsequent experience served to confirm it.

So, in closing this essay, as well as the one which precedes it, a final tying together of the two uncommon types of insight is called for. It may be asked, how can natural insight and spiritual insight be brought together? It must be assumed that this relationship is possible, since the effects of natural genius combined with a claim of the supernatural are occasionally seen. Such a juxtaposition would involve a capacity to use material means to express ends which are not material.

Imagine a person whose entire being is illuminated by spiritual expression and purpose. There have been such people. Let their originality, sincerity, and insight not be doubted. So what kind of person is this? First, there is the suggestion that this is an individual who is impressed with a strong compulsion to speak and act as she does. So much is this the case, that she appears to see everything in the profoundest spiritual terms. And she refuses to attribute her inspiration to herself.

Nevertheless, other human beings may be inclined to doubt her claims. So, for these claims to be made comprehensible to doubters, the spiritual compulsion which she has to express them

---

[64] For a philosophical analysis somewhat resembling this last comment, see "Lectures XVI and XVII: Mysticism," pgs. 381–386 in William James, *The Varieties of Religious Experience*.

The Immaterial Structure of Human Experience

must be translated into the language of a limited material being, which is what she is to an ordinary person's material understanding.

Now what stands before the skeptic is a possessor of a self-proclaimed spiritual insight and a compulsion to express it. But how is it expressed? There is but one way: the inspired "seer" must find metaphors in speech and action which will convey her conviction and translate its significance to others.

How does she do this? She accomplishes her mission through the power of natural insight, which is apparently inspired by that felt spiritual compulsion. Again and again she translates the spiritual mission which possesses her into a vision enunciated in terms of natural expressions and images which convey, and continue to convey upon future reflection, not natural but spiritual truths.

What is significant is that, for all the otherworldliness, the spirituality, of the message, it is a profound faculty of natural insight which makes its communication possible. That possibility arises because the seer is able to make the most extraordinary connections between disparate phenomena. She sees what others have not seen or have seen only in part. But through her special language those others soon learn to recognize what she sees, once she makes it clear to them. For the associations she puts together, however extraordinary, are natural.

55. The indeterminate mind. Any attempt to form a theory of the working of the human mind must consider whether or not that mind is determinate or indeterminate, caused or free. For there are consequences which result from making such a decision. So one must begin with a simple fact: the human mind is the foundation of all experience.

It is the box human experience comes in. Any analysis must begin with this fundamental observation. This is so regardless of whether one takes an immaterialist or a materialist view of reality. For, in the latter case, it is the mental representation of sensory experience which provides a means of interaction with that experience.

It should be further noted that this mind does not simply interact. It strives to create order out of its experience. Note also that, insofar as the mind is understood to function in a material world—i.e., insofar as it thinks in a finite manner about finite experience—it gathers both the materials and the structure of its imaginative and rational faculties from that experience.

Thus, given that the material world governs the structure of the mind's faculties—not the possibility of that structure, but the structure itself—what must be spoken of is not only those things with which the mind interacts, but the means by which it does so. So it can be seen that the mind is itself a part of its experience, insofar as the manner of its functioning is concerned.

This is to say that the faculties of imagination and reason are bound by the same limitations as the material world—i.e., those of finitude. For the instruments by means of which they function—that is, the rudely imaginative faculty of perception and those of the assimilation of perceptual content into more advanced images and concepts—are drawn from and limited by that world. So this discussion will concern itself not only with the mind's content, but with the structure of its instruments—i.e., the means by which the content is handled.

Imagination and reason rely upon an input of percepts into human awareness. In the maturing mind, they depend upon these percepts and their configuration within the phenomenal precipitate for the formation of images and concepts. Prior to this, a fun-

The Immaterial Structure of Human Experience

damental form of image making is involved in the initial configuration of extensions in the phenomenal precipitate from the associated percepts of the noumenal precipitate.

Since an image or a concept is a thought, and a thought is an extension of the mind, images and concepts are themselves integral elements of the phenomenal precipitate. For the phenomenal precipitate is composed of extensions, both those which are understood to be mental and those which are consigned to the physical domain.

So it is in this manner that the human mind functions according to the limitations wrought by finitude. These are limitations which characterize the material world, which is a finite world composed of finite percepts. It is in dealing with the limitations inherent in material awareness that the mind employs imagination and reason, or images and concepts, which are instruments limited in a manner similar to the material upon which they are employed.

The materials upon which they are employed are those of perception and those admitted to properly belong to the domain of thought. As a result of these limitations, and in the very act of apprehending these materials perceptually and intellectually, the human mind experiences itself as constrained by limitation. It imagines itself to be material.

Thus, in an attempt to position itself in the midst of such constraint, which it finds ubiquitous in its experience, it must bring meaning and purpose to that experience. So it seeks order. Furthermore, it attempts to discover an ordered explanation for itself as a limited entity in a limited world.

In other words, a mind operating within the environs of finitude is a mind contemplating finite entities. As it garners material from the array of finite percepts presented to it, and, as it forms extensions from this material, it experiences and thus regards itself as finite in its functioning. So such a mind is obliged to impose order upon itself as well as upon its experience.

The reason it is obliged to impose order in such an encompassing fashion is that finite entities must be related in some way. That is, they cannot remain disparate and unrelated if the mind is to act among them. This must be so if the mind is to think, let alone perceive, with any sort of purposeful recognition of what it thinks and perceives.

Thus not only must percepts (with the exception of the percepts of feeling and emotion) be ordered into extensions. But these extensions must be ordered into space, both physical and mental. For one must ask, how can meaning and purpose be found without an acknowledged interrelationship between the objects of the mind's activity? And, without meaning and purpose, how can the mind conceive itself?

Furthermore, how can a being, which recognizes itself as existing amidst an environment of change, function without a meaningful orientation to such a varying environment? Meaning and purpose are understood to direct perception and thought, as thought directs action. And, for a mind which is itself limited by finitude, any relationship between finite entities is an order. Thus the mind cannot function without order.

Insofar as the physical world is concerned, this imposed order is space and incremental time. But it is the accompaniment of feeling and emotion which provides value, or priority, in importance. They come to be associated with the extensions of space and time. But they are not themselves extended in space or time.

The objective phenomenal precipitate is that which is recognized as physical space and incremental time. The subjective

The Immaterial Structure of Human Experience

phenomenal precipitate is mental space (i.e., that which is recognized as thought). Mental space derives a measure of the sequencing of its thought—the pacing of its thoughts, one might say—in accordance with the incremental time of the objective phenomenal precipitate.

Now, if the mind is held to receive order from some source other than itself, namely from the finite world, which is the content of its consciousness and which it comes to view as limiting the function of its faculties, then it will not be understood to be free. Yet the mind continues to believe itself to be free. So, to maintain itself in freedom, the mind must conceive itself as not being dependent upon anything but itself.

It can only do this if it conceives itself as spirit—i.e., if it conceives itself as being as *in*finite (not finite), unbounded, and undetermined as spirit is, or, in other words, as its own consciousness is. Thus any metaphysical explanation intended to justify a free human mind must begin with the freedom of spirit. The mind must somehow be grounded in this freedom of spirit. It must therefore be an expression of spirit and a reflection of its character. For, since spirit is unbounded and infinite, there can be but one spirit. It is in this way that the mind must be conceived to be spirit.

Metaphysics is a theory of reality based on more than the immediate evidence of the senses. That is, metaphysics is an ordered explanation of the totality of experience, including consciousness. Yet the ordering faculty of the mind—its imaginative associations and its logic—is a product of the finite world.

Consequently, mind is not consciousness. It is what goes on in consciousness (and with the aid of consciousness) in relation to the limited, and therefore limiting, content of that consciousness. Since the mind draws its materials (its percepts) and its structure (its images and concepts) from the finite character of its content, it must be finite in function, conceiving of a world, including itself, which is finite. This is what distinguishes mind from consciousness.

Such a world must be ordered. For finitude demands order, as it demands relation. Order is the character of the relationship between finite entities. That there is a relationship is a condition which is necessitated by the fact that finite entities are delimited by one another. When they exist contiguously they fall into a relationship. It is that relationship which is given an order.

In other words, one limited entity implies another to demark its limitation. Where there is a plurality of finite entities, a relationship is formed among them. But not only is it formed. It is extended indefinitely in contiguous unity. This act of unification is a product of the unifying function of the intuition of simple unity. Thus this unity of limited entities forms a microcosm, a demi-universe, be it large or small, which, if its own limitation is to be demarked, must be bounded by another demi-universe, etc.

The mind therefore meets this demand, insofar as it can, with its ordering faculties of imaginative association (principally expressed in image formation) and reason (expressed in concept formation, propositions, and theory). For these faculties, or structures of the mind's functioning, are products of the mind's search for unity combined with its immersion in finitude. So it is according to these faculties that there must be an ordering of parts in any whole.

Order is therefore a meaningful consequence of any interrelationship of finite entities. And if this order undergoes change, it will, under these same auspices of a search for order, imply cause and effect as well. For the causal relation is that which is understood to provide a means of bringing about the change. Knowing

The Immaterial Structure of Human Experience

the means of change indicates an imposition of order on the change.

The causal relation does this by asserting that a ball previously identified as not being in motion has now been put in motion as a result of some effecting agency. The effecting agency is the cause, such as the principle of motion in a moving ball which makes contact with the stationary ball and is understood to cause its motion. The ball having been put in motion is the effect.

This causal relation, in turn, suggests a determinate field of activity: a universal and interconnected range of causation. For, given the ubiquitous character of change, and the need to bring that change under a unifying order, the concept of causation is enlarged to explain a continuous and unbroken tapestry of interrelated changes between objects. At least, this is the ideal, if not achieved in full. In other words, change, inasmuch as it can be brought under causal order, establishes a unity of interwoven relations. Such a tapestry acknowledges the fact that change, which is everywhere in human experience, is meaningful.

If a metaphysics of the mind devolves into a theory of some external source which causes the workings of the mind—i.e., if this metaphysics is an expression of the faculties of imagination and reason, which limit themselves to an incorporation and mimicking of material limitations—then the mind itself (inclusive or exclusive of consciousness) must be seen as a dependent part of some order. If it is a dependent part of some order, it is finite and determined. It is caused and not free.

The mind, then, is finite in operation. But, since it also functions under the auspices of spirit, or consciousness, it may at the same time be understood to be infinite in origin. Thus, initially experiencing itself as pure consciousness, it recognizes itself as uncaused spirit. But, because it functions by finite means in a milieu of finitude, it nevertheless begins to look for causes of itself. These causal explanations must be ordered. For cause is an ordering relation.

If the causal explanations are ordered—and they cannot be otherwise, since they are finite and involve relation—they bind the mind's sense of itself within that order. For they originate in experience of the material world. This is why a metaphysics for the source of the mind cannot be based on such a theory. It cannot be based upon an explanation of mechanism at all. For any such mechanism would deny the mind's essential character as free.

Thus, once again, a free mind must be understood to be the cause of itself. This must be assumed. For its irrefutable support lies in the direct experience of pure consciousness. Any attempt at a metaphysics of mind, which should be held to follow this assumption and therefore be based upon it, must declare the mind free. For such a metaphysics will locate the freedom of mind within consciousness itself.

It is in this way that the human mind is understood to be grounded in spirit. Spirit is free, infinite (not finite), immaterial, and unbounded. Thus the mind is likewise free in the character of its origin. And it is for the same reason that the human mind's finite workings—which are the faculties of imagination and reason—are not held to be an expression of its fundamental character. They represent a specific limitation of mind, in which it is understood to be "captured" by the percepts of its awareness.

56. The paradox of free will. The concept of free will would seem to present a paradox: Choice implies freedom. But freedom in its fundamental character is not constrained to choice. In other

The Immaterial Structure of Human Experience

words, a person is free to choose between A and B. But he is not free if he is constrained in his options or in having to choose.

In other words, he is not free if he *must* choose between this and that. Moreover, even if he chooses not to choose at all, he is constrained to choose. In this latter case, he abandons any consideration between A and B and chooses between acting and not acting. Thus he is bound on every side. In other words, if he is compelled to act under constraint, or if he is either constrained to act or not act, he is not free.

However, the stated set of relations is not valid. It does not present a paradox. For, since choice does not and cannot imply freedom, there can be no such paradox. It has nothing at all to do with freedom. Rather, choice implies limitation, compulsion, even a determinate order. The determinate order results from the fact that a choice between limited alternatives arises from the condition that the alternatives are limited in their individual character. Thus it leads to another set of limiting alternatives, ad infinitum. Whereas freedom implies a lack of limitation, compulsion, and ordered determination.

Furthermore, choice demands a limitation to two alternatives, however often this condition must be repeated to arrive at a final choice. That is, a choice between three or more alternatives is a choice between two, then a choice between the selected alternative and the next, and so on until the goal is reached.

Since three or more alternatives may be offered at once, this circumstance further indicates a limitation of the will. For, if it is to reach a desired result, the will is clearly constrained not only to choose, but to follow a string of choices. In short, it is consistently constrained to choose. It is constrained in the number of choices it can make in a single operation. And it is constrained in the reach of any choice, since one choice may not yet encompass the desired result.

Now this is an unacceptable limitation upon freedom. To be partially free is to be partially constrained. To be constrained in any way is not to be free. For the concept of freedom entails an unconditional absence of constraint. In other words, the will is free if it is unconstrained. If it is constrained, it is not free. It is thus one or the other. It is either free or not free. Hence the valid paradox (as opposed to the one just mentioned) that the mind, which would appear to be the seat of a free will freely choosing this or that, is only truly free when it is unconcerned with freedom, making no choices.

Accordingly, the mind can be considered free only when it is uncaused in its essential nature, not because it makes choices. This freedom may be held to be a valid characterization of mind because the faculty of making choices does not express the essential character of mind. Rather, such an employment of the mind as is occasioned by its making choices is an expression of limitation. It is a product of constraints placed upon the mind by the finite limitations of material reality. For the human mind's range of experience, insofar as that experience constitutes the content of mind, is material. Thus limitation becomes its reality. But it is only an apparent reality.

The human mind finds the operations of its faculties of imagination and reason to be enclosed within and conditioned by material circumstances. These material circumstances, exhibiting the character of finitude, are an inherent expression of constraint. As a result of its enclosure in these material circumstances, the mind forms such instruments of thought as it possesses from the constraints placed upon it by the limited character of its experience. But the mind also recognizes itself as immersed in that experi-

The Immaterial Structure of Human Experience

ence, as though a hangman's hood were pulled over it, and not as being a product of it.

Bibliography

Adriani, Götz. *Cezanne Paintings*, translated by Russell Stockman. Cologne: Harry N. Abrams, Inc., 1993.

Archimedes. "Measurement of a Circle." In *Euclid, Archimedes, Apollonius of Perga, Nicomachus, Vol. 11, Great Books of the Western World*, translated by Sir Thomas L. Heath. Chicago: Encyclopedia Britannica, Inc., 1952.

Aristotle. "Categories." In *Aristotle I, Vol. 8, Great Books of the Western World*, translated by J. A. Smith. Chicago: Encyclopedia Britannica, Inc., 1952.

———. "Metaphysics." In *Aristotle I, Vol. 8, Great Books of the Western World*, translated by W. D. Ross. Chicago: Encyclopedia Britannica, Inc., 1952.

———. "Physics." In *Aristotle I, Vol. 8, Great Books of the Western World*, translated by R. P. Hardie and R. K. Gaye. Chicago: Encyclopedia Britannica, Inc., 1952.

Baron d'Holbach. See Thiry, Paul Henry.

Bell, E. T. *Men of Mathematics.* New York: Simon and Schuster, 1986.

Berkeley, George. "The Analyst." In *The World of Mathematics, Vol. 1,* edited by James R. Newman. New York: Simon and Schuster, 1956.

———. "The Principles of Human Knowledge." In *Locke, Berkeley, Hume, Vol. 35, Great Books of the Western World*. Chicago: Encyclopedia Britannica, Inc., 1952.

———. "Three Dialogues Between Hylas and Philonous." In *The Longman Library of Primary Sources in Philosophy,* edited by Michael B. Mathias. New York: Pearson Longman, 2007.

The Immaterial Structure of Human Experience

Darwin, Charles. "The Descent of Man." In *Darwin, Vol. 49, Great Books of the Western World*. Chicago: Encyclopedia Britannica, Inc., 1952.

———. "The Origin of Species." In *Darwin, Vol. 49, Great Books of the Western World*. Chicago: Encyclopedia Britannica, Inc., 1952.

Descartes, René. "Discourse on the Method of Rightly Conducting the Reason." In *Descartes, Spinoza, Vol. 31, Great Books of the Western World*, translated by Elizabeth S. Haldane and G. R. T. Ross. Chicago: Encyclopedia Britannica, Inc., 1952.

———. "Meditations on First Philosophy." In *Descartes, Spinoza, Vol. 31, Great Books of the Western World*, translated by Elizabeth S. Haldane and G. R. T. Ross. Chicago: Encyclopedia Britannica, Inc., 1952.

Einstein, Albert. *Relativity: The Special and the General Theory*, translated by Robert W. Lawson. New York: Penguin, 2006.

Einstein, Albert and Infeld, Leopold. *The Evolution of Physics*. New York: Simon & Schuster, 1938.

Euclid. *Euclid's Elements*, translated by Thomas L. Heath. Santa Fe: Green Lion Press, 2010.

Frege, Gottlob. *The Foundations of Arithmetic*, translated by J. L. Austin. New York: Harper & Brothers, 1960.

Freud, Sigmund. "The Interpretation of Dreams." In *Freud, Vol. 54, Great Books of the Western World*, translated by A. A. Brill. Chicago: Encyclopedia Britannica, Inc., 1952.

Hahn, Hans. "Infinity." In *Vol. 3, The World of Mathematics*, edited by James R. Newman. New York: Simon and Schuster, 1956.

Hume, David. "An Enquiry Concerning Human Understanding." In *Locke, Berkeley, Hume, Vol. 35, Great Books of the Western World*. Chicago: Encyclopedia Britannica, Inc., 1952.

———. *A Treatise of Human Nature*, edited by L. A. Selby-Bigge. New York: Oxford University Press, 1973.

Isaacson, Walter. *Einstein: His Life and Universe*. New York: Simon & Schuster, 2008.

James, William. "The Varieties of Religious Experience." In *William James: Writings 1902–1910*. New York: The Library of America, 1987.

Kant, Immanuel. "The Critique of Pure Reason." In *Kant, Vol. 42, Great Books of the Western World*, translated by J. M. D. Meiklejohn. Chicago: Encyclopedia Britannica, Inc., 1952.

———. "Prolegomena." In *The Longman Standard History of Philosophy*, edited by Daniel Kolak and Garrett Thomson. New York: Pearson Longman, 2006.

Locke, John. "An Essay Concerning Human Understanding." In *Locke, Berkeley, Hume, Vol. 35, Great Books of the Western World*. Chicago: Encyclopedia Britannica, Inc., 1952.

Mahon, Basil. *The Man Who Changed Everything: The Life of James Clerk Maxwell*. Chichester: John Wiley & Sons Ltd., 2004.

Newton, Isaac. "Mathematical Principles of Natural Philosophy." In *Newton, Huygens, Vol. 34, Great Books of the Western World*. Chicago: Encyclopedia Britannica, Inc., 1952.

Plato. "The Dialogues of Plato." In *Plato, Vol. 7, Great Books of the Western World*, translated by Benjamin Jowett. Chicago: Encyclopedia Britannica, Inc., 1952.

Russell, Bertrand. "Mathematics and the Metaphysicians." In *Vol. 3, The World of Mathematics*, edited by James R. Newman. New York: Simon and Schuster, 1956.

The Immaterial Structure of Human Experience

Spinoza, Benedict de. "Ethics." In *Descartes, Spinoza, Vol. 31, Great Books of the Western World*, translated by W. H. White. Chicago: Encyclopedia Britannica, Inc., 1952.

Thiry, Paul Henry, Baron d'Holbach. "The System of Nature." Passages quoted in *The Philosopher's Way* by John Chaffee. Upper Saddle River: Pearson Prentice Hall, 2005.

The Upanishads, translated by Juan Mascaró. New York: Penguin Books, 1965.

Waterfield, Robin. "Parmenides of Elea." In *The First Philosophers*. New York: Oxford University Press, 2000.

———. "Zeno of Elea." In *The First Philosophers*. New York: Oxford University Press, 2000.

Index of Names

Archimedes, 193 (n. 33)

Aristotle, 8, 130, 363, 363 (n. 57), 366, 373 (n. 62)

Baron d'Holbach (See Thiry, Paul Henry)

Berkeley, 7, 8, 48, 53 (n. 18), 72, 72 (n. 21), 91–93, 119–121, 127, 129, 215, 215 (n. 38), 365, 365 (n. 58)

Cézanne, 184, 303

Darwin, 49 (n. 17), 373, 382, 427

Descartes, 1, 44 (n. 14), 91, 359, 360

Einstein, 12, 12 (n. 3), 208, 236 (n. 41)

Euclid, 6, 6 (n. 1), 7 (n. 2), 135, 135 (n. 28), 187, 187 (n. 31), 193 (n. 34), 427

Faraday, 94 (n. 25)

Frege, 12

Freud, 148

Hume, 7, 69, 69 (n. 20), 88, 91, 126, 129, 346 (n. 55)

Isaacson, 12 (n. 3)

James, 401 (n. 64)

Kant, 1, 3, 7–9, 12, 13, 20, 41, 41 (n. 9), 42, 42 (n. 11), 43, 43 (n. 12), 44, 47, 88 (n. 22), 91, 129–131, 153, 159, 258, 258 (n. 45)

Leibniz, 365

The Immaterial Structure of Human Experience

Locke, 28, 28 (n. 4), 42, 42 (n. 10), 93, 93 (n. 24), 129, 246 (n. 43)

Maxwell, 94, 94 (n. 25), 208, 257 (n. 44)

Newton, 7 (n. 2), 204, 365, 366

Parmenides, 21

Plato, 8, 12

Spinoza, 45 (n. 15), 216, 216 (n. 39), 217

Thiry, Paul Henry, Baron d'Holbach, 353, 353 (n. 56)

The Upanishads, 21

Weierstrass, 365

Zeno, 201

Glossary

Association of percepts – Impressions on the mind recognized as being in association with one another. These percepts appear in the mind in a close sequence. And the sequence is repeated.

Change – This concerns an object whose relationship to other objects in physical space is altered. Or the properties or qualities within it change. In either case, the change is a result of motion. For there is either external or internal movement.

Classification – An organization of properties into a concept by means of a definition. A classification has a nesting characteristic, which allows it to fully or partially include or exclude another classification.

Coalescence of percept – Impressions on the mind (i.e., percepts) which are not recognized as associated with one another, but in which a close sequential occurrence of impressions is recognized.

Concept – Properties brought together and limited by a definition. Concepts involve images. For properties are represented either by images or by concepts which are supported by images.

Consciousness – A condition of any kind of awareness.

Definition – Properties brought together and limited within a concept.

The Immaterial Structure of Human Experience

Emotion – A coalescence of percepts of feeling. There is more than one kind of feeling involved.

Energy – A quantitative recognition and measure of change.

Experience, imaginative – Imaginative images which appear in the mind. They may represent the perception of an object. Or they may be a result of free thought, resulting in the construction of new images in the mind.

Experience, intellectual – Concepts, statements, and theoretical systems formed from definitionally associated images representing properties.

Experience, physical – That which is represented by images in the mind, but which is understood to be perceived as an object or event in physical space.

Extension, mental – A thought. There are two types of thoughts: images and concepts. A thought is extended in the mind because its object is an image which either represents a physical object or something like a physical object. For example, not only do the images and concepts "a man" and "men" refer to physical objects. The more abstract, general, and inclusive concept "mankind" must also, in final analysis, reference something physical, namely human beings.

Extension, physical – An object in physical space. It is composed of an association of percepts (mental impressions), which in a physical object are its qualities.

Feeling – A percept (mental impression) which is not associated with other percepts.

Finite – That which is bounded, or limited, in all of its characteristics.

Focus – The means by which universal spirit self-limits itself in order to produce a material consciousness. Focus is the source of the intuitions of simple unity, plurality, and totality.

Human awareness – The content of the consciousness of an adult human being, exclusive of the subjective manner in which mental impressions are initially delivered to that awareness.

Image – An association of mental impressions (percepts) which exhibits the qualities and properties of a physical object, though it may not represent any known physical object.

Imagination – The image-forming faculty of the mind. Imagination underlies all processes of thought. For concepts are a unification of properties by means of a definition. These properties are represented by images.

Immaterial viewpoint – The view that all experience occurs in the mind and does not have a separate existence.

Immaterialism – The philosophy that all experience occurs in the mind. Thus there is no objective thing-in-itself independent of the mind.

The Immaterial Structure of Human Experience

Infinite – *In*-finite. Thus *not* finite. Not bounded, or limited, in any of its characteristics. This does not include the indeterminately large or the indeterminately small. For these are finite entities, which are indeterminate in some portion of their finitude.

Intuition of plurality – The second of the three intuitions. It is the means by which the finite mind recognizes limitation, finitude, and plurality. An example involves a recognition of more than one marble in which each is observed in individual distinction from another.

Intuition of simple unity – The first of the three intuitions. It is the means by which a finite mind recognizes a unity. An example is one marble recognized as a distinct entity.

Intuition of totality – The third of the three intuitions. It is a combination of the first two intuitions. It is the means by which the finite mind recognizes a unity of pluralities. An example would be a collection of five marbles recognized as a single collection.

Logic – The science of clear thinking. Logic makes use of the nesting interrelationships of concepts, or classifications. By this means, one classification may be fully or partially included in another. Or it may be fully or partially excluded from another. Where such a classification is repeated in two statements combining it with different classifications, the repeated classification may serve to bring the two different classifications into the relationship of a new and different statement. (See Syllogism)

Material viewpoint – The view that there is an objective realm of things-in-themselves located in physical space and incremental time.

Materialism – A closely related collection of beliefs which includes an objective existence of things which subsist independently of the person encountering such experience.

Memory – A mental record of past experience. In immaterialist philosophy no such record physically exists. Rather, impressions of past experience are repeated in the mind at times which are appropriate for the functioning of memory.

Nesting characteristic of a classification (See Classification)

Object, mental – An object of thought, as in a mental image. Such an object represents the perceptual characteristics of a physical object, regardless of whether or not it is understood to exist as a physical object. All concepts are dependent on these images.

Object, physical – That which is understood to be an object of perception. It is derived from an association of percepts (mental impressions) forming a physical extension and is experienced as existing in a contiguous relationship with other such extensions.

Objective reality – That portion of human experience in which objects and events appear to have an existence independent of the will of the perceiver.

The Immaterial Structure of Human Experience

Percept – A mental impression. This constitutes the most basic element among the perceptual content of consciousness. Percepts form the whole of material awareness.

Perception – The faculty involved in a recognition of material experience. One can be said to perceive a thought, a physical object, a physical event, or feelings. The term is generally used more narrowly to designate awareness of physical objects and events.

Precipitate, noumenal – The noumenal precipitate is the means by which mental impressions (percepts) are registered in human consciousness.

Precipitate, phenomenal – The phenomenal precipitate results from an instantaneous transformation of the associated percepts of the noumenal precipitate into the extensions (objects) of mental and physical experience. These extensions may be objects of thought or physical objects. Insofar as they are understood to constitute physical objects, the percepts are qualities of the object.

Predicate – That which is asserted of something else. In the statement, "dogs have big teeth," big teeth is the predicate which is being asserted concerning dogs.

Primary mind – Primary mind is universal spirit, which in turn is universal consciousness, or universal awareness.

Property – A classificatory characteristic of a concept. These are composed of percepts (which are qualities in physical objects) and are registered in the mind as imagery representing an object of perception or an object of thought. Usually in the plural, they are what a definition organizes into a concept.

Proportion – In this work, the word proportion is used to indicate a simple ratio: 3/4. This is different from the mathematical use of the term to indicate an equivalence of two ratios: 3/4 = 6/8.

Quality – A specific type of percept (mental impression), like the color red, when it is assumed to exist in a physical object.

Reason – A discipline of the mind, by means of which concepts are brought together through a continuing transferral of meaning. To be sound reasoning, it must follow the rules of logic. And, underlying both the concepts employed and the rules of logic which bring them together in a transferral of meaning, is the work of imagination through image formation and associations of images.

Representational viewpoint – That viewpoint which considers the mind as producing an image or images within itself of whatever it is assumed to have perceived. In immaterialist philosophy, the thing perceived has its origin as an image in the mind and does not exist apart from its mental representation. But there can, of course, be a representation of the representation.

Secondary mind – Primary mind, or universal spirit, functioning in such a manner as to self-limit itself in order to present the human mind with a limited awareness. It does this by means of focus.

The Immaterial Structure of Human Experience

Space, mental – When a thought has an object taking the form of an image, the image is an extension. In this it resembles a physical object, which is also an extension. But, whereas the physical extension (object) is experienced as existing in a contiguous relationship with other physical extensions, the mental object does not. Rather, it occupies mental space because the mental image is an extension and it is limited by sequence. Only one such mental object can appear in the mind at once.

Space, physical – Physical objects are extensions existing in a contiguous relationship to one another. Therefore, this simultaneity and contiguity of extensions creates a greater extension, which is a multiple of them all. This is space. An empty space, insofar as such a thing can be said to exist, is an allowance made by the mind for the imperfect fitting together of physical objects.

Spirit – Spirit is universal consciousness. There is but one universal spirit. Thus there is only one consciousness. Hence all other forms of consciousness are individual expressions of the self-limitation of this one consciousness.

Statement – In reference to the Aristotelian logic referred to in this work, a statement is a proposition. And a proposition is a declarative sentence linking two terms, a subject and a predicate, in a classificatory relationship.

Subject – That of which something is asserted. In the statement, "dogs have big teeth," dogs is the subject and big teeth is what is being asserted of the subject.

Subjective reality – In the most fundamental sense, which is that of the noumenal precipitate, it is the awareness of percepts, generally but not always, in association with one another. It consists of impressions on the mind. Subjective reality may also be described as the realm of thought, feeling, and emotion, as opposed to the realm of physical objects and events.

Syllogism – Three logically interrelated sentences in which one statement is the major premise, another statement is the minor premise, and the third is the concluding statement. There is a middle classification (the subject of the major premise and the predicate of the minor premise) which serves as a conceptual link between the major and minor premises. In the example below, the middle term is "big teeth."

> Big teeth are something to be feared. (major premise)
> All dogs have big teeth. (minor premise)
> Therefore, dogs are something to be feared. (Conclusion)

Theoretical system – A development of thought in which concepts are brought together in statements and statements are brought together in a system. Euclid's *Elements* is one such system. Darwin's argument for natural selection in *The Origin of Species* is another.

Thing-in-itself – That which exists apart from human consciousness. In immaterialist philosophy there is no such thing.

Thought (See Extension, mental)

The Immaterial Structure of Human Experience

Time, incremental – Time as recognized in the phenomenal precipitate. It is the form of time experienced by a mature human awareness. It is determined incrementally by means of changes in a distance relationship between two extensions, one of which is undergoing change in relation to the other.

Such a changing distance relationship between two extensions is compared to another similar relationship, the first being held as a standard for demarking the other. It is a comparative measure of motion. Thus the movement of a hand, or change in digits (which latter also involves change in distance) on a stopwatch is used to time the performance of a sprinter.

Incremental time can also be expressed in terms of a change within an extension, or object. This can be a chemical or physical change. It too involves motion, but *within* the object. So the same relations apply, but in a much subtler manner.

Time, non-incremental – Time as expressed in the noumenal precipitate. This time is generally only consciously experienced in infancy or very early childhood, prior to a mature formation of the phenomenal precipitate. It arises as a consequence of the sequence in which mental focus introduces percept impressions on the mind.

Understanding – Reason and judgment. A thought involving a concept, statement, or theoretical system. It is to be distinguished from imagination. But reason and judgment could neither exist nor make progress without imagination. Concepts are formed from imaginative images. Thus reason could not introduce new concepts without the work of imagination. Even the syllogism above (listed under syllogism) could not perform its transferral of meaning without underlying imaginative associations between concepts. For a statement as a whole is a concept, as well as the concepts within the statement.

Thus the conclusion of the above syllogism was reached by the subject of the minor premise being brought together with the predicate of the major premise to make a new statement, which is itself a concept, as well as being a relationship between two concepts. This transferral of meaning was accomplished by means of the association of two identical middle terms. Judgment, of course, depends on such reasoning. It depends upon deriving a conclusion from prior assumptions.

www.ingramcontent.com/pod-product-compliance
Lightning Source LLC
Chambersburg PA
CBHW070522010526
44118CB00012B/1050